CW01558426

Youth, Power,
Performance

Youth, Power, Performance

Applied Theatre
with Systemically
Marginalized Youth

Diane Conrad

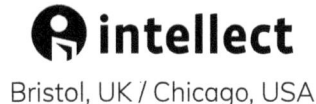 **intellect**

Bristol, UK / Chicago, USA

First published in the UK in 2025 by
Intellect, The Mill, Parnall Road, Fishponds, Bristol, BS16 3JG, UK

First published in the USA in 2025 by
Intellect, The University of Chicago Press, 1427 E. 60th Street,
Chicago, IL 60637, USA

Copyright © 2025 Intellect Ltd
All rights reserved. No part of this publication may be reproduced,
stored in a retrieval system, or transmitted, in any form or by
any means, electronic, mechanical, photocopying, recording, or
otherwise, without written permission.

A catalogue record for this book is available from
the British Library.

Copy editor: MPS Limited
Cover designer: Tanya Montefusco
Cover image: D. Conrad, 2010. Photo by Leslie Robinson.
Production manager: Debora Nicosia
Typesetter: MPS Limited

Hardback ISBN 978-1-83595-079-1
ePDF ISBN 978-1-83595-081-4
ePUB ISBN 978-1-83595-080-7

To find out about all our publications, please visit our website.
There you can subscribe to our e-newsletter, browse or download our current
catalogue and buy any titles that are in print.

www.intellectbooks.com

This is a peer-reviewed publication.

To Jack. Though I only knew you briefly, I feel the tragedy of your passing deeply. I want this dedication to honour the person you were meant to be and honour all those youth who struggle likewise.

Contents

Figures

Acknowledgements

There were a great number of individuals and organizations without whom/ which the applied theatre research discussed in this book would not have been possible.

I would first like to extend my eternal gratitude to all of the 200 or so youth involved in the various projects I facilitated over the years. It was my great honour to have been granted opportunities to spend time with these youth. Their commitment, strength, and imagination always impressed me and the insights they offered to the research were invaluable. I learned so much from them.

Thanks also to the organizations/institutions that generously made the time and space to collaborate with me on the research and provided access to the youth, including the inner-city high school, the rural Alberta high school, the youth offender jail, and the arts-based non-profit community organization serving street-involved youth. I especially want to thank those individuals associated with the organizations/institutions with whom I worked most closely: the principals and teachers, the corrections officers, and the outreach and social workers — those individuals whose established relationships with the youth smoothed the way for the projects' success.

I am grateful for my colleagues, collaborators, and mentors at the University of Alberta and from within the community who supported me and my work, the many graduate student research assistants who worked alongside me through the various projects, and the many, many applied theatre and drama education practitioners from around the world, whose work I learned from and drew upon to hone my own practice.

Thanks to the University of Alberta, the Social Sciences and Humanities Research Council of Canada and REACH Edmonton: Council for Safe Communities. Without their support and funding the work would not have proceeded.

Thanks also to the various book and journal editors and publishers who published my earlier writings about each of the projects discussed herein and the publishers and reviewers of this manuscript.

I extend a special thanks to the Gabriola Arts Council who granted me the Kasahara Gabriola Trust Artist Residency for fall 2022, which provided me time and space on beautiful Gabriola Island, British Columbia to work on this book. I am thankful to have had the opportunity to get to meet some community members, including some Gabriola youth.

Foreword:
Risk More, Dream Bigger,
and Connect Deeply

Mindy R. Carter

Collectively, the world is just beginning to comprehend the educational, social, and societal impacts of the COVID-19 pandemic on personal and collective socio-emotional, spiritual, and physical well-being. This is amidst an increased stratification of the wealthy and poor, who are contending with rising housing, food, and other costs. Alongside such realities are looming concerns about the impacts of Artificial Intelligence on job precarity, and the need to reckon with historical legacies of colonial frameworks and institutions that have undergirded the violence and systemic fallouts that have impacted the lived experiences of Black, Indigenous, and People of Colour. In these bleak times, such reckonings feel deeply connected to the environmental extremes such as ice storms, earthquakes, and floods that are occurring across the Earth.

How can anyone make sense of the enormity of our current realities? How can one contend with times such as these without feeling overwhelmed, afraid? Perhaps, returning to the self, to reflect and ruminate deeply, as some folks had the opportunity to do during COVID-19 lock-downs, is a way that one can consider where we/they have been, to respond to this moment in conscious, kind, and hopeful ways. This book represents a deep response in the arts education context, a response that is a beacon for our dark times, reminding others that a single life's work charted across time can make a difference to the individual, and to the communities that one is a part of.

Recently, Cindy Blackstock, member of the Gitxsan First Nation, who is a social worker, co-founder of First Nations Child and Family Caring Society, and professor at McGill University, iterated that 'academia and activism should co-exist', that we should not 'just publish another paper ... Let's do something' (cited in Rynor, 2023, para. 2 and 7). For Blackstock, one's work in academia must be tied to change beyond the *ivory tower*. Arguably, *Youth, Power, Performance: Applied Theatre with Systemically Marginalized Youth* is an example of how Dr. Diane Conrad's life work is also about connecting beyond academia through applied theatre.

'What is it about drama, or applied theatre processes specifically, that capture youths' imaginations for envisioning possibilities and increasing their sense of agency?' This question, at the centre of Dr. Diane Conrad's book, is a synthesis of the twenty-plus years of research that she has conducted across several research sites, contexts, and projects in the areas of applied theatre and applied theatre research. By offering examples of applied theatre as research practice, Conrad explores notions of social change, transformation, and empowerment through specific examples from her career, discussing the potential of empowerment through performance in a range of educational settings.

It is not often that a scholar takes the time, or has the opportunity, to reflect on their extensive research projects from the perspectives of an educator and artist, with almost 40 years of experience in these areas. As Conrad writes:

> Applied theatre is often focused as much on the participatory theatre process as it is on any theatrical product or performance (Kaplan, 2022; Santiago-Jirau, 2022). The roles of performer and audience are sometimes blurred with participants, at various times, taking on the roles of audience for their fellow participants' performances, and/or with audience members, at more formal performance events, sometimes invited to directly intervene in the action on stage. Applied theatre aims to address social issues relevant to the community with which it engages; it tells the stories of those people who have often been silenced (O'Connor & Anderson, 2015).

Youth, Power, Performance: Applied Theatre with Systemically Marginalized Youth offers several significant contributions to the field of applied theatre and beyond. Extrapolated from Conrad's book, the following offerings are highlights of her contributions, in the context of working with marginalized youth:

Collaboration: The collaborative nature of applied theatre creates a context in which youth can flourish. In Conrad's work, collaboration is discussed in relation to participants working in peer groupings that can sometimes be fraught with conflict. It is applied theatre that creates a supportive, non-judgemental s/place in which young people can work together towards a common goal.

Seeing oneself in a new role: Taking on a role helps one to experience distance from oneself, while simultaneously understanding the experiences of another. This autophenomenological space allows one to see something not only *as if* for the first time, but *for the first time* (Carter, 2022), and offers participants an opportunity to reframe not only their own lived experiences but to consider belonging in new ways.

Affective expressions: Drama and theatre offer actors opportunities to play, to be in their bodies, to engage socio-emotionally, and to put their own ways of thinking at stake. It takes risk and courage to express oneself through dramatic play, and the full expression of being that this engagement requires changes the individual deeply.

Claiming agency: When one shares their story and takes responsibility for their voice and actions, they are given an opportunity to claim/reclaim agency. Youth in this book are empowered in their own contexts as a result of being given a space to share their stories and to have them heard.

Dialogical performance: Through applied theatre, youth are provided opportunities to come to better understand their own life experiences and aspects of the lives and struggles of other youth in deeper ways.

Cultural production: Meaning-making through performing is a way of enacting resistance and hope. While applied theatre research cannot address youths' problems directly, it can raise awareness of injustices.

Tensions and ethical considerations: Conrad reflexively acknowledges the tensions and ethical considerations that arose during her applied theatre work, rather than ignoring them.

These seven strands represent some of the synthesizing ideas that Conrad's twenty-plus years of working with youth in applied theatre contexts have highlighted – as the ways that applied theatre can contribute to the empowerment of marginalized young folks. I believe that Conrad is calling all of us, through the examples she offers, to: Risk more, dream bigger, and to connect deeply with ourselves and others, by moving beyond community towards a disposition of being and belonging, where:

> at the core of community [is] belonging, or feeling connected in and through time…one of the great values of belonging to any group with a purpose is that we act with other people, for the benefit of other people, knowing that we could not accomplish anything without other people. (Clarkson, 2014, p. 73 in Carter, 2022, p. 114)

In *Smallest Circles First: Exploring Teacher Reconciliatory Praxis through Drama Education* (Carter, 2022), belonging is being with an ongoing commitment to hope (p. 117). Being while belonging is when:

belonging is the deep essential hope that one experiences in connection to all things. Anishenabeg. Affecting and being affected by experiences is not a choice, it is a part of belonging and offering one's own truth when the time for speaking or action is in season. (p. 119)

As I have theorized in my own work, using drama education with pre- and in-service teachers to foster agency, being and belonging is a movement beyond time and community that Conrad's work illustrates through the facilitation of close listening, attunement to the needs of a group, which sees power not as 'domination and control over others ... [but as] creative and life-affirming' (hooks, 1984, p. 84).

Perhaps because she identifies with being a potentially at-risk youth in her own childhood, Conrad is able to hold a space of love, care, and hope in her applied theatre projects with marginalized youth. Perhaps she seeks to be a light in the challenging times in the lives of those she works with so that she can learn what it means to connect more deeply with herself by working alongside others. Whatever the reason for the motivation of this work, it is an exquisite offering to the literature and body of work of applied theatre research with marginalized youth and beyond that encourages us all to risk more, dream bigger, and connect deeply in each moment we have.

Mindy R. Carter, PhD
McGill University

1

Considerations for Applied Theatre
with Systemically Marginalized Youth

This book will discuss five applied theatre research projects that I facilitated over the past twenty-plus years as part of my research program in Education at the University of Alberta. Over the years, I have written about each of these projects, which included my master's study at an alternative inner city high school (Conrad, 2002a, 2002b), my doctoral research at a rural Alberta high school (Conrad, 2004a, 2004b, 2005, 2006b), a pilot study (Campbell & Conrad, 2006; Conrad, 2006a) and a longer funded study (Conrad, 2010, 2012, 2013, 2016) with incarcerated youth, and a project with a non-profit, arts-based organization serving street-involved youth (Conrad, 2015, 2023; Conrad et al., 2015) (see Appendix 1 for an overview of all five projects). This book is a synthesis and expansion upon that work as I explore considerations for facilitating applied theatre with systemically marginalized youth. These include confluences and themes across projects as well as divergences relevant to particular groups and contexts. My understandings are informed by the accumulation of my practical experiences, alongside the writing of other scholars in applied theatre, education, and beyond.

My review of recent national and international literature by scholars working with marginalized youth, for the most part, confirmed my experiences. The literature I reviewed included reports on projects using various applied theatre approaches, sometimes combined with other arts forms (storytelling, digital storytelling, film-making, poetry, RAP) (Alrutz, 2013; Ansloos & Wager, 2020; Arteaga & Chavez-Arteaga, 2022; Barton-Farcas, 2022; Blight, 2015; Brendel Horn, 2017; Gallagher, 2016; Gallagher & Rodricks, 2017a, 2017b; Gallagher et al., 2017; Hughes, 2013; Kaplan, 2022; Lamparter, 2022; Linds et al., 2013; McCreery, 2001; Rhoades, 2018; Santiago-Jirau, 2022; Tate, 2022; Vettraino et al., 2017; Wager, 2015). I also reviewed some literature exclusively using other arts forms with marginalized youth (storytelling, poetry, drawing, RAP, music, media production) (Asakura et al., 2019; DeCarlo & Hockman, 2003; DeCastell & Jenson, 2006; Flicker et al., 2008; Marsh, 2012; Ottaway et al., 2009). These arts-based projects were facilitated by researchers in health/mental health, social work, education in mainstream and alternative contexts, and by theatre artists/practitioners. I also reviewed literature by youth work scholars reporting on non-arts-based interventions with marginalized youth, reporting on practitioners' successful strategies for working with marginalized youth, and/or reviewing literature on youth work with marginalized youth (Blanchet-Cohen & Salazar, 2009; Eichas et al., 2021; Gil-Kashiwabara et al., 2007; Iwasaki et al., 2014; Lavie-Ajayi & Krumer-Nevo, 2013; Sapiro & Ward, 2020; Smyth & Eaton-Erickson, 2009). The youth engaged in all these studies included street-involved/homeless, Indigenous, Black/Latinx/Chicanx/racialized, incarcerated/justice-involved, low-income/youth living in poverty, queer/trans/LGBTQ, urban, and/or immigrant/refugee youth, youth experiencing mental health challenges/trauma, youth who were sex workers, youth with disabilities, and youth in foster care. The literature confirmed my experiences in various ways – in terms of youths' realities, challenges encountered, effective processes and common outcomes, and also differed, at times, with the perspectives I share. I refer to this literature throughout the book as applicable.

What I share in this text, then, is grounded in practice and theory, but, like any scholarship, can only be tentative and partial. I acknowledge that my understandings are based on my limited experiences within the specific contexts in which I researched. As applied theatre practice is highly context-dependent, my insights may or may not have broader relevance. It is with this caveat that I venture to explicate what I have learned about doing applied theatre research with systemically marginalized youth and what I have come to recognize as the potential for youth empowerment that this work offers.

I invite you into this text by beginning with an introduction of myself. As I have learned from Indigenous traditions (Absolon & Willett, 2005), introducing oneself in relation to family and land is proper protocol. The term Indigenous in the Canadian context, I should specify, refers to the First Peoples of these lands – the First Nations, Inuit and Métis, who inhabited and cared for the land and their non-human kin prior to colonization by white Europeans. Particularly, in light of Canada's Truth and Reconciliation Commission and its Calls to Action (Government of Canada, 2015), Canadian institutions and individuals are compelled to take action towards mending relations with Indigenous peoples, which were severely damaged through settler-colonialism's betrayals and its ongoing effects, which continue to harm the lives of Indigenous peoples. And so, amongst other reconciliatory measures, clarifying my motivations for and investments in engaging with youth, including many Indigenous youth, through applied theatre research is appropriate. I begin by locating myself in relation to the applied theatre research I undertook.

Positioning Myself as Applied Theatre Researcher

I am a white, settler-Canadian cis-gendered woman. I am the daughter of parents who immigrated from Germany to Canada in the late 1950s just prior to my birth. I grew up in the Niagara region of Southern Ontario, which is Treaty 3 territory. I learned very little of the Indigenous history of this place growing up, but I am continuing to learn (Government of Canada, 2013a, 2013b; Native Land Digital, 2023; Noble & Filice, 2016). Treaty 3 (also known as the Between the Lakes Purchase – part of the Upper Canada Treaties) was finalized in 1792 and covers the Niagara region – territory of the Ojibway/Chippewa and Haudenosaunee Confederacy. This area was inhabited by Indigenous people for more than 8,000 years prior to colonization. An early group to inhabit the area were the Attawandaron, a political/cultural union of several Indigenous groups also known as the Neutral Confederacy. These were a peaceful woodland/farming people who formed a buffer, or neutral zone, between the warring Huron-Wendat (French allies) and Haudenosaunee Nations (English allies). It was one of the largest Indigenous societies in the area in the early 1600s totalling about 40,000, but was reduced by famine, war, and disease to 12,000, mostly dispersed by the 1650s. Currently no such Nation exists. My family's immigration became part of the legacy of settlers who displaced the Indigenous inhabitants and continue to live on and enjoy the benefits of this stolen land.

My father worked as a farm hand and a construction labourer. My mother stayed home to look after my four siblings and me. We were a working-class, immigrant family with no extended family in Canada to provide support and little in the way of extras to go around. While my family's newcomer and low socio-economic status in some ways negatively affected my well-being as a child and limited my prospects as a youth, nevertheless, I benefitted greatly, and still do, as a white European settler in Canada. I enjoyed, and continue to enjoy, many privileges. I had a stable home life, with loving, attentive parents and all my basic needs were met. Unlike many of the youth with whom I have worked, I did not suffer the effects of the overt and/or systemic racism or homophobia that prevails in our society. I acknowledge that the privileges I gained and continue to enjoy through the legacy of colonization and white supremacy cannot be understated. As a member of Canada's racially dominant and gender normative group, I easily gained the social and cultural capital I needed to succeed. I managed to finish high school without difficulty, to find employment as I needed, and with the help of some government funding to complete undergraduate and graduate level university studies. Upon completing my PhD, I secured a faculty position at the University of Alberta. For 26 years I have lived and worked in Edmonton, Alberta.

The Cree name for Edmonton, amiskwacîwâskahikan, is translated as Beaver Hills House (Government of Canada, 2015b; Ogg, 2015; University of Alberta, 2023). Historically, it was a traditional gathering place for many Indigenous nations including the Cree, Dene, Anishinaabe, Saulteaux, Nakota Sioux, Blackfoot, and the Métis peoples and continues to be home to many diverse Indigenous peoples. It is part of Treaty 6 territory. I have worked as a professor specializing in drama and theatre education at the University of Alberta for twenty years. During my graduate studies and during my brief sojourn in Canada's Northwest Territories teaching in two Dene community schools – on Treaty 11 territory (Government of Canada, 2013b), I gained some understandings of Indigenous histories, knowledges, traditions, and cultures, but still have much to learn. I feel honoured to have had opportunities to engage with many Indigenous youth in the Northern Alberta region through my applied theatre research.

In my time at the University, I also worked with hundreds of preservice drama teachers. Many of those students told me of their positive experiences with drama in high school, which motivated them to pursue a drama teaching career. What it is about drama that inspires young people is something I will explore in this text.

I was an enthusiastic drama kid in high school too. I was not interested in taking part in the popular high-school musical productions, however. My interests in drama lay elsewhere. I was part of a small group of students who took drama courses in high school, which overflowed into after school extra-curricular drama activities. Our drama teacher encouraged us to participate each year in the local high school one act play festival – an annual event in which high-school drama groups from across the province competed. While I enjoyed witnessing the work of and interacting with drama kids from other schools, I was not all that keen on the competitive environment. I remember one year, I appealed to our teacher, with the support of my classmates, to take up an offer from a local children's theatre group to work with us to devise and tour a children's show in place of our one act contribution. Our teacher reluctantly gave in. Devising and performing our own show was one of the most memorable and fulfilling high-school drama experiences I had.

Aside from drama and the socializing that happened at school, as for many teens, I found high school quite boring. I was always fairly good at school; for me, studying for tests and getting good grades did not present a satisfying enough challenge, though. Rather, I enjoyed tasks that required imagination and creativity and this is what drama offered. For me, joy in learning was never about getting the right answers, but about exploring possibilities, examining aspects of the human condition and their relevance to *my* life. Drama was not about memorizing facts or regurgitating information, as were most other subjects; it was about making sense of the uncertainties of life that were beginning to creep into my adolescent awareness. That's what drew me to drama more than anything. And besides, it was always lots of fun!

High-school drama, and the like-minded companions I found there, offered me a sense of belonging as a youth. I had a supportive environment both in school and within my family, but my youthful experiences were not without their share of boundary-testing and risk-taking. Eventually, as part of my doctoral research exploring the experiences of so-called *at-risk* (or marginalized) youth, I conducted an autoethnographic inquiry to help me understand how I too might have been deemed at-risk as a youth. It was an interrogation into my interest or motivations for doing the research I was undertaking that prompted the exploration (Conrad, 2003). My autoethnography recounted my experience of being back in Ontario one summer for a visit with a family for whom I had served as a sort of live-in nanny during my last year of high school. I had left some boxes of stuff in their farmhouse basement and I took some time, during my visit, to look through them. The artefacts from my youth that I unearthed there shook me into realizing that what I was really doing with my research was struggling to understand my own risky experiences as a youth. My group of friends and I, I recalled, were regularly engaged in recreational drug use and other youthful thrill-seeking behaviours. From a more sober adult perspective, I sometimes think back, with anguish, to the young woman I had been and reel at my perilous behaviour. I recall a few occasions when my well-being, even my survival, were at risk. In Chapter 7, for example, I share an instance of my youthful risk-taking involving substance use and reckless driving before a high-school dance (see Conrad, 2004c), which, had circumstances been slightly different, may very well have ended in my death. While the risks seemed minimal at the time, thinking back, I see now how precarious some of my youthful experiences really were.

Reflecting back to my own experiences as a youth that might have deemed me at-risk, the conditions that provoked my behaviours and the motivations for my teenage risk-taking, gave me insight into the youth population with which I was interested in researching. I wondered how I had managed to make it through adolescence and young adulthood relatively unscathed, while others regularly fell between the cracks. High-school drama, along with other supportive factors in my family and community, may very well have mitigated some of the risk that I encountered as a young person. My emic insight has proven invaluable in inform-ing my ongoing research program.

After high school, hooked on drama, I completed a Bachelor of Fine Arts degree in creative writing with play writing as my main interest, followed by a year of physical theatre training. I was, however, disappointed by the arts education I received as I found the attitude that I encountered there quite elitist, which was what ultimately led me towards pursuing a community-focused, applied theatre approach. When I chose to pursue an after-degree in Education, drama was, of course, the subject area I focused on. When I began graduate studies, again, my interests revolved around drama education. Those high-school drama experiences have had a life-long impact on me.

Between my Bachelor of Fine Arts degree and my Bachelor of Education degree, I spent five years as a volunteer teacher with World University Service of Canada in Lesotho, Southern Africa (Cobbe et al., 2023). While I did not have much engagement with drama during that time, my political education flourished through living and working in a region deeply affected by South Africa's Apartheid regime, and through interactions with members of the then still outlawed African National Congress. Upon completing my B.Ed, back in Canada, I sought a teaching position in Northwest Territories First Nations community schools. I spent three years living and working in two Dene communities, where I taught high-school drama, amongst other subjects.

It was graduate school that really allowed me to bring together my love of drama and my growing political commitments. Having been briefly (unofficially) exposed to Augusto Boal's *Theatre of the Oppressed* (1974/1979) during my B.Ed studies, I sought to develop my drama/theatre practice in that direction. Rather than focus on scripted theatre or theatrical production, my interest was in applied theatre – theatre that engaged community members as participants to explore their life experiences and issues relevant to their lives towards social justice ends. I began my graduate research in Education specifically interested in working with systemically marginalized or 'at-risk' youth (more on that term to come) – those youth who had been pushed to or found themselves living on the margins of our mainstream society due to social structural factors such as minority culture, gender, sexual identity, race, religion, socio-economic status, etc. From these beginnings, my interest in applied theatre with marginalized youth continued as the focus of my research program through my twenty-plus year academic career.

Now having introduced myself, throughout the remainder of this chapter, I will touch on a few key concepts or themes relevant to the work that is the focus of this book – the several research projects I have facilitated utilizing applied theatre with marginalized youth in various contexts including in alternative school settings, in a youth jail, and with an organization serving street-involved youth. Specifically, I touch on concepts central to the work beginning with some definitional discussion of *applied theatre* and *applied theatre research*. I then move on to describe the youth population that is the focus of this book and the challenges with terminology related to identifying such youth. I reflect briefly on issues related to my work with Indigenous youth, which I develop further in Chapter 5, and on the important distinction between symptoms and root causes/structural issues associated with youth behaviour. I explore notions of social change, transformation, and empowerment at the heart of applied theatre, and conclude by introducing the unique potential of empowerment through performance, which I also discuss in more detail in Chapter 6.

Throughout the book, when discussing the applied theatre projects undertaken, I often use the plural pronouns *we* and *our*. This is by no means intended to invoke the *royal we*, but rather legitimately reflects the fact that, though I was principal investigator for each of the studies, I was never alone in this work, nor solely responsible for decision-making. For every project, I researched alongside collaborators including teachers, institutional staff, community-based facilitators, graduate student research assistants, and, of course, the youth as co-researchers of their experiences, their contributions being integral to the work.

Applied Theatre and Applied Theatre Research

While it is a somewhat contentious term in the field of drama/theatre, I use *applied theatre*, as others have (Balfour, 2010; Nicholson, 2011; O'Connor & Anderson, 2015; Prendergast & Saxton, 2009; Thompson, 2003), as an umbrella term for a range of theatre practices that occur outside of traditional theatre buildings or theatre contexts with participants who may have little or no prior theatre experience. It encompasses such forms as theatre-in-education or educational drama/theatre, process drama, popular theatre, theatre for health education, theatre in hospitals, theatre for development, prison theatre, community-based theatre, reminiscence theatre, museum theatre, drama therapy, theatre for social justice, or sociodrama. Applied theatre stands in contrast to professional theatre or mainstream theatrical production. What applied theatre approaches have in common is that they all 'attempt to "apply" theatre skills to complex social environments' (Balfour, 2010, p. 55). Applied theatre is socially and politically committed theatre practice characterized by its intentions of efficacy in the real world over entertainment value.

As mentioned, the umbrella term *applied theatre* may include work in my field of drama/theatre education, within which there has also been ongoing discussion about terminology; distinctions are commonly (but inconsistently) made between *drama* and *theatre* (e.g. see Baker, 1973; Martin-Smith, 2005). As I understand this distinction, drama refers more specifically to practices that are *process* focused – where students/participants engage in dramatic play or performative exercises for their exploration/learning within the group, whereas theatre is more *product* focused – where the end-goal is a performance for an external audience. Both approaches have their strengths and weaknesses – for example, a process-based approach allows time for in-depth exploration, but may lack the motivating impetus that producing a performance product can inspire. And in truth, drama/theatre education practices often fall on a continuum between a focus on process and product, and, of course, there is always a process that builds towards any performance, so the dichotomy is somewhat artificial. The term *applied drama* (Prendergast & Saxton, 2013) has also recently come into use referring to applied theatre practices that are focused more on dramatic process.

Over my twenty-plus years as a drama/theatre educator and/or applied theatre practitioner, I have (and still do) alternately refer to my work as drama and/or theatre education, popular theatre, participatory or community-based theatre. Now, and throughout this book, I generally use the term *drama* to refer to my teaching practice with pre-service teachers and the term *applied theatre* to talk about my research approach.

As Thompson contended, applied theatre is 'a useful phrase for theatre that claims usefulness' (2003, p. 14) – although even the notion of *usefulness* is not without disparate ideological implications: Useful for what? The usefulness that I seek from my applied theatre practice is directed towards participants' – specifically youths' – personal well-being as well as social justice broadly conceived (as access, equity, participation, and rights for all). The extent to which applied theatre can achieve these lofty goals is part of what this text explores.

Applied theatre most often occurs with or within communities, in institutions or with special interest groups, with participants, who would not usually make theatre at all – the socially excluded or marginalized. Applied theatre is often focused as much on the participatory theatre process as it is on any theatrical product or performance (Kaplan, 2022; Santiago-Jirau, 2022). The roles of performer and audience are sometimes blurred with participants, at various times, taking on the roles of audience for their fellow participants' performances, and/or with audience members at more formal performance events, sometimes invited to directly intervene in the action on stage. Applied theatre aims to address social issues relevant to the community with which it engages; it tells the stories of those people who have often been silenced (O'Connor & Anderson, 2015). It is relational (e.g. see Ansloos & Wager, 2020; Gallagher, 2016; Hughes, 2013) in offering collaborative processes for listening, exploration, and creation. Its intentions are to raise awareness, to identify issues of concern, to analyse their conditions and causes, and to look for solutions towards generating change (Prentki & Selman, 2000). It is a theatre form that presents participants' real-life experiences, though often fictionalized, and performers often take on character roles that are close to themselves.

An applied theatre project begins with a clear intention established by, with, or for the community – to benefit the community with which it engages (Prentki & Preston, 2008), but the outcomes are highly unpredictable, since the processes are necessarily responsive to the needs and desires of participants.

The tradition of applied theatre that has most closely informed my work as an applied theatre facilitator is Augusto Boal's *Theatre of the Oppressed* (1974/1979). Dramaturge and theatre director, Boal developed his approach in Brazil in the 1960s in response to countryman Paulo Freire's popular education movement, which he discussed in *Pedagogy of the Oppressed* (1970/2000). At that time and in that context, Boal referred to his theatre techniques as rehearsal for revolution. I also drew upon David Diamond's *Theatre for Living* (2007) strategies, which he adapted from Boal's to better address the contemporary Canadian context.

Throughout this book, I describe the applied theatre projects I undertook and the sorts of activities engaged in with youth. While some of these activities may not be immediately recognizable as traditional Theatre of the Oppressed activities or even applied theatre activities, applied theatre was at the heart of all the work. As such, Theatre of the Oppressed has been a point of departure for my work, though I do not adhere to Boal's (1974/1979, 1992, 1995) strategies orthodoxly. For example, in Chapter 5, I describe a digital storytelling project I facilitated with incarcerated youth. While digital storytelling is not traditionally associated with applied theatre, others (e.g. Alrutz, 2013) have argued, and I would agree, that digital storytelling parallels the processes of applied theatre and can be seen as applied theatre praxis.

Inspired by my background, training, and experiences participating in and facilitating applied theatre, each study adapted processes and developed products based on Boal's and others techniques to meet the needs of that specific project, its context, and participants. I do refer to Boal's image theatre and forum theatre approaches in Chapter 3 and elsewhere, but I have adapted his techniques in practice to suit my own needs. Nevertheless, the philosophy that underpinned all of applied theatre processes I undertook was consistent with Theatre of the Oppressed – through the identification of issues by youth, the devising of theatre work based on their stories, critical analyses of the social contexts of their lived experiences, and the search for alternatives to the marginalizing circumstances of youths' lives.

Applied Theatre as Practice-based Research

Over the past few decades, a (post)qualitative (St. Pierre, 2011) approach to creative arts scholarship has emerged known as *practice-based research* or *practice-as-research* (Kershaw, 2009; in Canada this approach is also known as *research-creation*).

Practice-as-research within academic contexts seeks to abandon contrived divisions between thinking and doing, theory and practice. From this perspective, the processes and products of artistic creation can be seen as forms of research in and of themselves. In applied theatre, understood as practice-as-research, the devising of theatrical scenarios as well as performances or theatre events are inquiry processes, objects of inquiry, and/or outcomes of research. Practice-as-research may also include more traditional interpretive research outcomes such as journal articles, books, etc. In this vein, my approach to applied theatre research saw the creation processes and performances – as youth shared their knowledge with one another and with audiences – as research alongside the writing about our work together that I (at times with collaborators) authored.

Practice-as-research is consistent with the turn away from abstract theorizing or empirical positivism in scholarship, which arose in the mid-to-late twentieth century, towards a call for scholarship with more practical engagement in the world through practice or action. This trend also saw the emergence of participatory (Heron & Reason, 1997) or community-based research approaches, with which I also align my research.

Applied Theatre as Participatory Research

As a *new paradigm* research approach (Heron & Reason, 1997), participatory research is described as a means for producing knowledge, a tool for community dialogue, education, consciousness raising, and mobilizing for action (Park et al., 1993). It develops practical knowing in pursuit of worthwhile human purposes and practical solutions to pressing community issues (Reason & Bradbury, 2006). It is research *for*, *with*, and *by* participants accentuating the inherent human capacity to create knowledge based on experience (Fals-Borda & Rahman, 1991). Participatory research arose within community-development initiatives around the world in response to dominant scientific traditions that claimed neutrality, objectivity, and perpetuated colonizing attitudes to knowledge production (Hall, 2005). Participatory research also aligns with Indigenous research methodologies (Smith, 1999; Weber-Pillwax, 2004; Wilson, 2008) in focusing on relationality and reciprocity with respect and relevance for the community it serves.

Kidd and Byram's (1978) identification of applied theatre as a participatory research method – both involving a dynamic of critical reflection and action, or praxis – shaped my understandings. Both participatory research (or participatory action research) (Fals-Borda & Rahman, 1991; Hall, 2005; Park et al., 1993; Reason & Bradbury, 2008) and applied theatre are community focused and participant led. While some research approaches perceive conflict between research and advocacy, in both participatory research and applied theatre, advocacy on behalf of the community being served is inherent (Chatterton et al., 2007; Nicholson, 2005).

Specifically, I describe my work with youth as a youth participatory action research (YPAR) approach. Cammarota and Fine (2008) offered YPAR as a means for revolutionizing education – a model for engaging youth in research which aims to involve them in engaged praxis through participation in researching issues relevant to their lives. As one youth researcher in a YPAR study suggested, 'a lot of research is used as a stalling tactic in light of the fact that addressing the real problem with real solutions is a daunting task' (DeCastell et al., 2002, para. 2). YPAR offers an alternative research approach which has the potential to address the real material conditions of youths' lives. Researching *with* rather than *on* youth respects youths' perspectives and their right to be heard regarding matters that concern them, including research. YPAR is action oriented towards benefiting youth.

I offer a few examples of YPAR projects here to illustrate the approach: The Pridehouse Project (DeCastell & Jenson, 2006) partnered researchers in Education at two Canadian universities with a community organization, Pride Care Society in Vancouver, BC, to engage street-involved queer and questioning youth in an inquiry into their housing and support needs and to establish a basis for fundraising for dedicated housing for this population. The project used multimedia methods (video, website creation) for collecting data and disseminating research and included night-time excursions to give out food on the streets.

The Mothers on the Move (MOM) Oral History project (Guishard et al., 2005) partnered researchers from the Graduate Center, CUNY, with the South Bronx activist group MOM, which had, for thirteen years, been advocating for educational equity for their poor and working-class community. The study engaged community youth in collecting and disseminating oral histories of MOM members while investigating the achievement gap to raise their levels of consciousness around the issue and organizing a youth component to MOM to carry on its advocacy work.

Korteweg and Bissell's (2016) Tikkun research study developed an Indigenized YPAR as a decolonizing research methodology. The study featured the creation of an Indigenous youth-generated report, 'Feathers of Hope: A First Nations Youth Action Plan' (Provincial Advocate for Children and Youth, 2014), highlighting youths' needs in their own words and based on their own experiences. Kortewag and Bissell described their approach as 'a pedagogy of resistance or refusal and a method to build solidarity and a collective imagination of resilience and futurity for/by youth' (p. 15), focused on Indigenous youth 'reclaiming, recovering, and reimagining social and political power' (p. 15).

Iwasaki et al.'s (2014) interdisciplinary research in social work, public health, and human ecology worked with a group of youth leaders – the Youth 4 YEG

Team, identified by marginalized youth serving organizations around the city of Edmonton. The youth drew on their lived experiences to develop a framework for engaging marginalized youth as part of a larger project. Their framework included recommendations of arts-based activities as one means for promoting the framework's identified goals, including youth empowerment, learning, and relationship building, amongst others.

In addition to the examples above, Asakura et al. (2019) partnered trans artists with trans youth in a creative project of queer world-making; Flicker et al. (2008) used creative applications of technology (photography, video, music production) through seven projects engaging youth in health promotion. Participatory research approaches, including YPAR, commonly utilize arts-based methods, often incorporating alternative cultural forms that are already part of a community's life. Popular arts forms, creative media, and youth-friendly approaches offer powerful ways of engaging youth in meaning-making and knowledge representation building on their interests and capabilities.

Applied theatre can be seen as a method for participatory research through which community knowledge is generated and examined, as cycles of reflection and action are inherent to the process of devising and performing scenarios. It is an active and enjoyable approach for youth drawing on their personal stories and engaging them in embodied and emotional ways. As O'Connor and Anderson (2015) espoused, 'applied theatre, as a performance of hope and resistance, provides a unique opportunity for an aesthetic research form, one that challenges hegemonic structure and envisions the world as it might be' (p. 29). Applied theatre as YPAR creates the conditions for youth to become researchers of their lived experiences, amplifying their voices and perspectives. Of the five applied theatre projects I describe in this text, the project with the arts-based community organization serving street involved youth was the best example of applied theatre research as YPAR.

What Is Community?

As both applied theatre and participatory research are community-based practices, I share here a few thoughts on my understandings of *community*, followed by discussion of some other constructs relevant to the work which are discussed throughout this book towards offering some measure of conceptual clarification.

Applied theatre facilitator Diamond (2007) believed that 'community exists when a group of people share geography, values, experiences, expectations, or beliefs' (p. 47). Participatory researchers Iwasaki et al. (2014) defined community as 'a collective group of people that get together to create and maintain a supportive and reliable network in order to foster healthy, meaningful relationships' (p. 329).

Community, however, is a contentious concept – one of those terms that is often, but should not be, taken for granted. While the idea of community has much appeal – offering a sense of commonality and shared purpose – community has been critiqued as an ideal that denies difference (Young, 1986). This is a point well taken as shared characteristics within a group identified as a community may or may not be as significant as the differences amongst members of that community. Take a school, for example. A school may be described as a community based on the shared geography of the school building and the activities that occur within it, but individuals' experiences there will vary vastly depending on, for instance, their role within the school, or how well the norms of the school fit with their own socio-cultural backgrounds. Some individuals (i.e. youth) may even be members of the school community involuntarily, forced to attend because they are under the legal age to make the decision to quit. Carter (2022) in reflexively questioning the ideal classroom environment she had previously sought to foster replaced the notion of community, which both includes and excludes, with *a sense of belonging* – related to interconnection and hope.

I use the term community within this book to refer to an interest group comprising diverse individuals gathered to address a shared goal, or, more specifically to refer to a group of individuals working together in an applied theatre research project. I withhold judgement about whether or not the groups of youth involved with our projects and their support networks could authentically be considered communities. At times, any number of the individuals involved may have shared geography, values, experiences, expectations, or beliefs, and/or may have developed shared understandings, fostered healthy relationships or a sense of belonging through the processes of our work together, but I don't assume that this was necessarily so for all those involved. I acknowledge that even grouping the individuals with whom I worked under the common identifier: *systemically marginalized youth* is problematic as each individual and their circumstances were unique; nevertheless, I concede that to make any discussion possible, such shortcuts in terminology are sometimes necessary.

Systemically Marginalized Youth

A significant contribution that this book hopes to make is to discuss applied theatre research with a specific youth population that remains under-addressed in the applied theatre literature – specifically, marginalized youth, or, the term I have recently begun to use: *systemically marginalized youth* (Sweenie et al., 2022). I understand the systemic marginalization of youth as occurring through various processes, not of youths' own making, by which they are pushed to the periphery of mainstream society – socially disadvantaged or excluded (see also Gil-Kashiwabara et al., 2007; Iwasaki et al., 2014; Sapiro & Ward, 2020), leaving them with limited access to resources or physical and mental/emotional support, acknowledging that experiences of marginalization may be fluid as youth move in and out of the margins (Blanchet-Cohen & Salazar, 2009; Eichas et al., 2021). This youth population, due to the precarious nature of their lived realities, can be challenging to access and it can be challenging to sustain their engagement for a research project. Throughout the book, I offer insights into the lives of the youth with whom I worked based on the stories they shared and suggestions for work-ing with this youth population as well as discussion of some of the outcomes of our work together.

For scholars who strive to be conscientious and socially critical, the language used to speak or write about our work can never be taken for granted. In the social sciences, the language and terminology we use to identify, categorize, label, or talk about our fellow human beings as research participants, in order to discuss the work we have done with them, are never value neutral. Terms often come with assumptions or stigma that need to be acknowledged, problematized, and mitigated as best as possible. As Austin (1975) claimed, speech acts are not only descriptive, but performative; they can have definitive effects upon the realities they attempt to describe. Such is the case with the language used – the language I use – to talk about youth.

The Problem with Language and Labels

As I alluded to above, I began my doctoral research with an interest in explor-ing the notion of *at-risk* which was so commonly applied to youth. At-risk is a problematic label that is applied somewhat indiscriminately to youth in the fields of education, social work, health care, criminal justice, etc. I wondered: Who is at-risk and how do we know? At risk of what, exactly?

In the literature, the label at-risk seemed to imply the *bad kids*, those who were unmanageable, who refused to conform to society's expectations of them. Concerns about youth being at-risk were often fuelled by neo-liberal economics – a fear that youth would fail to become productive, contributing members of our capitalist economy, or by misguided morality – a fear that non-conforming youth would be a threat to our peaceful democracy (Giroux, 2022; Tanner et al., 1995). With such language comes stigma, a deficit view of youth that creates a vicious cycle – a spiral of low expectations, internalization of negative attitudes, learned helplessness, and self-fulfilling prophecies, all detrimental to youths' well-being (Howard & Edelman, 1985; McLaren, 1998; Tanner et al., 1995). Once labelled at-risk, youth behaviours often live up to the label.

The literature in education described youth as at-risk of dropping out of school (Baruth & Manning, 1995; Tanner et al., 1995) – which was my particular interest within an educational context. In healthcare (Gascoigne & Kerr, 1996), youth were also described as being at-risk of physical and mental health concerns through engaging in behaviours such as substance abuse, risky sexual activity, or drinking and driving, and/or youth were described as at-risk of involvement with the justice system (Juvenile Justice Comprehensive Strategy Task Force, 2000) through illegal activities such as violence, gang involvement, reckless driving, graffiti writing, etc.

I understood the label at-risk and the act of labelling as problematic from the outset. The literature applying this label to youth seemed to suggest at-riskness as a quality inherent to the youth. A long list of *risk factors* (Developmental Research and Programs Inc., 1995) that underpinned the notion of at-risk seemed to blame the youth, their families, or communities for youths' failure to conform to societal expectations. The list of risk factors was so long, in fact, that all youth might be said to be at-risk in some way or another. Risk factors were accompanied by *protective factors* at individual, family, and community levels that were said to help support youth resilience. Social-structural factors were initially not addressed in the literature, and the term *resilience* too, assumed a quality inherent to the youth themselves (Werner & Smith, 1982) – some youth being more resilient than others, again supporting a deficit view.

Later literature began acknowledging factors inherent to practices of schooling and social-structural factors that put youth at risk (Howard & Edelman, 1985; Tanner et al., 1995). Scholars began to suggest alternative terminology such as youth *put* or *placed* at-risk (e.g. *Journal of Education for Students Placed at Risk*, 2022; Hanley, 2001) to shift the blame for youths' struggles away from the youth and onto existing social conditions. More recently the definition of resilience too has expanded to consider environments as resilient (Unger, 2012), or as resilience involving 'overcoming adversity, whilst also potentially subtly changing, or even dramatically transforming, (aspects of) that adversity' (Hart et al., 2016, p. 6).

Unlike some initiatives with marginalized youth (Eichas et al., 2021; Iwasaki et al., 2014), my applied theatre research sought not to socialize youth to the current status quo – to assist them in becoming so-called contributing members of society (Lavie-Ajayi & Krumer-Nevo, 2013) – but rather to engage them in both exploring their lived realities and critically analysing the social structures that contributed to their marginalization (Gallagher, 2016).

For my doctoral research (Conrad, 2005), I worked with youth at a rural Alberta high school with a large Indigenous population to explore, from their perspectives, their behaviours that might deem them at-risk and I sought their insights into how the label at-risk positioned youth. Through the course of our work together, they told me that they neither liked the label, nor identified with it – in fact, they said they found it offensive. They insisted, instead, that their behaviours were a matter of choice. They claimed they chose to engage in such behaviours for their own reasons – often for social status amongst their peers or for the enjoyment it provided them. They helped me to re-frame the notion of at-risk as risky or risk-taking behaviour (more on this to come). *At-risk* took away youths' agency, while acknowledging their capacity to choose gave them back a sense of agency.

From working in schools, I moved on to two projects with incarcerated youth. If ever there were youth at-risk of detrimental outcomes, I reasoned, certainly they included the youth already embroiled within the justice system. Moreover, youth had previously told me that schools were sometimes like prisons for them (see also Giroux, 2003). Perhaps incarcerated youth could offer me further insights into risky youth behaviour. If stigmatization around the label at-risk initiated a detrimental cycle in youths' lives, even more so the label *young offender* and the experiences of incarceration. While the justice system attempts to protect youths' identities from public disclosure to avoid future negative effects, such experiences undoubtedly follow the youth throughout their lives.

In my subsequent study with a youth organization serving street-involved youth, terminology was also an issue. The term *street-involved* had replaced more demeaning or inaccurate terms such as *street kids* or *homeless youth* (Makofane, 2014; Phelan et al., 1997). The Alberta child welfare system used the term *high-risk* to identify youth whose life struggles moved beyond only being in danger of risk, to youth leading lives characterized by risk and vulnerability. The Alberta government defined high-risk youth as youth aged 14–22 whose drug and/or alcohol use interfered with their daily functioning, whose decisions jeopardized their safety, who lacked healthy adult connections, and who experienced multiple residential placements or multigenerational child protection involvement (Smyth & Eaton-Erickson, 2009). Based on our experiences with that project, we added that the youth also struggled with mental health issues, often were or had been involved with the criminal justice system, were under-housed, experienced poverty and/or racism, and had negative experiences at school which led to them being pushed out, all of which made their survival highly precarious. It's also important to note that such marginalization is often intergenerational, with the children of marginalized adults being especially vulnerable.

As terms such as *at-risk* and *high-risk* are ultimately detrimental when applied to youth, for the reasons I discussed above, I tried to avoid applying this language to the youth. These labels, and the discourses from which they emerged, did however have some value in raising awareness of the dire predicaments some youth faced and highlighted the urgency warranted in addressing their needs. I sometimes used such terms in my applications for funding for our projects or when I spoke with policy makers, for example, to draw attention to youths' circumstances. It was language to which funding bodies, service organizations, and the public responded and so served a purpose. Conversely, in my scholarly writing I problematized terms such as *at-risk* and *high-risk* based on youths' responses. As I mentioned, in my doctoral research, the youth ultimately rejected the label *at-risk*. In the project with street-involved youth, which we called Uncensored, for which we devised and performed workshops to educate service providers, in an evaluation video the youth created (Youth Uncensored Evaluation Video [YUEV], 2012), one youth commented on the label *high-risk*. He said, 'I wouldn't call myself a high-risk youth, just a youth who doesn't have as much as other youth' (00:04:56–00:05:08). Other youth described their life circumstances similarly:

We're all so used to shit piled over more shit, over more shit and people giving up on us and it's really fucking shitty. (00:11:30–00:11:38)

[Youth like us have had] shitty cards handed to them in life … Not everyone has mommy and daddy to tuck them in at night and tell them it's fuckin' okay. A lot of us are really alone and scared. (00:20:54–00:21:10)

A lot of people that live good lives or lives that have been privileged, they don't understand what we go through … They don't realize that even waking up in the morning is hard, stepping your foot out into a school is hard, taking a bus is hard, anything is hard when you don't got what most people do. (00:31:40–00:32:12)

For the Uncensored project, one of the scenes we created, based on youths' experiences, which I describe in detail in Chapter 3, specifically spoke to the problem of labelling.

Recently, I began tentatively using the term *marginalized* to describe the youth with whom I worked, but this term still seemed to focus too much on the youth as being somehow implicated in their marginalization. Other terms taken up in the literature to describe this youth population include socially, economically, politically marginalized or historically marginalized (Gallagher et al., 2017), underserved, disenfranchised, or pushed to the margins (Vettraino et al., 2017), and silenced and/or dispossessed (O'Connor & Anderson, 2015). Then, I came across the term *systemically marginalized youth* (Sweenie et al., 2022). I prefer this term for the way it squarely places the blame for youths' marginalization on existing social structures. The addition of the adjective *systemically* satisfies my commitments to youth advocacy, so it's the term I prefer for now and will use in this book.

Working with Indigenous Youth

When I began my academic career, I never specifically sought to work with Indigenous youth, though, as I learned early on, my interest in working with at-risk youth within the northern Alberta region where I lived and worked meant I was likely to encounter some Indigenous youth. This proved to be the case with approximately 60% of the youth I worked with for each of the projects identifying as Indigenous. The tragic reality was, and still is, that in the region many Indigenous youth and their families and communities suffer the intergenerational and ongoing effects of colonization and genocide – the systemic racism inherent in our settler colonial society (Tuck & Yang, 2012).

When I found myself engaging with many Indigenous youth, it was important that my work respond to this reality. The Indigenous youth naturally raised issues related to their Indigeneity and Indigenous culture, history, and issues through our applied theatre work and while the research was not able to do anything directly towards redressing ongoing settler-colonial injustices, as small symbolic actions (Robinson & Martin, 2016), our work might be said to have responded to youths' struggles through opening spaces for Indigenous youths' perspectives and desires to be heard (Ansloos & Wager, 2020; Conrad, 2020). I speak more to my experiences as a white settler-researcher working with Indigenous youth in Chapter 5.

Symptoms Versus Root Causes

Much research focusing on the circumstances of youth marginalization (Bell & Bell, 1993; Eichas et al., 2021; Institute of Medicine & National Research Council, 2011), and likewise the efforts by service providers working with marginalized youth that I encountered, only responded to the symptoms of youths' behaviours – those behaviours deemed to be deviating from the norms and expectations of mainstream society. I have heard corrections workers, for example, refer to substance use as the *root cause* of criminal activity; I heard comments such as 'the kids got high on drugs and caused mayhem'. In reality, likely, both the drug use and the criminal activity were responses to deeper underlying issues. Substance use, I have learned, is often a form of self-medication (Tate, 2022) – a sort of anaesthetic (Buck-Morss, 1992) used to numb the pain of youths' challenging lives. As one youth who worked with our project with street-involved youth expressed: 'A lot of us are really alone and scared and only have a crack pipe to turn to' (YUEV, 2012, 00:21:09–00:21:11).

Likewise, criminal activity is often symptomatic of socio-economic injustices. I'm reminded of a story shared by a participant during my research in the youth jail. I wrote the following dramatized version of the youth's story in a play, entitled *Athabasca's Going Unmanned* (Conrad, 2012), about my research experience:

> When I's 12 … My little brother 8 'n my sister 14 … Mom used to take off with her boyfriend, eh? They'd be gone days. No grub in the house … My sister would cry … We used to dream 'bout sometimes … cheese burgers … Sometimes I'd take my little brother to the supermarket … We'd get a cart 'n go up 'n down the isles fillin' it up with all the stuff we liked … Just like we're suppos' to be there … No one ever noticed us … Figured mom's around somewhere … When we got all we wan'ed … Pushed the cart out the door … And soon as we're around the corner we'd run like hell all the way home … *(Laughing)* We'd have all the grub we wanted for a few days … Did that so many times 'n never got caught … That was six years ago … Since then I been into every kinda crap you c'n imagine. (p. 116)

This story illustrates that what we commonly consider criminal activity is sometimes youths' only means of survival.

While there are, no doubt, youth at-risk who are white and from relatively affluent homes, research indicates and my research confirmed that social structural factors are the root causes of youths' struggles, which is particularly true for Indigenous youth. The principal factors that put youth at-risk are low socio-economic status (poverty) and racial-cultural minority status (systemic racism) (Gil-Kashiwabara et al., 2007; Lavie-Ajayi & Krumer-Nevo, 2013; Machamer & Gruber, 1998; Tanner et al., 1995). I have learned, through my experiences working with systemically marginalized youth, that they have indeed often lived much of their lives suffering the effects of intergenerational poverty and racism including abuse, neglect, substance use, violence, and crime. Take for example Indigenous gangs which pose threats to communities across Canada's prairies and often engage youth – often the younger relatives of gang members, as their front-line soldiers in committing crimes as forms of initiation into the gang and/or because youth garner lesser sentences when caught. These gangs are products of inequity; the majority of the Indigenous gangs were, in fact, founded inside prisons (Friesen & O'Neill, 2008) and recruitment and training often occur within prisons and jails. To me the co-relation between poverty, racism and criminal activity becomes painfully evident – demonstrating how toxic environments spawn resistant behaviours (Foucault, 1991).

So long as interventions to youth behaviour are only always problem-focused – addressing only the evident symptoms of youths' undesirable behaviours leaving the root causes – the structural issues, unaddressed, the challenges associated with systemically marginalized youth will not be resolved (Eichas et al., 2021). Rather, what is needed is honest social critique along with interventions directed at the structural levels of society. So long as youth, their families and communities continue to struggle under conditions of poverty inherent to our neoliberal, capitalist economy and continue to suffer from overt and systemic racism deeply ingrained in our colonial social structures, the issues associated with youths' marginalization will continue. While applied theatre research cannot address these problems directly, it can raise awareness of these injustices, as I have attempted to do through my research.

Social Change, Transformation, and Empowerment

Education and scholarship focused on social change – in particular the sort of critical pedagogical work promoted by scholars/practitioners such as Paulo Freire (1970/2000) and Augusto Boal (1974/1979), whose work I draw upon, has not been without its critics (e.g. see Bowers, 2008, from an eco-justice perspective; and Ellsworth, 1989, from a feminist perspective). Likewise, critiques around concepts such as *social change, transformation*, and *empowerment*, central to this work, are legitimate and need to be considered. An overarching critique about concepts and the terminology used to discuss them is that terms are sometimes so widely utilized that their meanings become ambiguous – they can mean whatever a speaker or author wants them to mean. I encountered this some time ago within my own Department at the University (see den Heyer & Conrad, 2011). In dialogue with my colleagues around our educational goals, it became apparent that we could not reach a consensus on what we meant by social justice, how social justice is achieved, or what role education might have in bringing about social justice.

Terms lose value if used indiscriminately and can be potentially harmful when applied uncritically. As such, the concepts of *social change, transformation*, and *empowerment* are, admittedly, grounded in western modernist/humanist traditions and need to be scrutinized. In the field of applied theatre, such terms are sometimes taken-for-granted and steeped in good intentions without adequate reflection on what they mean in practice (Freebody et al., 2018).

Social Change

Inherent to the grand narratives of western modernity is a belief in the myth of progress – that human society is ever evolving towards a more ideal future state (Wessels, 2013). The process of progress, in this view, involves a more-or-less linear trajectory of change from less than ideal towards *the ideal*. Inherent, but unspoken, within this discourse is the assumption that there is a single, universal ideal that we all can and should work towards – specifically, an ideal shaped by the colonial values of western civilization (Donald et al., 2012; Korteweg & Bissell, 2016; Tuck & Wang, 2011). Dominant theories of change are predicated on this linear view in which a *problem* is identified, interventions are planned and facilitated to overcome the problem, outcomes are evaluated based on the ways initial goals/ objectives have or have not been achieved. Such change can be seen to happen at various levels: at the micro (individual), the meso (family, community) and/or the macro (society) levels. These linear views of progress and change, however, don't seem to accurately describe the complex and messy processes of life and social interaction that we actually experience. Alternately, complexity theory (see Capra, 1983; Davis & Sumara, 2008; Diamond, 2007), based in a post-modernist paradigm, offers a useful lens for understanding complex phenomena such as social change, education, community, and applied theatre processes. Complexity theory or systems thinking posits that 'systemic change cannot be externally directed, but occurs as a result of the self-organising interactions and relationships within the system' (Durie & Wyatt, 2013, p. 174). Interactions and accompanying feedback loops create change within nested systems based on both facilitating and constraining influences. In this view, change, at all levels of the social collective, is constant, unpredictable, and inexorably interconnected. Complexity thinking offers a theory of social change that is emergent and dynamic.

It is true that definitionally, applied theatre may seem to follow a linear trajectory of progress in its focus on identifying problems and looking for solutions, but in practice, applied theatre processes are anything but linear; they are often unpredictable, messy, and chaotic (Ansloos & Wager, 2020). What, then, is applied theatre's role in creating change? If applied theatre presumes some problem to overcome, how does it avoid approaching its work and participants from a deficit perspective (Freebody et al., 2018)? What sort of change do applied theatre practitioners hope to nurture?

Change in applied theatre, as I understand it, is never presented as advancement towards a singular or prescribed solution. Rather, the pursuit of change is an exploration of expansive, as-yet unimagined possibilities – consistent with a complexity theory world-view. The problems identified are never seen as deficits that reside with/in individuals, but are seen as symptoms of unjust social conditions, the solutions to which are open for negotiation. While a project may begin with some issue to address or a general topic for exploration, because the process is dialogical in nature, in which participants are the authorities, its impacts or outcomes are unpredictable (Thompson, 2003) – change may take various forms. In applied theatre, social change always begins at the micro level, through interactions between individuals (Diamond, 2007; Gallagher, 2016; Hughes, 2013). We can hope for subtle change (shifts in perspective, new awareness, raised consciousness) as participants engage in exploration of issues relevant to them. There may be impacts within the larger community if participants share their learnings through dialogue and/or performance. I like to believe there may even be ripple effects as the new understandings of participants and/or audiences influence attitudes within the larger society, but any particular change is never guaranteed.

Transformation

Within scholarly discourses, the term *transformation* is sometimes used interchangeably with *change* (Freebody et al., 2018); for others, transformation is considered more profound – a more encompassing, more extensive, or radical sort of change. Change is described as changes in behaviours and responses, whereas transformation is considered fundamental change, in beliefs and values, for instance – a paradigm shift. Some argue that it is such individual or community-based transformations – major changes in interpersonal relations – that are needed to make any substantial social change (Diamond, 2007).

I used the language of *transformation* in my research proposal and application for funding for the applied theatre project I proposed with youth in jail. I titled the project 'The Transformative Potential of Drama in the Education of Incarcerated Youth', because it sounded impactful and perhaps spoke to the perceived urgency of change needed for this population. The research sought to avoid future negative outcomes of youths' behaviours but exactly who (the youth?) or what (the social structures?) needed transforming was deliberately left ambiguous. The grandiose title ultimately succeeded in garnering funding and access to the research site. I personally don't subscribe to distinctions made between degrees of *change* or *transformation*.

While the quest for some change or other is implied in applied theatre, I prefer to move away from the language of change altogether; I do believe, as complexity theory suggests, that change, for better and/or worse, is constant. Rather, what I seek through the applied theatre work I undertake is justice for youth – both individually and as a social group – but even this is not a straightforward goal. Justice, whatever that might look like, is not something that will be achieved through a single applied theatre project or even a lifetime of such projects. The best I hope for is that my applied theatre practice might facilitate some small steps towards greater justice for systemically marginalized youth by creating spaces and offering opportunities for them to reflect on and express their experiences – perhaps to find, claim, or re-claim their voice, agency, or power.

Empowerment

Modernist notions of *power* assume that some individuals in society have power, whereas others do not, and that there are processes by which the balance of power can be changed. It is assumed that those with greater power, which includes authority figures, experts, and professionals, can either exercise their power to dominate others or can use their power to facilitate others in vulnerable positions in gaining power. Alternately, post-structuralist notions of power (Foucault, 1994) do not understand power as necessarily good or bad; rather, power takes many forms. Power can be exercised as domination and control over others, but can also be creative and life-affirming (hooks, 1984). Whatever the form, power is not an object that one can possess (or not possess) or simply transfer to another. Poststructuralism sees power as constantly circulating within human relationships; power relations are not fixed, but fluid and dependent on context. Even those in positions of marginalization, then, always already have access to or the potential to access some forms of power, whether they recognize it or not. Individuals can and do exercise power, to greater or lesser extents, to shape their present lives and their futures, at times as resistance to more centralized forms of power (Foucault, 1991).

Those who work with vulnerable populations, such as applied theatre facilitators and/or academic researchers, are often seen to be in positions of power in relation to those with whom they work. The processes engaged in are meant to *empower* individuals, but how do we imagine this empowerment occurs and to what ends? As discussed above, progress-oriented theories of change, the myth of linear progress – from oppression to liberation or marginalization to empowerment, have been critiqued as following a western colonial logics (Donald et al., 2012; Korteweg & Bissell, 2016; Tuck & Wang, 2011), which have proven to be detrimental.

Iwasaki et al. (2014) defined *empowerment* for their research with marginalized youth as the 'means to enable youth to recognize their abilities and potentials by helping them develop the confidence to implement positive changes in their lives' (p. 324), but this definition seems to imply that the power to empower youth lies with facilitators. As an applied theatre practitioner, I contend that the most I can do is to create a set of conditions through which individuals might experience moments of what they might define as empowerment. It is up to the youth to determine for themselves if and how empowerment has occurred – for them to perhaps have envisioned some way(s) to gain greater access to power for themselves or some increased measure of control over their lives towards creating conditions for flourishing in their own lives.

I do not assert that the road from marginalization to empowerment is straightforward, definitive, or once and for all. The journey to empowerment is much more complex than that. If power is fluid, then it ebbs and flows through all our interactions. It is up to individuals to exercise power for themselves if and when they deem appropriate, within situations that allow it, and in ways relevant to them. I acknowledge that power may look and feel differently for different individuals. This power may come in the form of a greater sense of control or agency in one's life, or the power derived from a feeling of being seen and heard, or through increased confidence to act.

As applied theatre facilitators, we also need to be vigilant in reflecting on how power circulates within our own practices. Without critical reflection, our intentions to provide opportunities for others' empowerment can easily slip into exercising our will to power in ways that control, manipulate, or speak for others. We also have to be clear about the extent to which we can claim empowerment as an outcome within the constraints of the contexts in which we work. Our roles within and the expectations of the institutions within which we work might limit opportunities for empowerment, as might the restricted timeframes within which we engage participants. Moreover, our practices will always exist within larger social structures that may continue to disempower others (McLaughlin, 2016).

Social change, transformation, and empowerment are claimed to be amongst the goals of applied theatre, but how do we know if our work has achieved these? Of all the projects I describe in this book, formal evaluation of the impacts or outcomes of the work was only ever undertaken for one project. For the project with street-involved youth, an evaluation of outcomes for service providers was conducted by an external evaluation service (Evaluation & Research Services [E&RS], 2011) and an evaluation of youth outcomes (YUEV, 2012) was conducted by a sub-group of the youth who were active participants throughout the process. I include findings from these evaluations throughout the book. Other claims that I make about potential impacts or outcomes of the research are anecdotal based on my observations, on my interpretations of the work we produced together, and on our conversations. In any case, for any of the projects I discuss, I do not claim that any particular change, transformation, or empowerment occurred. I do not believe that as a facilitator or researcher there is any way to know for certain that/if such elusive, unmeasurable expectations have ever been met. It is only the participants themselves who might be able to attest to what effects the work might have had for them – perhaps within the immediate process of doing the work, or perhaps only retrospectively. I do raise the hope that the potential for empowerment may have been present through youths' participation in applied theatre, whether in a moment of invigoration resulting from performance or through a seed planted that might manifest into a youth claiming more power, control, and agency in their lives (Hughes, 2013).

The Power of Performance

Critical performance studies scholars (Conquergood, 1985, 1998; Fabian, 1990; Turner, 1982) understand rituals (weddings, funerals, etc.), games, sports, storytelling, as well as moments of conflict in everyday life, everyday interactions, the performances of social roles, and performative speech acts (Austin, 1975), as instances of cultural performance. Human interactions, it has been argued, are always performative (de Certeau, 1984; Schechner, 1985, 2003; Turner, 1986) as we adapt and shift our roles and expressions of self appropriate to different contexts and with different people. In this way, performance is an inherent part of our everyday lives and a natural way for us to explore our identities, realities, and make meaning of the world.

The arts and particularly theatre in representing everyday cultural performances are all about power and politics in the interpersonal domain (e.g. CBC Radio, 2020). The radio program cited above quoted *New York Times* theatre editor Heller: 'What makes theatre inherently political is that it's an art of conversation and it's an art of being in a room watching people talk to each other and work issues out' (para. 4). Similarly, Alrutz (2013) suggested, 'the collaborative and interactive nature of theatre works to construct and perform relationships between self, others and society' (p. 46). An exploration of human relationships and the power dynamics always circulating within those relationships – a micro-politics – is the heart of theatre whether or not larger political issues are addressed. Theatre makes power and relations of power visible, whether through process drama exercises in classrooms, in the production of plays, or in applied theatre within community settings. Relationships of power, always complex and fluid, are dramatic themes for exploration.

With power explicit in acts of performance, in both the content of theatrical explorations and inherent to the processes involved, performance becomes a powerful medium for learning about ourselves and society – through exploring power dynamics between people and the structures of power circulating all around us. Youth involved in applied theatre processes, then, are engaged in meaning-making, in cultural production (Gaztembide-Fernandez, 2013), in storying and re-storying their lives, in creating counter-stories that rehearse potential approaches they might take into their everyday lives (Gallagher & Rodricks, 2017b; Lavie-Ajayi & Krumer-Nevo, 2013). In these ways, applied theatre adheres to the precepts of critical pedagogy – to Freire's (1970/2000) notion of reading the *world* in order to transform it. Freire believed that education was never neutral, but like applied theatre involved politics, art, and knowledge. I further discuss the empowering potential of applied theatre for youth in Chapter 6 and the potential role of applied theatre in social change, for social justice in Chapter 8.

Concluding Introductory Thoughts

To conclude this chapter, I offer a few thoughts on my aspirations for this book overall. My aim is for this book to offer insights for academics engaged in applied theatre research, in education, and/or in other youth work disciplines, and for applied theatre practitioners within various contexts with an interest in working with systemically marginalized youth. The book may also have relevance for drama education instructors in higher education and/or for high-school drama teachers with an interest in applied theatre. I expect that the chapters will have varying relevance for different readers as some chapters focus more on practical considerations while others are more theoretically oriented.

In the chapters that follow, I draw on the applied theatre research projects I undertook throughout my academic career to explore considerations and processes for working with systemically marginalized youth populations through applied theatre. In this chapter, I have introduced myself and discussed some key concepts related to the work described throughout the book. In Chapter 2, I will discuss considerations for accessing systemically marginalized youth populations and sustaining their engagement within an applied theatre project. Chapter 3 looks at applied theatre processes that I have found productive with this population. In Chapter 4, I discuss how my applied theatre processes were adapted specifically for the context of incarceration. In Chapter 5, I look at my experiences working with Indigenous youth through applied theatre. Chapter 6, at the heart of the book, examines the dynamics inherent to drama/theatre processes by which applied theatre might offer youth moments of empowerment and thereby supporting advocacy by and for youth. Chapter 7 explores some of the tensions I encountered and the ethical considerations that must be pondered when conducting such work. Finally, in Chapter 8, I offer concluding reflections on how, over my twenty years of deeply engaging in this work, I have come to see the potential of applied theatre research as a form of vital social performance.

I am honoured by the opportunities I have had to facilitate youths' engagement with applied theatre throughout my academic career. When I first began my faculty position many years ago, I recall a colleague asking me if I was sure that an academic career was right for me. Based on my doctoral work, he knew I was interested in the practice of applied theatre with youth. I assured him (and myself) that I would be able to build a research program that would allow me to do applied theatre work while simultaneously engaging with it academically. It has not been a straightforward journey, nor has it been without its challenges. I am left wondering, now, towards the end of my career, if my research has had any impact. I have to believe that my work has had some, albeit possibly fleeting, positive outcomes for the youth involved, and that my writing about the work may have some lasting value for other applied theatre facilitators, as well as for educators, researchers, and youth workers – amongst whom, conventionally, 'programs and services have generally been designed *for* youth as opposed to *with* youth' (Blanchet-Cohen & Salazar, 2009, p. 6, emphasis added). I am pleased that my research program has been possible.

In the chapters that follow, I focus on both the applied theatre strategies I employed and the youths' perspectives that emerged through our work together. I hope that the text will provide food for thought as well as practical advice for all those who work with systemically marginalized youth.

2

Engaging Systemically Marginalized Youth in Applied Theatre Research

I want to dive into my discussion of applied theatre work with systemically marginalized youth with an acknowledgement that everything I share in this book is based on my limited personal experience as an applied theatre facilitator and researcher with youth in the Northern Alberta region. As applied theatre is highly context dependent and every context is distinct, my claims may or may not apply to other contexts. Yet, I hope that my experience has given me some insights that might be valuable for others. As my primary discipline is Education, many of the examples and anecdotes I share are from high-school settings. I also draw on my experiences working with incarcerated youth and with street-involved youth, which included many Indigenous youth from the area.

It will become evident through my discussion that follows that attempting applied theatre work with systemically marginalized youth is not for the faint of heart; it is fraught with challenges (e.g. see Blight, 2015; Smyth & Eaton-Erickson, 2009; Wager, 2015). However, as seasoned applied theatre practitioner Thompson (2003) noted, 'applied theatre thrives on the barriers, the compromises, the problems, the delays, the setbacks and the restrictions. These are what make the practice, not what breaks it … we should welcome the fraught, dirty and difficult nature of applied theatre' (p. 145).

A Reality Check: What You Might Expect

I presume that some of what I share here in terms of expectations when working with marginalized youth will resonate with the experiences of others who have done similar work, but I don't presume to speak to all contingencies. The *reality check* I offer may conform, more or less, to other/others' realities.

Systemically marginalized youth exist within our school systems, in our jails, and on our streets. They are by definition overlooked, often invisible, but make no mistake, they are there, often in the most unlikely of places. I remember an undergraduate student I taught early in my career at the University of Alberta in the teacher education program. He was a mature student, so he came with considerable life experiences already. He was from a small Alberta town and had plans to move to a rural community to teach within the Catholic school system. He complained when I spent some of our class time together talking about my research with so-called at-risk youth. As he wasn't expecting to encounter any at-risk youth where he was going, he deemed my insights irrelevant. Just a few months into his teaching career, however, he e-mailed me to tell me about what he was encountering. A student in his small rural Alberta Catholic school had committed suicide; the tragic stories of that youth's life and the lives of other youth in the community began coming to light. He was distraught by the difficult realities faced by the youth he was teaching. I was saddened, but not surprised.

Systemically marginalized youth may be the quiet sulky ones; they are quiet, perhaps, because they don't want to draw attention to themselves. The student who falls asleep in class or never finishes their homework, we label lazy or unmotivated. They may be falling asleep in class, however, because they've been up all night caring for their younger siblings while their parents are at work or because their sleep is disrupted by their parents' all-night partying (one of our projects created a scene about this) if they have homes to go to at all. They may not complete their homework because they're busy attending to their survival needs – working or scavenging to feed themselves or looking for someplace to sleep that night. (I met a youth who was finishing high school while sleeping in a tent year-round.) Alternatively, these youth may be the ones who are aggressive and act out. We label them trouble-makers, the bad kids. Who knows what is going on with them in life. They may be acting out because they are physically, sexually or psychologically abused at home or on the street, or just plain angry that life has dealt them such an unjust hand. I would be angry too. The most tragic case that I encountered during my work with this youth population was that of a 12-year-old girl whose mother's addiction led to abuse too horrible to detail here. It's hard to imagine a child having to survive such circumstances. Some youth who are mistreated in these ways by those very adults who are meant to care for them and/or youth who suffer other sorts of life struggles turn to alcohol or drugs as a form of self-medication (Tate, 2022), to help them numb the pain of their harsh realities. Substance use in such cases is not *the problem*, but *a solution* to their problems albeit temporary and ultimately detrimental.

For the project I facilitated with street-involved youth, it was often the case that youth had left their family homes due to poverty, abuse, and/or their parents' intolerance of their lifestyles – their gender identification or sexual orientation, for example – the situation at home being so untenable that leaving was the best option, if they hadn't actually been kicked out (e.g. see Ansloos & Wager, 2020; Ottaway et al., 2009). The youth found themselves without secure housing, on the streets or struggling to make a home for themselves and sometimes for their own young children too. While not all of the youth I worked with over the years displayed all of the characteristics ascribed to the most vulnerable youth (Smyth & Eaton-Erickson, 2009) they were, tragically, all too common.

All that said, it's important to note that not all youth who are unmotivated, prone to causing trouble or taking drugs, are systemically marginalized; likewise, not all systemically marginalized youth are unmotivated, cause trouble, or take drugs. Without making unwarranted assumptions, as facilitators we need to keep in mind the harsh realities of some youths' lives – realities that are sometimes beyond our worst imaginings. We must be prepared to respond to such realities if we wish to engage youth through applied theatre.

Accessing Systemically Marginalized Youth Populations

Accessing any youth population for applied theatre work can be challenging as youth generally constitute an underserved or gatekept group. Access is even more challenging when the youth are amongst those marginalized by our society. These youths' lives are precarious; they are often transient and understandably preoccupied with other things such as their survival. Often, for good reason, they have grave distrust of adults and institutions (Ansloos & Wager, 2020; Gallagher, 2016; Iwasaki et al., 2014; Sapiro & Ward, 2020). For the projects I facilitated, I depended on adult care-givers/administrators/gate-keepers already working with the youth in some capacity to negotiate access. Those adults who successfully work with these youth populations and have built trust with them are justifiably protective of the youth; they won't allow just anyone to interact with them because naïve or negative attitudes on the part of short-term facilitators can do more harm than good. So, to access these youth there is often a period of having to prove oneself required (Lavie-Ajayi & Krumer-Nevo, 2013) – along with clear articulation of one's motivations that align with those of the collaborating individuals/organizations.

In Chapter 1, I shared my story of potentially being *at-risk* as a teenager and of my realization that this is what motivated my research interests. This personal history, which I shared openly in my doctoral research and when/as appropriate with those adult care-giver administrators/gate-keepers with whom I sought to negotiate access (and later with youth), went some way in giving me a small measure of insider status towards understanding and being sensitive to the experiences of the youth with whom I was proposing to work. As well as sharing my personal experiences, I was explicit (again, as appropriate) about my socially critical perspective of the contexts of these youths' lives. I was always clear that I did not place blame on the youth for their circumstances, but was seeking to better understand the social structural circumstances that led to their marginalization. I was interested in researching with youth towards seeking solutions – not for ways for youth to better fit within existing societal norms, but for ways for society to better accommodate the needs of the youth.

Below, I briefly describe each of the applied theatre projects I facilitated – which I discuss in more detail throughout the book, in terms of what it took to gain access to the youth in order to illustrate the effort required. To facilitate accessibility for the reader, I have included an appendix (see Appendix 1) with an overview of each of the five applied theatre research projects I discuss in terms of focus, location, and the participants involved. The reader can refer to these descriptions as reminders of each projects' details as they are mentioned if they so desire.

Five Applied Theatre Research Projects

When researching in schools – as schools regularly receive requests to do research, there are usually processes in place for accessing students. When I began my graduate research in Education, I sought to access potentially at-risk high-school students. New to Alberta, I worked with my supervisors at the University, who knew school principals and teachers, to assist me in finding the sites suitable to my interests. For my master's research, I worked in an alternative inner-city high school with two small groups of students new to the school as part of their orientation period. I negotiated with the school's administrators to find a fit between my research interests and the needs of the school. My work with these students took place over two four-day intensive sessions. These students had dropped out or been pushed out of their regular high schools and attended this school in hopes of completing their programs. I designed an applied theatre project focused on media studies for which students earned Career and Technology Studies (Alberta Education, 2009) credits in media production.

For my doctoral research, I opted for an Alberta high school in a rural, northern community. The school served students from the small municipality as well as Indigenous students from several Cree reserves in the area. I spent one month living in the rural community and worked every weekday with two drama classes to explore with students their experiences that might have deemed them at-risk. While I knew that not all the students in those drama classes would be at-risk,

I expected there might be some whose experiences resonated with the sorts of experiences I was interested in exploring and I was not mistaken.

Following the school projects, since the youth in schools had told me that schools were sometimes like prison for them, I sought to work with incarcerated youth. I thought if there was ever a place where I would be certain to find youth at-risk it would surely be in jail. I wondered what applied theatre could offer them. For a pilot study, a colleague and I contacted the facilitator of the Community Transitions Program at a young offender centre in the region. She was happy to have us come in once a week over a six-month period to work with the youth as part of her program. Subsequently, as a newly employed faculty member at the University, negotiating access for a longer three-year federally funded study took an entire year. I began by speaking with the facility's head administrator who was highly sceptical of applied theatre research and unwilling to allow me to proceed. She was afraid that the loosely structured and spontaneous nature of applied theatre would *raise issues* that the facility's staff would be unable to control. They seemed to be more concerned with security – with keeping a lid on the pot, than they were in offering the youth opportunities for educational programming. The programming that was available to the youth at the centre was, for the most part, prescriptive and generic – rather than engaging and personally relevant. As one youth later told me, the Anger Management program he was pressured to attend just made him mad!

Unsatisfied with the initial rejection of my proposed research, I went to the Alberta Government's Office of the Solicitor General, the body that would ultimately have to approve my research in any case, to see if I'd have better luck there. It was fortunate for me that the person in charge of correctional services for youth was sympathetic. He had a family member doing a PhD in Education at the time so he understood the nature of educational research, trusted my motivations, and saw value in the work I was proposing. Nevertheless, it took several meetings with him to work through details of the project followed by conversations between him and the centre's administrator and more meetings between the administrator and me to convince her to allow me in. Once receiving approval at these two levels, I still needed an existing program willing to partner with me. The corrections worker who ran the centre's Native Program expressed interest in my proposal. This individual, a Métis woman, was happy to have me come in to work with interested youth as part of her after school extra-curricular program. Her ongoing efforts and support allowed for a productive applied theatre project. It was delightful to work alongside her for weekly visits over three years. Underlying tensions with the administration continued, however, and erupted from time to time when, for instance, they heard about issues raised through our work that they deemed potentially disruptive. Challenges similar to those I encountered in working within a youth carceral institution are echoed in the literature (Kaplan, 2022; Lamparter, 2022; Tate, 2022).

The project I conducted with the organization serving street-involved youth was the project for which my values and commitments and those of the partner organization were best aligned. Gaining access to this youth population, however, took a good ten years of community-building efforts. Shortly after arriving in Alberta, I learned about this Edmonton arts-based, non-profit organization. I was impressed by the success they were having supporting a challenging population and excited by the art the youth were producing. I began attending public events that the organization advertised, visiting their facility and talking with staff. Slowly, I got to know key staff members. I shared some of my previous research with two of the organization's outreach workers who recognized and appreciated the alignment between our efforts. Eventually, I also joined the organization's board of directors, where I served in the role of secretary for a number of years.

During my time with this organization, I proposed a research study, which the organization approved, but for which our application for funding was unsuccessful. A short time thereafter, one of their founders and primary outreach worker approached me with an idea for a project. Based on his experiences and the experiences of a social worker with whom he worked closely, he identified the need to educate service providers who worked with the youth about the youths' experiences; of course, I suggested we do so through applied theatre. The service provider groups we targeted included social workers, educators, healthcare providers, law enforcement officials, etc. – those who were positioned to regularly provide support for or engage with the youth. It was ideal, for the success and sustainability of the project, that it was initiated by leaders in the organization. We began the project based on the identified urgent need, then applied for funding and fortunately were successful.

A Note on Ethics Review

For academic research within a university context in Canada, rigorous ethics review by an internal committee is always required to ensure that participants are not harmed, that any potential minimal discomfort or inconvenience is appropriately mitigated and to ensure at least some tangible benefit for participants – and rightly so. Canadian research university ethics review boards are regulated by the Government of Canada's Tri-Council Panel on Research Ethics which lays out policies for ethical conduct for research involving humans as well as other types of research. Additionally, some school boards, government organizations, and community groups have their own formal ethics review processes. The Office of the Solicitor General, for example, administered an ethics review prior to granting me approval to proceed with my research in the youth jail.

For research involving youth, it is not policy, per se, but common practice, especially in working with youth in institutional contexts such as schools, that youth 18 years of age and older are considered adults, and therefore can give consent for their participation in research, whereas youth under 18 can give assent for their participation with consent ultimately required from a parent or guardian. The youth I worked with across all projects ranged from ages 12 to 24, with the majority being 16–18 years old, so for youth participants under the age of 18 parental/guardian consent was required. Such consent, however, was sometimes challenging to acquire as many of the youths' contacts with the adults in their lives were tentative. For the Uncensored project, for example, several of the youth with whom we worked were in care with our social worker collaborator as their guardian, so he could provide consent. I mention all this here, as ethics approval is part of the process of gaining access for research with marginalized youth that also takes time and careful consideration. Formal ethical oversight is important and time consuming.

Terms of Engagement

Attending to Youths' Needs

Maslow's (1943) hierarchy of needs, not inconsistent with more recent assets-based research in youth development (e.g. see Granger, 2002), which attempted to understand motivations for human behaviour, posited that individuals will focus on meeting their primary needs before progressing to more advanced needs. The foundational level of Maslow's hierarchy pyramid begins with physiological needs (air, water, food, shelter, sleep, clothing) and safety needs (personal security, employment, resources, health) as an individual's most basic needs that must be met. It then moves on to the need for love and belonging (friendship, intimacy, family, sense of connection), then esteem (respect, self-esteem, status, recognition, strength, freedom), and finally, at the pinnacle of the pyramid is the need for self-actualization (the desire to become the most one can be). Many systemically marginalized youth don't have even their most basic needs met on a consistent basis. This is where engaging systemically marginalized youth in any project must begin. Without first meeting their basic needs, youth won't be able to fully engage in other activities (Ansloos & Wager, 2020; Ottaway et al., 2009; Tate, 2022).

In the alternative high-school setting in which I facilitated my master's project, the school staff were very attentive to ensuring youth were supported with meals while at school and assisted them with accessing services that provided other necessities such as housing, healthcare, transportation, etc. The students in the rural Alberta high school had relatively stable home lives, so their subsistence needs, as far as I was aware, were met. In the youth jail, the youths' housing and meals were, as a matter of course, covered. I made a point of bringing in snacks each time I visited as a small show of my appreciation and as reciprocation for the youths' participation.

The non-profit youth organization's objectives, along with providing arts programming, involved supporting all of the youths' needs from food and transportation, to assistance with accessing services related to employment, housing, healthcare, legal aid, etc., to timely crisis intervention and beyond. This level of wrap-around support for the youth continued throughout our applied theatre research project, which was supplementary to the organizations' regular programming. We invited youth to come to my studio at the University each week for our sessions. Since we were successful in garnering funding, we directed the majority of those funds to the youth. We successfully petitioned the University's ethics board that small honoraria for youths' participation were appropriate, since their attendance at our sessions would take them away from otherwise attending to their needs; we offered youth $15 per hour for each session they attended (Ansloos & Wager, 2020). We also provided food each week along with bus tickets or transportation to and from the University, and child care as needed. The project also earned income by charging service provider groups who booked the workshops we offered and these funds were divided amongst the youth who performed. (I provide further details about these workshops in sections to come.)

Along with meeting some of youths' basic needs, youth also received support from facilitators. For the Uncensored project, our team of facilitators included two of the organization's outreach workers, a social worker from Child and Family Services, graduate students in psychology and arts education (whom we employed as project manager, and research assistants) and volunteers, all of whom worked alongside me. These trained and experienced individuals were always available to support the youth as needed. On one occasion, for example, a young woman who worked with the project had a run-in with campus security. Having apparently been *banned* from campus due to some earlier incident, she was accused of trespassing. She came to us with campus security in tow distraught that she would no longer be allowed to participate. This instigated our writing of a letter to campus security on the youth's behalf, in which we confirmed the youths' active participation in our project and questioned the ethics of banning a young person from a public institution of learning. Our letter successfully advocated for the youth's continued attendance on campus.

On other occasions during the project, a youth would sometimes arrive at a session in crisis (e.g. in a manic mental state; in a rage over a dispute with another youth; having just had their child taken away by social services; having suffered physical abuse by a partner; or having just been kicked out of their residential placement) (see also Hughes, 2013). As an applied theatre facilitator, I would not have been able to deal with such crises on my own. In these instances, the presence of professionals trained in crisis intervention was critical. Likewise, in doing applied theatre around potentially sensitive topics, there was always the possibility that issues could have arisen that might have triggered distressing or volatile responses, in which case, having trained professionals on standby was also essential.

The project facilitators served as mentors for the youth and the youth involved also formed bonds with each other, all of whom became part of their support network towards fulfilling Maslow's (1943) need for belonging. The following youth comment from the youth evaluation video (YUEV, 2012) for the Uncensored project indicated the sense of connection and belonging that the project offered them:

> I've gotten so many awesome mentors out of the Uncensored group that I'm so thankful for and it's totally enriched my life. Everyone in Uncensored is my friend. They're like a family now to me. Those guys are awesome. I look forward to coming here every week. It's something I'm so thankful to have in my life. (00:32:37–00:33:10)

These were some of the ways we attended to youths' physiological needs and beyond. Arguably, the street-involved youths' participation in our project provided them a limited opportunity for some support and income towards meeting their basic needs. More importantly, perhaps, as I hope to illustrate through this book, for all the projects I will discuss, youths' engagement – through working communally and positioning the youth as experts regarding the issues we were exploring, the applied theatre work offered them some sense of belonging as well as recognition and self-esteem on the road to self-actualization.

Building Trust

As I mentioned earlier, systemically marginalized youth, often for good reason based on their prior experiences, are distrusting of adults. Any hope of facilitating a successful applied theatre project requires at least some measure of trust. The time it takes to build trust with these youth and the value gained through taking the time needed to do so should not be underestimated (Barton-Farcas, 2022;

Blanchet-Cohen & Salazar, 2009; Gil-Kashiwabara et al., 2007; Kaplan, 2022; Sapiro & Ward, 2020; Tate, 2022). Gaining access through existing institutions/ organizations and programs offered me openings for building that essential trust. For my projects, the schools' teachers, the jail's program coordinators, and the youth organization's outreach workers were vital for making introductions to the youth and assuring them that I might be someone to whom they could extend an iota of trust. The adult collaborators' participation alongside me for of all the projects was vital.

My early interactions with each of the groups of youth always involved a period of presenting myself to them in sincere and humble ways. Power differentials between the youth and me – between youth/adult, student/teacher-researcher, incarcerated/free-to-leave-the-facility, street-involved youth/employed, middle-class professional – could never be entirely evaded, neutralized, or transcended (D'Arcangelis, 2018), and it's essential to acknowledge that this was so. Nevertheless, some measures could be taken to mitigate, in small ways, some of those divides.

In my work in schools, I was never their *teacher*, but only a visiting academic/ graduate student and applied theatre facilitator. I negotiated with the schools, consistent with university ethical expectations, to ensure that the projects I facilitated did not involve my formal assessment of students' work. In the young offender centre, I was not their jailer nor judge. I assured the youth that I would not think less of them for anything they chose to share through our work together. On the contrary, I was interested in learning about their experiences and perspectives and in supporting them in any way I could. My work was intended to educate others about and advocate for youth in their circumstances (Arteaga & Chavez-Arteaga, 2022; Barton-Farcas, 2022; Lavie-Ajayi & Krumer-Nevo, 2013).

I was always very open about my motivations for my work and about me personally, to the extent that this was appropriate. I remember during my doctoral study at the rural Alberta high school, I told the students about my interest in and previous work with marginalized youth, though I deliberately avoided using the label at-risk so as not to overly direct the discussion from the outset. One of the students suggested that I had an interest in working with what he termed *bad-asses*, implying that I had come there in search of bad-asses too. When I asked the students if they were bad-asses, some said no, but many were proud to lay claim to that identifier, responding enthusiastically that yes, they were *bad*! I confessed that I had been a bit of a bad-ass as a youth myself. However, when they asked me how bad I had been, as a novice researcher, I was afraid of disclosing too much; I still clung to some of my assumed authority. Nevertheless, my hint at having been *bad* as a youth was enough to open the way for them to share some of their bad experiences, always in fictionalized form, however thinly veiled, during our applied theatre process. Subsequently, I was at times more candid with youth about my prior experiences, which I came to realize had been relatively tame when compared with some of theirs.

Building trust between youth and an applied theatre facilitator – perhaps more productively described as working to develop a relationship as an ally or accomplice (Indigenous Action Media, 2014) with the youth – is never a given and never absolute. It takes time to prove oneself through consistently supportive behaviour and through living up to any promises made. Trust has to be built individual by individual from the ground up and maintained throughout a project.

Equally essential is building trust amongst the youth themselves. There is no guarantee that the youth in any group will trust each other. I learned that we should not delude ourselves with visions of pre-existing trusting and caring communities amongst youth, whether in a classroom setting or on the streets. There may be underlying tensions amongst individuals based on their prior experiences. The pre-service teachers in my classes often come with a desire to create idyllic *safe spaces* in the drama classrooms they will teach based on their (mostly white middle-class students) own high-school drama experiences. Literature from the perspectives of marginalized others (e.g. racialized, Indigenous, LGBTQ+), however, tells us that entirely safe spaces are an illusion (Anzaldúa, 2002). We can only hope to create *safer* spaces through community-building efforts and ongoing, open dialogue. I advise my pre-service teachers to aim instead for creating *brave spaces* (Arao & Clemens, 2013) where honest and challenging conversations can be had across differences.

I've occasionally encountered long-standing and deeply held grudges amongst certain youth within a group that were not necessarily apparent from the outset. These are almost impossible to overcome within the context of a project – beyond the realm of what a project can or perhaps should attempt to tackle. Yet, such circumstances need to be mitigated, somehow. It's possible that agreements can be reached to temporarily set aside beefs in order for the work to proceed. Youth will sometimes self-select in or out of a project or a session based on who else is in the room. Adults who know the youth well can help to dispel conflict or de-escalate conflict if it arises. I witnessed this once when an outreach worker had to leap across a table to pre-empt a fist fight, when one youth told an unfavourable story in which another youth's cousin was implicated. Another time, we learned after the fact, a youth had brought a knife to the session and was prepared to use it if another youth had been in attendance.

There are never guarantees that trust can be built or maintained throughout a project. It requires open communication and ongoing processes for checking in with all those involved. When trust is broken, it needs to be re-built. I remember an occasion in the youth jail when I overheard two youth talking about their sports program. They exchanged stories about how rough the corrections worker/sports program coordinator was with them while playing indoor hockey. They detailed a litany of injuries they'd endured, caused by him. Naively perhaps, I felt that this was something I was obligated to report. My notification to the administration gave rise to an investigation, which the youth interpreted as me jeopardizing their highly valued sports program. The Native Program coordinator generously intervened on my behalf to ensure the youth that I had had the best of intentions in caring for their well-being. I apologized to the youth for interfering, promised to mind my own business, and thankfully all was forgiven.

Non-Judgement

Vital to building trust with youth is the need to extend them a non-judgmental attitude (Blanchet-Cohen & Salazar, 2009; Iwasaki et al., 2014; Linds et al., 2013; Ottaway et al., 2009; Santiago-Jirau, 2022; Sapiro & Ward, 2020), which is counter to how marginalized youths' lifestyle predicaments are commonly perceived. For instance, many organizations that serve youth have strict policies about substance use – specifically, they disallow any drug or alcohol use on site and/or do not allow youths' participation if they are under the influence of any substances. This is certainly the case in schools, where the banning of substance use is almost taken-for-granted and perhaps rightly so given the nature of these public institutions in serving the needs of a broad cross-section of society. This, however, doesn't stop youth from coming to school under the influence or even indulging in substance use at school. (In high school, I frequently indulged during my spare period in the middle of a day.) If caught, youth suffer dire consequences such as suspension or expulsion from school and/or involvement with the criminal justice system. In Chapter 3, I share a scene created with high-school drama students which speaks precisely to this point.

Even community-based organizations serving youth often explicitly declare their prohibition of substance use. I recently encountered a teen drop-in program whose rules for participation stated: *No drugs, no thugs*, associating substance use with criminal activity. (Such criminalization of youth behaviour is something the youth in jail commented on in a scene we created, which I share in Chapter 4.) Such policies, which pass judgement on youth behaviour, likely pre-empt any engagement by systemically marginalized youth – those perhaps most in need of such programs. In any case, it is often not the substance use itself that creates problems, rather, the effects of particular substances (e.g. alcohol vs. cannabis) combined with confrontation by adults that lead to undesirable responses.

The youth organization that I worked with for the Uncensored project, I feel, took the right approach in relation to youths' substance use. Their practice was informed by the philosophy of harm reduction (Canadian AIDS Society & Canadian Harm Reduction Network, 2008; Mate, 2008; Smyth & Eaton-Erikson, 2009), which focuses on preventing harm, rather than an all-or-nothing eradication of undesired behaviours and is particularly relevant in addressing issues of addictions with youth (MacMaster, 2004; Poulin, 2006). The organization certainly didn't encourage or openly allow substance use at their facility, but neither did they maintain a no-drugs policy. They did not turn youth away if they arrived under the influence, so long as they were there for legitimate reasons, were working productively, and/or not disrupting others from doing so. If the need arose to address an individual's substance use, that was done on a case-by-case basis. Rather than making general assumptions or judgements about youths' substance use, as needed they worked to address the youth's issues underlying their substance use, or if necessary arranged for admission to a drug detox or rehab program. Systemically marginalized youth sought and received this organization's much-needed services and attended their programs because they knew they would not be judged. The practice of not judging youths' behaviours, which our applied theatre project also adopted, extended to other areas of the youths' lives as well. We understood substance use, criminal activity, disconnection from family, and so on, not as qualities inherent to youth but as symptoms of systemic oppressions which led to their life challenges (Eichas et al., 2021; Sapiro & Ward, 2020).

Similarly, in our work with youth in jail, youth were never judged based on whatever prior actions may have led to their incarceration. I recall, during the first instance I worked with incarcerated youth for our pilot project, when we happened to learn that one of our most friendly and enthusiastic participants had perpetrated a horrendous crime that had been reported in all its gory detail in the local papers. I was initially deeply shocked. It took some time for me to reconcile the pleasant young man we had met with his crime. When we returned to the facility the week following, I was unsure how I would react to seeing the youth again, but once in his presence, the smiling, playful youth before us took precedence; it was this individual young man who claimed our care and attention, not the criminal actions he had committed. The crime was something he had done – under some set of circumstances that we could not fathom; this was not who he was while engaged in our applied theatre process.

Marginalized youths' behaviours are regularly judged by the adults they encounter. As one service provider who participated in our workshop evaluation of the Uncensored project admitted: 'I, as I am sure many people are, am guilty of judging a youth by how they look … assuming that they are only going to give me grief' (E&RS, 2011, p. 16). Youths' life challenges are compounded by the social stigma they face associated with their behaviours, feeding into a detrimental cycle. Extending a non-judgmental attitude, then, is absolutely essential for engaging meaningfully with systemically marginalized youth in any context.

Flexible Expectations

Related to being non-judgmental is the need for flexible expectations and processes – the need to give up control and respond to the context when working with systemically marginalized youth (Blanchet-Cohen & Salazar, 2009; Blight, 2015; Hughes, 2013; Kaplan, 2022). Schools, other institutions, and even families often have fairly rigid expectations to which youth are expected to adhere and which they commonly rebel against. I recall the lengths I went to as a youth to work around such expectations. In working with youth already marginalized by institutionalized structures, to engage them in an applied theatre project that hopes to mitigate their marginalization, applying rigid expectations would be counter-productive, even oppressive. In my research, I always attempted, as best I could within the given context, to allow youths' engagement on their own terms.

In the school settings and especially in the youth jail, in which I worked, many expectations were already definitively set in place. Such institutional expectations as well as cramping youths' style often constrain the freedom of expression needed for effective applied theatre processes too. I had to, in order to work within those institutional settings, of course abide by their expectations or at least only subvert them in innocuous ways. This was another reason the work with the non-profit youth organization, which had more fluid expectations, was more successful.

Even as a young high-school teacher, I rebelled against schools' norms. Rather than have students call me Ms. Conrad, as expected by the school for the authority it implied, I preferred just being Diane to them. I knew students were on my side when they called me Ms. Conrad in front of the principal and other teachers and just Diane when we were alone. I also found it challenging to enforce *no swearing* rules or *no hat* rules at school because I found such rules arbitrary at best, and downright classist and colonizing at worst. No swearing rules, for example, very common in public school settings, perpetuate certain values which may or may not correspond with the values of the youths' families or communities. While middle-class parents may very well teach their children not to swear, we can't assume that these values are shared by all our students' families. Some parents themselves might use language deemed unacceptable by schools. I always felt it unconscionable to ask students to mind their language, when their parents might be using that same language at home; it felt as though I was telling students their parents were unacceptable by school standards. It's no wonder that such students might be resistant to schooling. Alternately, I developed a nuanced approach to language use in my classrooms, which I also used in my applied theatre facilitation. I made a distinction between using swear words to emphatically express oneself or using swears appropriately within the context of a drama scenario, versus swearing at someone, deemed verbal abuse or hate speech, which was never acceptable under any circumstances.

Expectations for youth engagement in the applied theatre projects I facilitated were always flexible. I encouraged youth to participate to the extent and in the ways they felt comfortable (Blight, 2015; Santiago-Jirau, 2022). As a facilitator, I always had an agenda of work to accomplish for each session, to which we would more or less adhere based on how the youth present that day were feeling. Just being physically present was enough of an accomplishment for some youth at times. It's important to note here that regular attendance at applied theatre sessions with systemically marginalized youth is not a given (Blight, 2015; Gallagher, 2016; Hughes, 2013; Wager, 2015). This would be highly problematic in most mainstream theatre contexts where each participant is given a particular role (with possibly an understudy in place) such that the work would be unable to proceed effectively if one or more individual were absent. Even youth who had wholeheartedly committed to participating, due to the precariousness of their lives, were regularly drawn away from attending, often due to circumstances beyond their control. For example, a youth's long-standing medical appointment might have been suddenly re-scheduled, with no one having bothered to consult the youth about their timetable on the assumption the youth would not be doing anything important.

A marginalized youth's attendance at school might be sporadic as days are missed or classes skipped. Even in the youth jail, amongst a literally captive audience, attendance at our sessions was unpredictable. A youth might unexpectedly have gotten released or transferred. If a youth had been involved in some violation or had accumulated a number of minor infractions that week (they were assessed on a daily point system for behaviour that awarded or revoked privileges), they might have been dorm confined or prohibited from attending extra-curricular activities as punishment (Kaplan, 2022; Tate, 2022). In my work with the youth organization, attendance fluctuated from up to 25 youth at any given session, to as low as five or six. For all the projects I facilitated, our processes had to accommodate for irregular attendance and for other anticipated or unanticipated contingencies. I discuss some of these accommodations in describing details of specific projects throughout.

Through all of our work together, I knew the youth were capable, resilient, and resourceful but I always kept my expectations minimal to avoid adding stress to their already challenging lives. Ideally, youth would have participated fully in all aspects of our processes; however, circumstances demanded flexibility regarding their engagement to maximize the benefit for them. For the Uncensored project with street-involved youth, for example, if a youth was present, but not up to following our agenda for that day, we welcomed them to just observe or engage in other related creative activities of their choosing such as drawing or writing. We always had materials available and also made space for them to share with the group if they wanted. We accepted that youth might be there just for socializing, or just for the honoraria money, or for the food (Tate, 2022), as even these forms of engagement met their needs within a positive environment. Our hope was that if they weren't pressured, they might choose to engage further on their own terms when they were ready, as was the case with one youth who described his initial experience thus:

> How I got involved with Uncensored was my friend invited me. This is when everybody used to be part of Uncensored. I thought, well I've got nothing else to do on a Tuesday, might as well check it out. So, I went to check it out. I liked it. The first time it was kind of annoying because there were so many people. Everyone was being really loud. I didn't know what to do. I started drawing. (YUEV, 2012, 00:09:59–00:10:20)

This youth eventually did join in our theatre devising, became a core performer, and took part in the project evaluation. Flexible strategies prioritized benefits for youth over the project agenda in ways that enabled youth engagement based on their interests and capacities while the project benefitted from the expertise of diverse participants.

Flexible Intentions

As an educational researcher, I always began the applied theatre projects I facilitated with a set of questions in mind, framed around my scholarly interests and what I saw as the general aim(s) of the project. These were necessary starting points for negotiating access with gatekeepers, for ethics review applications and for funding proposals, etc. While *questions* as starting points – versus puzzles or hunches, for practice-as-research are sometimes seen to 'imply a limit to their potential answers' (Kershaw, 2009, p. 112), I found that questions devised to be open and flexible were able to serve my needs and accommodate the needs and interests of the research partnerships. I share my research questions for each project below to illustrate the kinds of overarching intentions that applied theatre research with marginalized youth can address. My questions were always Education focused, since this was my primary discipline and often addressed both the topics under consideration as well as the methods to be explored. I substituted, here, the term *applied theatre* for other terminology (drama, popular theatre, participatory drama) that I had previously used to refer to my work. The sophistication of the questions evolved along with my emerging research acumen.

For my master's research at the alternative inner-city high school, the research question was: *What is the relationship between youth and media advertising and how can I use [applied theatre] to draw out and question students' meanings or understandings toward finding appropriate ways of teaching media studies?* For my doctoral study at the rural Alberta high school, I wondered: *What are the perceptions of youth regarding their experiences that may deem them at risk and how can [applied theatre], as pedagogy and as research, be used to explore youth experiences?*

In the youth jail, for the pilot study, my colleague and I asked: *How can [applied theatre] help understand the experiences of young offenders toward finding appropriate approaches to meeting their needs? What are the contingencies of enacting [applied theatre] to bring about personal growth and social change in the context of a young offender facility?* For the longer funded study in jail, the research questions were: *How can [applied theatre] contribute to the education of incarcerated youth to avoid future negative outcomes of their at-risk behaviours? What are the educational needs of incarcerated youth to help them make positive change in their lives? What [applied theatre] practices can best contribute to meeting those needs? How can spaces be created within institutions such as prisons and schools for transformative processes to occur? How can we assess the benefits of [applied theatre] intervention in that context?* Following the three years of research with youth in the jail, I had proposed to write a play as an arts-based form through which to disseminate my research insights to a diverse audience. As I sat down to begin writing the play, which I entitled *Athabasca's Going Unmanned* (Conrad, 2012), I found that character relationships, scenarios, and dialogue seemed to flow almost effortlessly onto the page. The playwriting process inexplicably translated my three years of lived, embodied experience of doing applied theatre with the youth in jail into a research outcome that, though entirely fictionalized, at least to my mind, responded well to the questions I initially posed to guide the research. I share many of the applied theatre activities we engaged in with the incarcerated youth to address these questions in Chapter 4.

For the study with the arts-based youth organization serving street-involved youth, the initial questions, developed with the organization's collaborators, focused on outcomes for service provider audiences of our workshops: *How can we educate service providers to better prepare them for working with high-risk youth? What are effective methods for doing so? What is the role of youth in this process? What is the role of the arts in this process? To what extent are service providers receptive to such an educational undertaking?* As the study progressed and we witnessed that the project was also having great benefits for the youth involved, a final phase was added to the project focused on assessing outcomes for the youth, asking: *What are the benefits for youth collaborators in the study? What effective methods are being employed to facilitate these outcomes? What role do arts interventions play in this process? What are the effects of engaging youth as research collaborators? What are the effects of positioning youth as educators of service providers who work with them?* For this study we conducted formal evaluations for both phases that explicitly addressed the research questions. These included exit surveys, follow-up surveys, and a focus group with service provider audience members conducted by an outside evaluation service (E&RS, 2011), and a youth created evaluative video (YUEV, 2012) and T-shirt design (see Figure 3.4) for the evaluation of youth outcomes facilitated by two graduate research assistants. As principal investigator, I deliberately kept my distance from both evaluation processes so as not to inadvertently influence their outcomes.

I made note, here, of the questions that were starting points for my university-based research, because applied theatre facilitators whether associated with academic research or not, formally or informally, likely always come to a project with any community group with some intention or other in mind and these intentions are significant for initiating and giving shape to a project. Ideally, in applied theatre research, the impetus for the work comes from the community group, as I described it did for the project with the youth organization where the questions emerged from our initial conversations.

Researchers within academic settings are expected to develop ongoing research programs based on their disciplinary interests. For applied theatre and/or participatory research approaches, the need to set questions in advance, however, may be constraining. Nevertheless, as the questions above, mostly devised by me, illustrate, they are focused on drawing out participants' knowledge and are broad and general enough to accommodate whatever issues participants might raise and however the applied theatre process might unfold. Within the framework of these initial questions, for all the projects I facilitated, it was the youth who guided both the content of our explorations and the ways in which our processes proceeded. They made decisions about which scenarios we developed and worked with, what issues we would address, what meanings we made of them, whether or not we would perform, and what we would perform. Details about the nature of the processes we engaged in are the topic of the next chapter.

Concluding Thoughts on Engaging Marginalized Youth

As I prepared to write these concluding thoughts on engaging marginalized youth, I reflected on a community-based youth workshop I had facilitated the previous day in a small community in which I was a temporary resident. It served as a poignant reminder to me about the key considerations for engaging youth in applied theatre. The workshop took place within a community new to me, with youth whom I had never met before. I had the luxury of a very small group, but they were at the younger end of the age range (12–13 year olds) of youth with whom I usually engaged. As always, I wasn't sure what to expect or how the youth would respond. I had jotted down a few of my go-to activity ideas, but didn't overprepare. As I suspected, ultimately, it was my responsiveness to the situation, not my preparation or experience that won out.

I listened to the youth. I checked myself when my experienced theatre artist's brain told me a youth's choice wasn't *dramatic* enough. I listened and responded when they told me they found an activity awkward; when they told me they wanted to explore one aspect of an activity, but not take it any further; when they called for something more active; when they rejected one of the established rules of a game or wanted to play a game of their own choosing. I offered up the activities I had prepared, shifted gears as appropriate, changed up activities frequently to match their levels of attention and interest, and went along with what the youth suggested. I was impressed with what we managed to achieve, and the fun the youth had considering this was our first, brief encounter. Ultimately, successfully engaging youth, I was effectively reminded, is about meeting their needs, not about adhering to my agenda.

3

Applied Theatre Processes for Working with Systemically Marginalized Youth

In Chapter 2, I discussed some fundamental considerations for engaging systemically marginalized youth populations in applied theatre – primarily focused around the need for non-judgement, responsiveness and flexibility. In applied theatre work with marginalized youth, the theatre processes, the workshop and performance strategies engaged in also needed to be flexible with the youth, their well-being, needs, and desires at the centre. I've already mentioned the fact that in the work I facilitated, our processes needed to accommodate irregular attendance, which would present a major obstacle for a traditional, mainstream theatre process; our alternative processes always kept this consideration in mind.

The processes described below did not necessarily unfold in absolutely linear fashion. As an applied theatre facilitator, I always begin a project with community-building activities and such activities are regularly re-visited throughout the process, with drama games and exercises serving as warm-ups for or interludes during each session. Likewise, the storytelling, devising, and rehearsing phases are recursive, often overlapping or revived as needed. Applied theatre processes often culminate in performance, but not necessarily.

Community-Building

Drama and theatre projects or programs, whether focused on play production or applied theatre, whether set within school contexts, partnering with institutions or community organizations, with youth or adults, even if the participants know each other well, generally always begin with exercises for community-building (Ansloos & Wager, 2020; Eichas et al., 2021; Gallagher, 2016; Iwasaki et al., 2014; Wager, 2015) – to establish a sense of cohesion, to the extent that this is possible,

47

to develop common intentions or expectations within the group for the project. Since theatre-based explorations can be quite intense – physically, emotionally, and intellectually demanding, there's always a need to begin by developing a sense of comradery, a shared sense of purpose, and some common understandings around ways of working in collaboration with one another. In typical theatre terminology, the notion of *ensemble* is commonly deployed to describe a tight knit group of actors who perform together. With a group of systemically marginalized youth, the aim of developing a strong sense of ensemble or even a cohesive sense of community may be a stretch; the level of trust and commitment required to achieve such goals may be unrealistic. Nevertheless, attempts to build at least some measure of agreement within the group and a willingness to work together are important.

Guidelines for Working Together

Within school contexts, drama teachers often work with students to create a set of ground rules or guidelines for a group's work together. In schools, students are sometimes thrown together for a drama course and forced to participate even if drama was not an option of their own choosing, and they are subsequently graded on their achievements. If youth are not present because they want to be, creating a sense of common purpose or authentic engagement can be challenging, so making a set of basic expectations explicit is helpful. Some common guidelines that I have devised over the years, which I also share with my drama teacher education students include: respect others' privacy; commit to fully engaging in activities; be willing to take creative risks; be open to questioning your beliefs; be willing to give and receive constructive feedback; don't always go for the laugh, and so on. (See Appendix 2 for a set of guidelines that I developed with my drama education classes over the years.) Such guidelines, especially when developed in collaboration with group members at the outset of the process, can go some way towards building common, agreed upon expectations.

When working in extra-curricular or out-of-school contexts, youth who participate are usually present because they have chosen to be there and they are free to opt out if they so choose. Within a research context, of course, following ethical guidelines, participants must always have the option to withdraw from specific aspects of the work or to withdraw from the research altogether at any time. In some research models that involve groups of participants, such as in classroom contexts, it is possible for participants to take part in the group activities, but have their contributions excluded from the research. In applied theatre research, this is very challenging since individuals' contributions are not necessarily always distinguishable in group devised work. In such cases, the extent to which individuals' contributions can or cannot be withdrawn must be made clear at the outset. I am always sure to inform participants that any contributions they make must be freely offered for the group to make use of in any ways the group sees fit. That said, we would always respect individuals' requests to alter details that made them uncomfortable.

In working with systemically marginalized youth, beginning with ground rules or guidelines is not the best approach. Marginalized youth are often in the positions in which they find themselves precisely because they have resisted the rules and expectations imposed upon them, so adding more rules would be inadvisable. As a facilitator, then, I might have *guidelines* in the back of my mind as our work unfolds and I may invite youth to consider specific aspects of these guidelines as the need arises; I would more likely frame them as common theatre practices to develop, rather than as guidelines to follow. In my experience, if youth aren't forced to participate, when they don't appreciate or aren't interested in what's happening in any given exercise or session, rather than behaving in ways that disrupt the process, they will simply just step aside or leave altogether. If, in any of our projects, a youth's behaviour ever became disruptive for whatever reason – likely as a cry for attention, the behaviour was addressed by an adult collaborator from a perspective of care or harm reduction (Hughes, 2013; Smyth & Eaton-Erickson, 2009), focusing on what the youth needed in that moment.

Preparatory Drama Activities

Drama and theatre facilitators all have a wealth of drama games and exercises in their back pockets – what Boal (1974/1979) called his arsenal of theatre techniques, to call upon for every occasion (e.g. see Boal, 1992; Pura, 2002, Spolin, 1986). These games and exercises are so common that their origins have often faded into obscurity; any game might be known by various different names and have multiple variations. (See Appendix 3 for an index of games, exercises, and activities mentioned throughout this text.) Such games and exercises are used very purposefully at different stages of a process to prepare participants to engage together, as warm up or cool down for sessions, to practice specific skills, or as entry points for moving into exploration (Blight, 2015; Kaplan, 2022; Linds et al., 2013). They are more than just frivolous fun and games, though they are often lots of fun too (Kaplan, 2022; McCreery, 2001). As Thompson (2011) noted about the significance of games, 'there is a "filling" of the body with an overwhelming energy during games … [game playing] stimulate[s] an aliveness that spills out into an immediate engagement with others in the room' (p. 54). Game playing, then, is both individually enlivening and socially engaging. Games are essential parts of the process of learning to express oneself effectively using the tools of the theatre: one's body and voice, improvisation, character, situation, story, etc., and to do so within a social context.

Applied theatre sessions commonly begin with getting-to-know-you games. Even if participants already know each other, they get to know each other in new ways through participating in activities that ask them to play together, to work collaboratively on a task and sometimes to share personal details.

In drama activities that ask participants to share aspects of their lives, participants are encouraged to take creative risks (Lamparter, 2022; Linds et al., 2013; Wager, 2015), but are advised to share only what they are comfortable sharing – to care for their own well-being. At a conference I once attended – the one and only time I ever met and took a workshop with Augusto Boal himself, I had the honour of sitting beside him at our shared dinner table one evening. I took this opportunity to ask him a burning question I had as an educator-researcher working with youth. I asked him what he felt the role of the applied theatre facilitator was in caring for the well-being of participants since applied theatre can often veer into uncomfortable territory. He stated that it wasn't about the facilitator, that it would be paternalistic for a facilitator to assume the responsibility of caring for others' well-being, and in fact extremely arrogant for a facilitator to think that they could do so. Participants need to take on that responsibility for themselves, he insisted. I took his advice to heart. While I certainly never disregard participants' well-being, I do remind them to take care of themselves and invite them to let me know if there's ever anything I can do to support them. Of course, no one should ever be forced to share something they don't want to share.

In relation to participants caring for themselves, many drama/theatre activities involve participants touching each other – whether the touch is as limited as putting a hand on another's shoulder or as intense as falling backwards into another's arms for a trust exercise. Based on their prior experiences, participants will have varying levels of comfort with touch. At the beginning of any work with a new group, I always remind participants to confirm others' consent before touching them (Shawyer & Shively, 2019) – by simply asking the other person if they're okay being touched in a specific way. In fact, this has become common practice in educational, recreational, and other contexts, especially when involving young people as awareness around the inappropriateness of some forms of touching has become heightened. I remind individuals to be clear about their boundaries and take care of themselves in relation to touch.

When working with marginalized youth, particularly if they have little or no previous drama experience, considerable time is needed to achieve a level of comfort with performance and so taking time with all these preparatory activities is essential. On the other hand, youth may feel that games are frivolous, a waste of time, and they'd prefer to get right down to work. It's useful to let participants know that the games and exercises are valuable strategies for building community and developing necessary skills (Linds et al., 2013) – perhaps letting them know what particular skill or attitude each game is practicing. Games are never just frivolous filler, but a balance appropriate to the group does need to be struck.

Ritual: Along with play, ritual (Turner, 1982) comprises the evolutionary basis for what we now call drama or theatre. Communities through time immemorial have practiced rituals to consolidate group values and a sense of identity (Arteaga & Chavez-Arteaga, 2022; Linds et al., 2013). Drama and theatre processes generally involve a number of ritualistic type practices. A circle formation, for example, is common for many drama games and exercises and for group discussions or reflections. Speaking circles are also consistent with Indigenous protocols (Graveline, 2000). In both instances, the circle aims for democratic interaction – to include all individuals within the group on an equal basis, so that each can be equally seen and heard. Time set aside at the beginning and ending of sessions for brief check-ins and check-outs with participants is common, as is taking time out for snack breaks or for reflective journaling. Drama activities might also include developing unique group rituals, such as breathing and relaxation exercises to begin class or a repeated gesture and chant to practice right before a performance, similar to what a sports teams might do before a game. Establishing rituals appropriate for a group assists with building a sense of group cohesion and belonging. Rituals can be as simple or as elaborate as needed.

Name Games: Whenever I begin working with a new group, I commonly begin with name games. Although participants may know each other's names, we shouldn't assume so. Also, it is important, in my opinion, to be able to call individuals by their preferred names, so as a facilitator I need to learn names as quickly as possible. Teachers have many tricks to learn students' names. Using simple names games, I've been able to learn twenty or more new names after just one session. My favourite name game associates a person's name with an adjective and an action that describe them: Standing in a circle, I ask each participant, one at a time, to say their name, along with an adjective that begins with the same letter or sound as their name (alliteration) and which describes them. I also ask them to strike a pose with their whole body to illustrate the adjective (e.g. Daring Diane with a strong stance and a raised fist indicating daring). I remind students to focus on adjectives that present them in a positive light, so they are remembered for one of their strengths. To play this game, the first person performs their name/adjective/action once and then the rest of the group copies them. Then, the second person performs their name/adjective/action, the rest of the group copies them, and then also repeats the first person's name/adjective/action, and so on. For each round, we begin with a new person's name/adjective/action, and then go back around the circle repeating each person's name/adjective/action in order. The game continues until everyone around the circle has had a turn. By the end of the game, the whole group is repeating everyone's name/adjective/action around the entire circle. Through repetition we begin to learn the names. I always make note of each individual's adjective and action alongside their name at the end of the session to provide me with memory prompts.

Introducing Personal Stories: To introduce the practice of sharing personal stories, which is a key element in applied theatre (Barton-Farcas, 2022; Lamparter, 2022; Tate, 2022), it is appropriate for community-building activities to begin with sharing personal stories in low-risk ways. An approach that I've taken for this asks participants to bring in a personal object of significance to them, or to simply grab a significant object from their bag/purse/pocket and then share a personal story about that object with the group. Another common strategy involves pairing participants with each individual sharing with their partner their responses to a set of pre-determined questions (e.g. Where did you grow up? Did/do you have a beloved pet? What is your most memorable family occasion?) Once each partner in the pairing has had a chance to share, back in the large group individuals are asked to re-tell their partner's answers as a story, in as much detail as possible, as if it were their own story. This demands that partners listen attentively to each other's responses. I have also introduced such personal storytelling exercises by having participants draw, collage, or dance some aspects of their life experiences to share with the group.

Physical and Vocal Warm Ups: Since performers' creative tools are our bodies, making the most of those tools is central to the art form of theatre. In Boal's (1992) *Games for Actors and Non-Actors*, he introduced activities in sections of the book under the headings: Feeling what we touch; Listening to what we hear; Seeing what we look at. He believed that our modern lifestyles obstruct us from closely attending to information received from our senses, which the art of theatre can restore. Through this approach awareness of the significance of our senses and the embodied nature of drama/theatre is highlighted. Many drama games and exercises focus on fine-tuning our senses of perception, requiring us to be fully in the moment. The personal storytelling exercise in partners described above, for example, demands careful listening in order to honour our partners' stories, which also supports the development of empathy. Other games and exercises, likewise, work at optimizing the tools at our disposal, becoming aware of and moving beyond our personally and/or socially ingrained habits (e.g. women are socialized to stand with a slight arch in their backs to accentuate certain body parts, which, however weakens one's stance), honing our physical and vocal skills, expanding our repertoire of ways of moving and vocalizing, and freeing us of our inhibitions, which can be empowering.

Focus Activities: Another theatre skill honed through practice is the ability to stay focused in the moment – a much-needed skill for successful performance of any kind. This is especially significant for young people who are easily distracted. There are many drama/theatre exercises that attend to developing focus. A game that a young man who participated in the project in the youth jail taught me, which became a favourite with many of the groups I've facilitated, including my drama education students, involved ball throwing. For this game, I prefer to use hacky sacks (small round bean bags), which are soft enough not to hurt anyone when thrown, yet substantial enough to be easily throwable over a short distance. I have a set of ten hacky sacks that I use for this game. The group stands in a circle and establishes a throwing pattern beginning with one ball: I begin by throwing to a person across the circle: A then throws it across the circle to B, who throws to C, who throws to D, etc. until everyone in the circle has thrown once and received once – no repetition is permitted for this game. The last receiver throws to me (the first person to throw) and the pattern is complete. I ask participants to do all this in silence and I remind them that we are all responsible for ensuring that each pass of the ball is completed successfully. We begin the throwing pattern again and once it is well underway, I add a ball, then another, then another, until ten hacky sacks are flying, in pattern, back and forth across the circle at the same time. Participants really only need to remember (1) who they receive from and (2) who they throw to, but they must be hyper-alert and focused at all times in order to catch another ball coming their way in the midst of all the balls in play. The activity is simple enough, but hysterically fun, highly energizing, and demanding of razor-sharp focus. I sometimes jokingly tell my drama education students that this game will comprise their final exam!

Youths' engagement in simple drama games can also reveal much about them as a group. During our pilot project with youth in jail, for example, we introduced a common drama game we called 'Who's the Leader?' For this game one participant volunteers to temporarily step outside of the room – to be the guesser. The others in the circle choose a leader and that leader initiates a small gesture (e.g. a wave of the hand) which is copied and repeated by all the others in the circle. The leader inconspicuously changes the gesture from time to time with all others copying. The objective of the game is for the copying of the gestures and the changes from gesture to gesture to be as seamless as possible so as not to reveal, to the guesser, who has initiated the gesture. When the guesser returns to the circle, their aim is to watch the action to try to determine who the leader is.

Prior to playing this game in the jail, I had played it many times before with many different groups, so I knew it could be quite challenging to identify the leader. For the incarcerated youth, it seemed to be no challenge at all. Guesser after guesser was able to accurately identify the leader almost immediately and not because the players weren't being discrete. My colleague and I conjectured that given the context these youth must have always been on high alert, hyper-vigilant in scrutinizing one another's actions in order to navigate the thorny social dynamics of the place.

Exploring Power Dynamics: As explorations of power are inherent to theatre, as I discussed briefly in Chapter 1, many applied theatre exercises play with power. Boal's (1992) *Games for Actors and Non-actors* introduced several games that very specifically explored power dynamics (see e.g. The Great Game of Power and Columbian Hypnosis). For Boal's Columbian Hypnosis (which I call just Hypnosis), for example – a game which I utilize regularly both in my applied theatre research and in my drama education instruction, one member of a pair begins by taking on the role of leader slowly leading their partner around the room with the palm of their hand an inch or so in front of their partner's face. The follower is instructed to unquestioningly follow the leader's hand wherever it takes them – up or down, around the room, backwards or forwards, while maintaining the distance between their face and their partner's open palm. After a few minutes of play the roles are reversed. The unequal power dynamics being explored through this game are visceral.

In other theatre contexts, status games, which also explore power hierarchies amongst individuals, are common. It's useful in an applied theatre project where power is central to the exploration to work explicitly with power games to begin to help participants identify power and its various manifestations.

The Fun Factor

The enjoyment that participants experience through engaging in applied theatre is a fundamental element of the work and should not be under-valued (Thompson, 2003). Humans of all ages seek enjoyment in their lives and we should welcome it whenever, wherever it can be found. The joy that occurs through applied theatre activities comes from the sense of play that is unleashed when acting out, when bodies, minds, emotions, and imaginations are fully engaged. The playful *as if* world of performance is reminiscent of the make-believe play that we engaged in effortlessly and joyfully as children. There is always joking, laughter, and fun involved in applied theatre, even when exploring the most challenging of issues (more on this in Chapter 6). Pleasure comes from the shared experience of working communally towards a common goal – as collaborative engagement in productive action brings an increased sense of power and agency. Pleasure also comes from a release of tension or nervous energy around the challenging issues being explored, from the freeing feeling of uninhibited expression or from the experience of performance itself – the exhilaration that comes from taking the risk of putting oneself on display.

Thompson (2008) argued that in assessing the benefits of applied theatre, the real question to consider is not whether the work has effected change, but whether it has had an *affective* response in the community with which it has engaged. The creation and expression of joy, he argues, and I would agree, should be considered an end in itself. Moreover, Thompson (2011) also argued that the desire to replicate an enlivening experience, such as the embodied joy experienced through play, can be an impetus for seeking social justice. So, the enjoyment of play and our pursuit of social justice are not mutually exclusive.

For young people, enjoyment in a positive, productive environment is generally very welcomed. In particular for marginalized youth, whose day-to-day lives are filled with struggle, the opportunity to freely play and laugh is a great benefit in itself. It is the enjoyment that youth gain from participation in applied theatre, I believe, that hooks youth and keeps them coming back for more.

In a recent series of youth workshops I facilitated, I noted how some of the youth would arrive sullen and grumpy, but as soon as we started in on some games, their moods changed. If working towards making positive change in their lives is also a source of enjoyment for youth, it's a win-win for all. It is what the youth themselves seek and what I, as an adult facilitator, wish for them. When I hear laughter in a group I am facilitating, I know that vital work is being accomplished. I will further discuss the power of joy or affective response in Chapter 6 as I explore the potential applied theatre has for supporting positive change or empowerment in the lives of youth.

Brainstorming

Following introductory and community-building activities, getting down to devising work with a group often begins with the brainstorming of ideas for exploration.

As I mentioned, while I generally come to a project with an idea of the overarching intention of the work, it is the participants who inform the specific topics to be explored through initial brainstorming of ideas and issues from their perspectives. I ask youth to brainstorm ideas around how the project intentions relate to them, or how they understand the issue(s). For the projects I discuss in this book, our brainstorming sessions sometimes occurred as round-table discussions, with researchers taking notes, or alternatively through other creative exercises, such as one I call 'Graffiti Wall', where youth write words, phrases, slogans, song lyrics, etc., or sketch illustrations on a long strip of mural paper to express their issues and understandings.

After viewing and analysing the Graffiti Wall brainstorming activities completed by the two drama classes at the rural Alberta high school where I researched, the students synthesized that their issues were determined by their rural environment. Their risky experiences, they surmised, were all about the fact that they lived in a remote, isolated location, and so the starting point for our exploration became *Life in the Sticks*, a phrase that featured on one of the Graffiti Walls they created (Figure 3.1).

In a Graffiti Wall exercise with the youth in jail for the pilot project, one youth drew a stick-figure image of a strip-search: a youth bending over saying *ouch*, with a corrections worker standing behind the youth saying *shut up*, one hand holding the youth's arm and the other presumably searching the youth for contraband (see Figure 4.5). In their explanation of the image, a youth told us of a cruel joke with a football reference that an intake officer liked to make to intimidate the boys upon their arrival at the jail during an initial strip-search: You may be coming in a tight end, but you'll be going out a wide receiver. The provocative image the youth offered and their explanations informed our interpretation of what the youth had shared. We could only image the anxieties they must have faced in their experiences of incarceration.

The street-involved youth, through several brainstorming round-table sessions, identified seven specific themes that they felt were significant areas warranting further exploration towards educating service providers about their experiences. These were relations with law enforcement, educational issues, access to healthcare, the social services system, worker-client relations, family dynamics, and other youth experiences. We subsequently shared stories and devised scenarios for each of these categories. For all the projects, initial brainstorming sessions became the jumping off points for further exploration.

Informal Conversation: I'll mention here, briefly, some other informal sources of insight into youths' experiences. Often, during applied theatre processes, time is taken out from theatre activities for breaks, to share food, for reflective journaling,

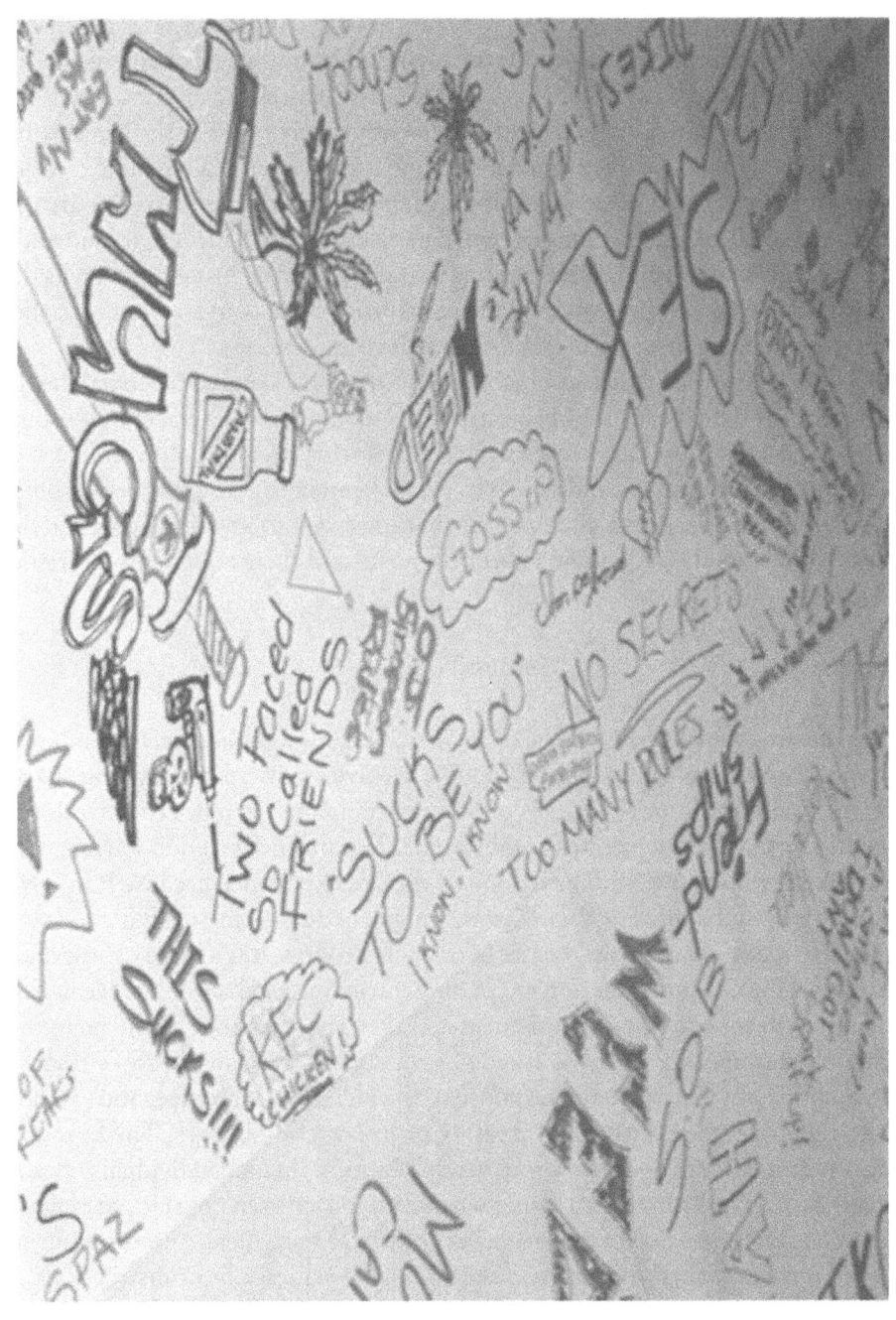

FIGURE 3.1: Graffiti wall from the Life in the Sticks project, 1999. © D. Conrad.

or to work on crafting artefacts to serve as props for performances or as alternative outcomes of the research. I've found stories or understandings that emerge during such activities particularly authentic since they arise entirely unsolicited. Youth get chatty when their hands are occupied with creative activities. For the Uncensored project, for example, we once spent some time sitting around a big table creating content for *zines* (small do-it-yourself magazines) – collections of youth-created anecdotes, collages, poems, images, word games, etc., to distribute to audiences (Figure 3.2). The informal conversations that occur during instances such as this can be fascinating and informative. Elements from these conversations can then be re-visited during more formal sharing or devising sessions.

Also very informative are glimpses into youths' lives shared on social media. At the start of the Uncensored project, we decided to create a Facebook group. The youth were all on Facebook at the time, so this became a convenient way for the project facilitators and youth to easily keep in touch. I originally joined Facebook for this very reason. It was fascinating to get to know the youth in this alternative way – through their Facebook posts and their comments to friends and family.

Image Theatre

Image theatre, one of Boal's (1974/1979, 1992) techniques that has been adapted in various ways (see e.g. Diamond, 2007), involves participants making shapes with their bodies and/or the bodies of other participants – similar to what drama teachers know as frozen pictures or tableaux. Image theatre is a good starting place for working with youth who have limited theatre experience because it involves minimal risk and skill. For this reason, I also encourage my drama education students to make use of image theatre in their classrooms. It is a low-risk approach because (1) the original intention in creating the image need never be revealed, so is therefore never subjected to judgment, (2) those participating in the image are not required to speak, or may be asked to speak only a word or phrase or respond with a simple physical action in response to the facilitator's prompt, and (3) there are no right or wrong answers in creating or interpreting images. The beauty of images is that they are open to various interpretations. (In fact, individuals offering images should avoid miming an action when entering a frozen position, so as not to suggest one interpretation of the image over others.) Image theatre occurs in silence except for participants' responses to the facilitator's questions or instructions.

Images are usually created to depict a character or characters in a scenario, although at times it may be appropriate to depict objects, attitudes, or qualities, or individuals representing attitudes or perspectives. To create or sculpt the images, depending on the context, participants can use their own bodies – for

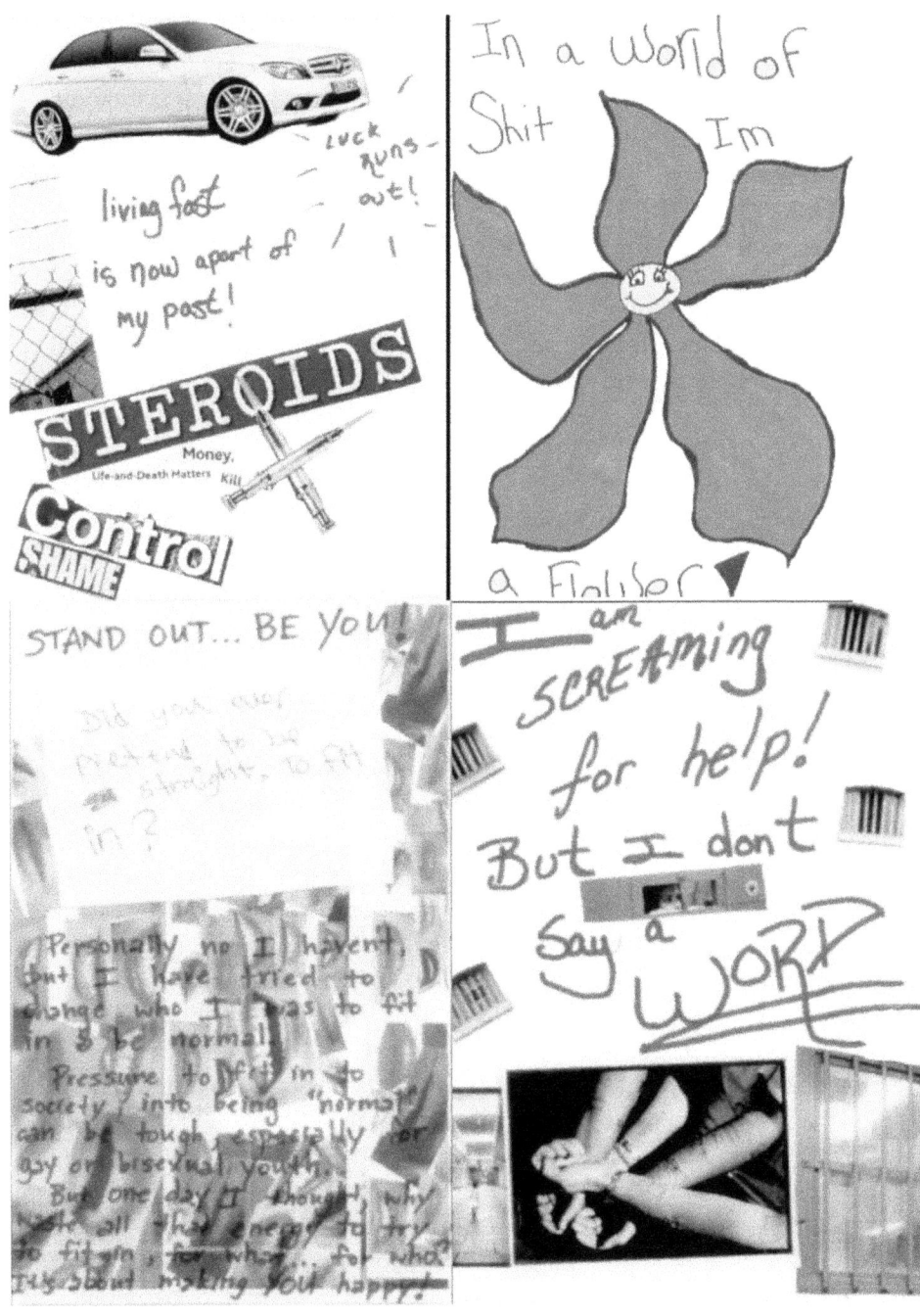

FIGURE 3.2: Pages from a youth created zine for the Uncensored project, 2012. © D. Conrad & iHuman Youth Society.

which they simply strike a physical shape or position and hold it, or they can sculpt other participants' bodies (as though the bodies were clay) through various means depending on comfort levels. Sculpting techniques include, (1) moulding – through which the sculptor gently manipulates another's body to shape their various body parts (with consent to touch them); and/or, (2) if participants are not comfortable with touch, for example, through mirroring – for which the sculptor takes a shape which the other copies (this works especially well for facial expressions); and/or (3) marionetting – for which a string is imagined to extend between the sculptor's hand and the sculpted person's body parts, like a marionette, with the person being sculpted moving into shapes accordingly. The initiator of an image can sculpt others' bodies and can also place themselves into the image. Participants in an image are asked to remain motionless, but invited to unfreeze and shake out as needed before returning to their positions as the interpretive work continues.

Sculpting in image theatre is done in silence with no explanations regarding the sculptor's intentions. Diamond (2007) spoke about the power of not naming images thusly: 'By not naming images we start to break down the artificial barriers between the individual consciousness and that of the group. In doing so we bridge the mind/body gap and start to awaken the group consciousness' (p. 98). In interpreting an image, attention should be paid to details, to the positions of all body parts, to any tension in the body, to facial expression, and distances and positions between bodies for images with more than one body. Every detail of an image is significant and scrutinized for possible interpretations as the work proceeds.

Once an image has been created, the facilitator can use various methods to bring to life or animate the images to engage those participants within or outside of the image in its interpretation. The various animation strategies I use are adapted from Boal (1992) and Diamond (2007). For example, as the facilitator, I may tap a participant or each participant in the image in turn on the shoulder and ask them to say a word or phrase which speaks to what they are thinking or feeling (Thought Bubble) as the character they imagine they are depicting within the image; or a word, phrase, or sentence indicating what they would say (Dialogue Bubble) to another character in the situation they imagine; or what they are thinking but would never say aloud (Secret Thought). Initial ideas, thoughts, feelings, or motivations can be further developed through giving participants a few seconds to formulate a silent inner monologue (Inner Monologue), and then asking them to continue speaking their monologues aloud. Other animation strategies include Stepping into the Future, for which participants make one movement or gesture towards what they want on the clap of the facilitator's hands in order to visualize a characters' motivations in the given situation; and Wide Shot, which broadens out from the image to see who/what else might be influencing the situation to consider external influences or social forces acting upon the characters in the scenario. (Social forces are most effectively portrayed as persons representing the social forces influencing the character.)

As well as questioning those within the image, the facilitator can also question those observing, asking them to make suggestions about what a character in the image might be thinking or feeling, what the relationships are between characters in the image, and what the image might be about. All participants' answers will inform others' understandings of the image. Each participant in an image along with those observing from outside may have a different idea about what the image is about, who the characters are and their relationships to others in the image, and that is fine. Ultimately, through the animation process one or more possible scenarios may emerge as participants begin to hear and respond to one another. A consensus regarding what the image is about may be reached, or may not. The role of the facilitator is to use the animation strategies to draw out participants ideas in order to engage in embodied discussion of the issue(s) being explored. (See Appendix 4 for an example of an image created and animated with one of my drama education classes.)

The strength of image theatre is that it is a way to begin generating ideas without any wrong answers. From the images created and the animation strategies explored, full scenes with movement and dialogue can easily be developed. I often begin image theatre activities by having participants create images randomly and then after some time I insert a theme relevant to the intentions of the workshop.

Turning Games into Exploration

A strategy that I've found very effective, especially for shorter workshop sessions, when time doesn't allow for an extensive process or when participants are hesitant to share, is to begin with a game and then layer in content to begin the process of exploration. Image theatre games work well for this.

Complete the Image: Complete the Image is an image theatre game (Boal, 1992) that begins with two volunteers moving into the centre of the circle, taking a position of shaking hands, and freezing in that position. The game proceeds with one member of the pair exiting the handshake image, while the other holds their same position. A new volunteer then enters to *complete the image* by adding their body to the scene to create a new image, with the added requirement of having to justify the body position of the remaining original participant as something other than a handshake scenario. The game then continues with the other original participant leaving the scene and another volunteer joining to complete the image and so on. Each new image will conjure a new scenario.

To begin the process of interpreting an image, as the facilitator, I question those outside of the image about what they *see* with a focus on details – describing the actual details of what they see in relation to body positions, facial expressions, etc., then I move on to asking them how they *interpret* the image based on what they see. I emphasize the distinction between describing details and interpreting (or analysing) those details to encourage participants' careful attention to the nuances of a performer's body shape, position, facial expression, etc., and how those details could be read by an audience to justify an interpretation. This game illustrates to participants how even the minutest of details communicates something in theatre. For example, the initial image of the handshake is never neutral; the two people are shaking hands in some very specific way (e.g. they are standing quite far apart with straight arms, one character has a slight smile, etc.) that reveals something about the characters, their relationship, and the scenario. In the interpretation phase, I ask observers questions such as: Who are these people? What is their relationship? Who has more power? What is happening here? What is each person thinking? What might happen next?

As the image making continues, as the facilitator, I will introduce additional layers of information for participants to consider in creating and interpreting images. Once the game is well established, I might offer a prompt: From now on all the images are in relation to such and such an issue or theme. And the workshop exploration has begun. Image theatre animation techniques can also be used to unpack the images in this game.

Three Things: Another game that I have used successfully with youth for moving from a basic image theatre-based game into thematic exploration, I call Three Things, although it goes by other names. The game involves making images of objects rather than people, though it can be adapted to include characters too. It begins with one volunteer coming into the circle and making an image of a thing and declaring what they are: e.g. 'I am a tree'. A second volunteer adds to the image with their body in the shape of another thing that somehow relates to the first object: 'I am the sun'. Finally, a third person joins: 'I am a bird'. All three things in the image need to be in relation to each other somehow. Once the three things have been created, the round ends, and a new round begins with three new volunteers. Again, once the game is established, I will layer in a theme: e.g. All the images from now on are about life in your community. At this point the things created often include people. Then I ask participants to interpret the image of the three things, by using animation strategies and/or asking questions such as: What's going on here? What does this image say about your community? Such questions are posed to begin discussion and exploration.

Images of Youth Leadership: Several years ago, while I was conducting research in a Northern Dene community, I was invited to facilitate an applied theatre workshop for a youth conference they were hosting. This was the same community in which I had taught many years previous. It was an honour to be back in the community and working with some youth who were the children of the students I had taught all those years previous. The conference was organized by a young woman from the community and focused on youth leadership. I was happy to offer a series of drama workshops for the conference, but knowing little about what youth leadership in a remote Dene community might entail, I opted to engage the youth in exploring their understandings of youth leadership.

Over the course of a Saturday, I worked with four groups of 10–15 youth from the region for a series of four 1.5-hour sessions. For each session, following some quick introductory and warm up games, I asked the youth: What does youth leadership look like in your community? Youth volunteered to create images of youth leadership using their own and fellow participants' bodies, following the processes described above, which we animated to generate shared understandings. The images that the youth devised and their explanations of how those images illustrated youth leadership in their community were very insightful; they shared understandings of youth leadership that I would never have envisioned.

A graduate research assistant, who joined me for the workshops, took photos of each image the youth created and recorded notes about all that the youth said about each image. Each session generated three to four images and various scenarios for each image. At the end of the day and for the following day, my research assistant and I proceeded to collect all the materials from the workshops into a comic book, depicting how the youth understood youth leadership in their community. We used a photo editing program to clean up the original backgrounds of the photos, drew in backgrounds and objects relevant to the scenarios the youth had devised, applied a comic filter to turn the photos into cartoon images, and added text (youths' words) in speech and thought bubbles. For the closing event of the conference on the Sunday evening, I was able to share the comic book back to the community to show the youth, their parents, and other community members what the youth had achieved through the workshops – what youth leadership meant to them.

While this applied theatre project was not part of the research I was conducting, it was a knowledge generating activity for, by, and with the community youth. It demonstrates the versatility of the image theatre approach for exploring and disseminating community issues.

Storytelling

In the subsequent phase of an applied theatre project, based on initial brainstormed findings, I may invite youth to share stories from their life experiences related to the project theme(s). Personal storytelling is a potentially empowering process (Ansloos & Wager, 2020; Barton-Farcas, 2022; Blight, 2015; Gallagher, 2016; McCreery, 2001; Ottaway et al., 2009). As Alrutz (2013) suggested,

> performing one's personal story can and does constitute the making and disruption of systems of power. To tell your story for a public, to share your (perhaps marginalized, new, unpopular or uncomfortable) narratives, has the potential to affect how each of us sees the past, participates in the present, and imagines the future. (p. 44)

I always advise youth, from the outset, that they should carefully consider which stories they are willing to share and to share only those stories that they are comfortable sharing with the group. If they are willing to share a story, I suggest, they also have to be willing to have us possibly work with their story or aspects of their story in our ongoing devising. In effect, they have to offer up that story for the group to make use of, adapt, or not use at all, as the group sees fit. Youths' stories, then, on whatever theme or issue is being explored can be collected and recorded.

Individual stories, if they resonate with the group, can be utilized to move directly into devising, or stories can be accumulated for later analysis and use. Ideas and experiences that emerge from stories can be collaboratively examined and sorted through; stories can be grouped based on recurring issues or themes that resonate with the group as the basis for devising scenarios. The following is an example of a scene created in this fashion for my doctoral research.

A Collective Story Exploration: The Bus Trip

As I mentioned earlier, the theme that emerged from our brainstorming for the project at the rural Alberta high school was Life in the Sticks – the youth believed that their risky behaviours were due to the fact that they lived in an isolated, rural environment. From this starting point, the students began sharing stories about how that theme was evident in their life experiences. One student recalled a story about an incident that had occurred at the school the previous year involving an instance of rule-breaking. Others in the group were also aware of this incident, but none of them had actually been directly involved, nor had any of them been privy to all the actual details of the event. Nevertheless, the story resonated with the group.

As they collectively shared, a group of senior students had been on a school outing by bus. On the way home, some students had drunk alcohol on the bus, but had not been caught in the act. The school's administration had somehow learned of the incident after the fact. It resulted in suspension of several students involved and the expulsion of the identified instigator of the illicit activity. For those students not already aware of this bus trip incident, they could imagine the scenario well enough to contribute to the devising process.

In analysing this incident, rather than just talking about it, we immediately put it on its feet, in fictionalized form. We created the bus as the setting for the scene from rows of chairs. Students volunteered to play various characters in the scenario. We played out the situation through improvisation, with me as facilitator stopping the action intermittently to ask questions, to dig into students' understandings of the perspectives and motivations at play. In my discussion of the scene below and elsewhere in the book, the names of the individuals mentioned were the pseudonyms that the students gave their characters within the scenes, and the dialogue is what emerged from within our discussions, which I documented in the form of scripted descriptions of our work for my doctoral dissertation.

The bus trip story spoke very poignantly to my interest in youth experiences that might deem them at-risk. In this case, the youths' choices to engage in the activity of drinking alcohol on the bus put youth at-risk of being suspended or expelled from school. In our work with this scenario, which we titled 'The Bus Trip', the story took on a life of its own. It did not matter, for the purposes of our exploration of youth experiences, whether or not the details of our story corresponded to what actually happened. The students had no problem bridging the gap between the thinly veiled fiction we enacted and their authentic perspectives about what happened in the actual incident, or how they understood what happens in such cases generally.

Our exploration revealed that the students felt the motivation for the risky behaviour of drinking alcohol on the bus was, for the instigator, about being *cool*. For others who joined in the activity, it was about maintaining friendships and status amongst their peers. Overall, it was about alleviating the boredom of the long bus trip home. When the student portraying the character who initiated the illicit activity was asked why he had done it, Shadzz said, 'I don't know, just for the rush I guess'. Other students concurred.

The students believed that the only reason the authorities learned of the incident was because one of their peers had told them about it. The students expressed disdain for this peer informant. When asked how they felt about informers, Shadzz said, 'Informers? They're rats!' Lady responded, 'They suck!' They also talked about wanting to teach *the rat* a lesson by beating them up. Through their responses in character, the students positioned themselves at odds with the governing school authorities and articulated their own sense of justice. This was indicated by Shadzz's claim, 'But rules are made to be broken. You have to break the rules once in a while', and Daryl's response, 'Let them worry about their own rules. If they didn't find out we were drinking …'. They concluded that since no real harm had come from drinking on the bus, the instigator's expulsion from school was not warranted.

Our version of the story – our scene, became a representation of reality that allowed the right aesthetic distance needed for our in-depth analysis (Barton-Farcas, 2022). For instance, the youth believed that someone on the bus must have informed the administration about the incident, but this was never confirmed. In our fictionalized re-enactment one youth, in a moment of improvisation, willingly took on the role of the despised informer, which allowed for the discussion about youths' perspectives of peer informants as rats. Students believed that if their peer had not informed the administration, the illicit act would never have been found out; for them, this raised the question of whether a rule would, in essence, have been broken if the authorities had remained uninformed. They understood that from the perspective of the school's administration rules were needed and that informers helped to enforce those rules, but they strongly disapproved of peer informing. They felt that justice had not been served in this case, that the punishment of expulsion had been too harsh.

'The Bus Trip' story proved to be fertile ground for eliciting interesting insights regarding students' perceptions of the motivations behind youths' risky activities, peer group relations, their perspectives on rule-breaking, their relationship to the authority of the school, and their idiosyncratic or situated sense of justice.

Devising

Through the phases of community-building, brainstorming, and story-telling, applied theatre processes are much the same for most groups with which a facilitator might engage. I have found that the latter stages of the process involving theatrical devising – the collective creation of a theatre piece involving improvisation, directing and play writing (Prendergast & Saxton, 2013), rehearsing and performing, when working with marginalized youth require the most flexibility and adaptation. Following Boal's (1974/1979) approach, the work I devised with youth often took the form of short three-to-five-minute scenes. Some applied theatre practitioners prefer to create longer performance pieces, but I have found such short scenes effective for concisely raising the issues we hoped to address, keeping the logistics of performing them manageable, and putting the focus on interaction/discussion with audiences.

From the stories youth shared, fictionalized scenarios were collaboratively devised, often by beginning with an image and/or through improvisation – as we did with 'The Bus Trip' scene described above. These fictionalized scenes were sometimes based on one story, but were often compilations – composite stories (Barton-Farcas, 2022) based on similar themes with, for example, the setting from one story combined with one or more character types from other stories, and an incident from yet another. To devise a scene, we generally always began by talking through what we wanted a scene to accomplish. Participants volunteered to play characters, got on their feet, and began acting out the scenario to see what might happen. The improvisation process was intermittently interrupted by questioning or side-coaching from the facilitator to interrogate character intentions and motivations, to check on the plausibility of how events were unfolding, and to garner youth insights and suggestions. Following each devising session, we would talk about and record what we liked about a scene, what hadn't work, and what needed further refining. Once we settled on a scenario that we felt worked well, we loosely sketched a scripted outline for the scenario – indicating scenario structures, characters, key dialogue based on youths' improvised words, and some stage directions – only those details needed to tell the story. This version of the scenario became the scene we rehearsed (or re-improvised) and used for performance – as a forum theatre scene, for example.

Forum Theatre

Forum theatre, another of Boal's (1974/1979) Theatre of the Oppressed approaches, involves devising and presenting short activating or *problem* scenes on the topic being explored. A forum theatre scene, as mentioned above, is a short scene, often no longer than five minutes or so, that presents a problem. Unlike in a typical play, where conflict is satisfyingly resolved at the end – catharsis achieved and the world returned to order (Brecht, 1957/1964), a forum theatre scene ends at the high point of conflict, and is left intentionally unresolved. The performers present the scene for an audience once through and then replay the scene again and again inviting audience members to intervene by stopping the action and actually coming onto stage to replace characters to try out various strategies towards eliciting more positive outcomes for all.

For our forum theatre presentations, I always took on the role that Boal (1974/1979) termed the *Joker* – to facilitate audience interventions and lead the ensuing discussions around the interventions' success or lack thereof. Following an intervention, I would ask the audience intervener: What was your idea? What were you trying to do? How did it go? Did you get what you wanted? To the youth performers I would ask: How was that for you? Did it make things better for you? I would ask probing follow-up questions to dig deeper into the issue(s) being explored. And finally, I would ask the audience: What did you see happening on stage? This is a highly interactive theatre form that is excellent for initiating dialogue.

When Boal (1974/1979) developed his forum theatre model, he originally worked only with those deemed *oppressed*. At the time, in the 1960s, these were Brazilian peasants seeking to overcome the oppression they suffered at the hands of the landowners. Both actors and audience members, in Boal's early practice, were from amongst the oppressed group. Boal allowed audience members, whom he called *spectactors*, to replace only oppressed characters in the scenes on the grounds that oppressed individuals can only change their own behaviours; they cannot change their oppressors. In the circumstances in which the form was developed, this approach was undoubtedly appropriate. In contemporary western contexts, the distinction between oppressors and the oppressed is not always so clear-cut; we can be either/both oppressors or oppressed at various times and in various circumstances. Current adaptations of forum theatre (e.g. Diamond's, 2007) commonly allow any characters in a scene to be replaced because everyone in the scene could be seen to be *struggling* in some way or other. Intervening in any one of those struggles might enable a more positive outcome overall. Weinblatt and Harrison (2011) also used forum theatre with those in positions of privilege, those who may be seen as oppressors, 'convinced that all of us are culpable and responsible for uprooting social injustice' (p. 21).

In our project with street-involved youth, we developed a unique approach to forum theatre as our performance strategy. Street-involved youth were clearly positioned as the ones who were struggling, and the service providers were framed as those in need of making changes in their service to youth. The service providers were the intended audiences of our scenes, so, using Boal's (1974/1979) terminology, our project brought the *oppressed* together with their *oppressors* for dialogue. Our scenes depicted encounters between youth and service providers that failed to adequately address youths' needs. We invited our service provider audience members to replace only service provider characters in our scenes to try out strategies for engendering more positive outcomes for the youth. In most cases, the service providers attended our workshops because they had a vested interest in better serving youth, though we did at times encounter resistance (I'll offer an example of a resistant audience in Chapter 6). The following is a forum theatre scene we devised for the project with street-involved youth that became one of our most effective scenes.

Confronting Labels and Labelling: One scene we devised for the Uncensored project with street-involved youth, which we entitled 'Labels', was based on a recurring theme in youths' stories: they felt they were seen by service providers only as the labels applied to them in their files (Lavie-Ajayi & Krumer-Nevo, 2013), rather than as unique individuals in need of support. In devising this scene, we sought some way to visualize the labels for optimal effect. As the facilitator/dramaturge, I came upon the idea of creating a set of actual physical labels – 12″ × 6″ brightly coloured placards with bold text bearing some of the common labels applied to youth. As identified by the youth, these included such labels as Drop Out, Drug Addict, Thug, FASD, Suicidal, etc. A clip was affixed to each label so that it could be attached to a youth performer's clothing.

The scene began with two service providers sitting at a table. These could be two social workers, two teachers, two medical professionals, etc., depending on our audience for any given workshop. A youth stood in the middle of the stage with a hoodie covering their bowed head. As the service providers began speaking about the youth, looking through the youth's file, as one was preparing to hand over the file to the other, other performers clipped label after label onto the youth at centre stage. At the end of the scene, when the new service provider went to meet the youth for the first time, all the audience could see was the youth covered head to foot with labels (Figure 3.3). In this way, we introduced a visual element to our performance, which powerfully hit home the premise of the scene. The 'Labels' scene became one of our most impactful scenes which we adapted for various service provider audiences to suit the context.

'Labels' was not a typical forum theatre type scene because of its symbolic element – the physical labels being applied to the youth. When replaying the scene, in eliciting interventions, service provider audience members would usually replace the service provider character in the scene who was newly receiving the youth's file. The intervening audience member would commonly avert the discussion with the original service provider, preferring to meet the youth before looking at their file. Then a conversation with the youth would occur (sans labels) allowing the service provider to get to know the youth on a personal level, which the youth agreed would offer a more congenial approach.

We used forum theatre approaches for other projects as well. For the project at the rural Alberta high school, we performed 'The Bus Trip' scene and other similar scenes devised with the youth in forum theatre style for an audience of other students at the school where the project took place and we also travelled to a neighbouring community to perform for an audience of high-school students there. In the youth jail, we devised a forum theatre scene based on a newspaper article (I discuss this scene further in Chapter 4), though we did not have the opportunity to solicit audience interventions for that scene.

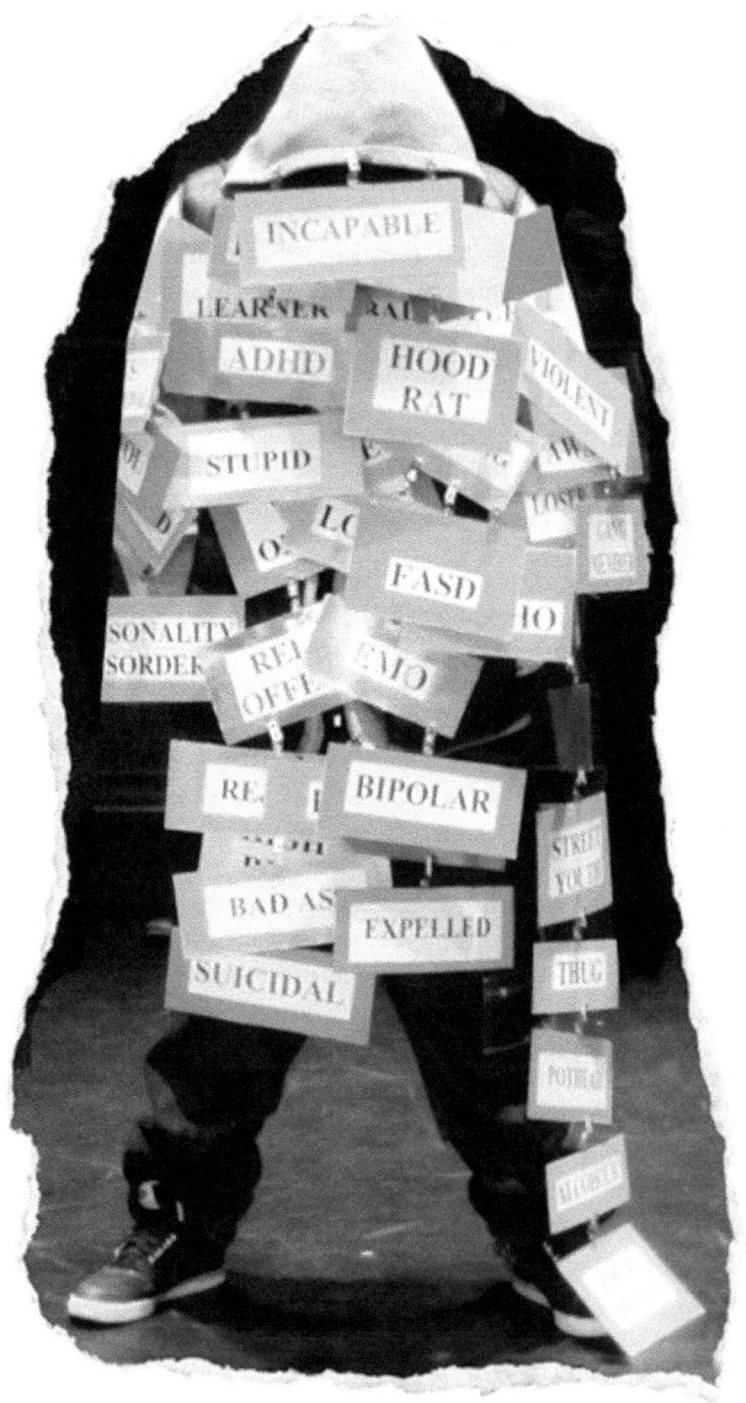

FIGURE 3.3: From the Labels scene, Uncensored project, 2010. © D. Conrad & iHuman Youth Society. Photo by Leslie Robinson.

Rehearsing and Performing

Not all of the applied theatre work with youth that I facilitated led to performance. Often, the brainstorming, storytelling, and devising processes offered plenty of opportunity for valuable exploration and meaning-making. If a scene that a group created was being prepared for performance, during rehearsals I asked youth to familiarize themselves with the minimalist scripted outlines we'd crafted, indicating only characters and their relationships, settings, situations, and some key points of dialogue, and then we'd re-create the scenes anew each time through improvisation (Kaplan, 2022; Rhoades, 2018). We never expected youth to memorize dialogue. This was key as the need to memorize lines, which would be an expectation in mainstream theatre settings, could have been oppressive to youth already struggling in life (Kaplan, 2022; Wager, 2015) and would likely have dissuaded some youths' participation altogether. Rather, we emphasized those particular details that were needed to tell the story we wanted to tell. Roles were always flexible, based on who was present at any given time (given that attendance was sporadic) and who wanted to try which role. We asked performers to commit to performances, but sometimes, youth who had committed didn't or were unable to attend a rehearsal or even a performance, often for reasons beyond their control. We always needed to be prepared to make changes. We often found ourselves having to change up roles (such as the gender of a character) and details of scenes at the last minute based on who was or wasn't there. To accommodate such last-minute changes, loose structures and flexibility were paramount.

For forum theatre performances, we generally did well in preparing the youth for what they could expect. We spent time during rehearsals explaining forum theatre and simulating potential audience interventions, but on one occasion during the Uncensored project we fell short. The project was well underway; we had already presented several workshops, so the process was familiar to most. A young woman had just joined the project and was eager to perform. She rehearsed scenes with us, so was prepared in that respect, and while we had explained forum theatre to her, we neglected to adequately prepare her for the interactive process. She was unprepared to have our stories questioned, plus that workshop was for the most challenging audience we encountered (more on this experience in Chapter 6). The youth did an outstanding job performing, improvising during scenes, and sharing during talk-back, but this young woman was emotionally exhausted by the end. In the evaluation video, she expressed being caught off guard:

I wasn't very well prepared for my first workshop 'cause we, like, rehearsed our scenes and stuff like that. I was like 'okay cool, I get to do these scenes', but then we did the whole intervention kinda thing, like where we talked to the audience and

I had no idea that was coming. So, that was really interesting. It was kinda over-whelming at a point, like, 'cause people are very stubborn. (YUEV, 2012, 00:28: 01–00:28:29)

Nevertheless, as she explained, the experience was positive overall and she was an enthusiastic participant throughout the remainder of the project.

In performances, youths' energy and enthusiasm always took centre stage. Our emphasis on improvisation honed youths' skills at being in the moment to respond to any twists and turns that their fellow performers introduced. Youth always had great fun performing and added their own flair to any role; it seemed they gained much enjoyment from the rush of performance. It always amazed me how they were able to pull off stellar performances regardless of how chaotic the rehearsal process might have been or how underprepared I may have felt they were. They never disappointed. The impact and power of their presence were always palpable, which confirmed Kidd's (1984) claim that applied theatre,

> may lack the polish of professionalism but it will make up for this with the authen-ticity and concern of people who live the situation they are presenting … Lack of technical skill will be overcome by great energy and vividness. (p. 8)

When the youth got onto stage in front of audiences, they fully embodied their expertise and their right to be seen and heard.

The semi-improvised quality of the performances also accentuated the play between the fiction of the scenes and youths' lived realities as the lines between fact and fiction blurred. In the forum theatre interventions and in talk-back with audiences, youths' responses were always astute and insightful. They alter-nately spoke as their characters from within the contexts of the scenes, always informed by their personal experiences, or as themselves speaking about their own lives. Given the platform, the youths' intelligence, wit, and talents really shone through.

Critical Reflection

Reflection is an important aspect of any applied theatre process as experience only makes sense through reflection (Bailin, 1993). As alluded to throughout this text already, *lived experience* is a valued form of knowledge in applied theatre. Individuals' life experiences, upon which the creative processes of applied theatre draw, as well as knowledge gained through the direct experiences of participating in drama/theatre activities, are embodied, emotional and intuitive. Bringing that knowledge into the cognitive realm – to one's conscious awareness, to make meaning from experience – requires ongoing reflection (Ansloos & Wager, 2020; Linds et al., 2013). Moreover, within an applied theatre project, where social issues and power dynamics are being actively explored, *critical* reflection (Gallagher, 2016; Iwasaki et al., 2014; Lavie-Ajayi & Krumer-Nevo, 2013) is a necessary component entailing not only description of what was experienced but also analysis of its implications within the broader social context.

Individual reflection is vital and even more so collective reflection. Reflecting as a group allows for the construction of shared meaning from experience, through comparing and contrasting participants' experiences, through interpreting, questioning, and challenging one another's deeply held assumptions. As Freire (1970/2000) noted, only through critical reflection can we counter dominant taken-for-granted beliefs and come to understand the whys and wherefores underlying our realities. To optimize what youth participants gained in terms of personal development and/or social learning, then, critical reflection on the drama experiences during all stages of the process was essential. Through reflection, critical questions were asked about what was shared, improvised, devised, or performed and/or how it was received by an audience – how these related to the intentions of the project, towards developing self-awareness and socially critical perspectives.

For the applied theatre projects discussed in this book, reflection was an integral part of all stages of each process. Critical reflection began through clarifying the intentions of the project, in identifying the issues to be addressed and in discussing the particularities of those issues. Through reflection, participants could begin to articulate their understandings of their then current realities and envision how their struggles could be overcome.

Following a group's participation in a game or activity, I always take a few moments to draw out learning from what was experienced during the game/activity and its significance. This is something I emphasize with my pre-service drama education students too: We don't play games in drama just for the sake of playing games, but rather, games are selected intentionally for what they can teach and this intended learning needs to be made apparent. After playing the Hypnosis game described above, for example, I always ask participants what they experienced in the game, in order to make their embodied learning explicit: How did it feel to be the leader? How did it feel to be the follower? Which role did you prefer? Why? What strategies did you use or avoid as a leader or follower? Why? How is what you experienced in this game symbolic of your real-life experiences? What does this game teach us about power?

In the sharing of personal stories, refection upon one individual's story always elicited others' related stories in response, which allowed for comparing and contrasting of experiences to get to the bottom of the power dynamics at play.

Reflection also occurred in collaboratively deciding how to compile individual personal stories into fictionalized scenarios for presentation. In the devising processes, we identified the details of the stories that spoke most clearly to what the youth wanted to say. Likewise, in rehearsal and preparation for performance, reflection was ongoing through assessing how our message did or did not come across and what would strengthen the scenario.

In Image Theatre, reflection is inherent in the animation process as the facilitator asks participants to interpret what they see in an image. Further, reflection occurs as participants enact responses (e.g. to the facilitator's prompts) based on their interpretations. In forum theatre too, reflection occurs through probing the effects of audience members' attempted interventions – how and why an intervention was successful in alleviating characters' struggles or not, and reflection also occurs during talk-back sessions with audiences.

For the Uncensored project, the video that the youth created (YUEV, 2012) as a form of arts-based evaluation of the outcomes of the project from their perspectives reflected upon their experiences prior to and their experiences of joining the project – their reasons for joining and for staying with the project; their experiences of being involved in the project – both the benefits they gained and the challenges they encountered; how they experienced their interactions with workshop audiences and what this meant to them; what overall effects they felt the project had for them, for other youth in similar circumstances, and for service providers or the services they provided. In segments of the video, the youth described the Uncensored project in a word or phrase as artistic, creative, my best friend, unpredictable, educating us all, paying my phone bills, buying my groceries, and allowing me to take risks. In other segments of the video, which the youth called *word on the street*, the youth interviewed people they encountered around the Faculty of Education building. They asked: 'What do you think would happen if a bunch of street kids got together and told social service providers how to do their job better?' Responses included:

I think that it'd be really cool to have street kids come talk to [service providers] because it kinda drives that human connection ... I need to forget about all that other stuff, all the ... things I may have learned about ... risk factors in school and all that theoretical stuff, and actually ... put a face to the population that [I'm] going to be working with and hopefully become more empathetic and more passionate about [my] job and take more pride with what [I] do as well. Overall, I think it would be a great change. (00:13:15–00:13:41)

You know ... these kids have had to learn how to become ... street psychologists ... they're so savvy and they know a lot. So, if the ... service providers were really open

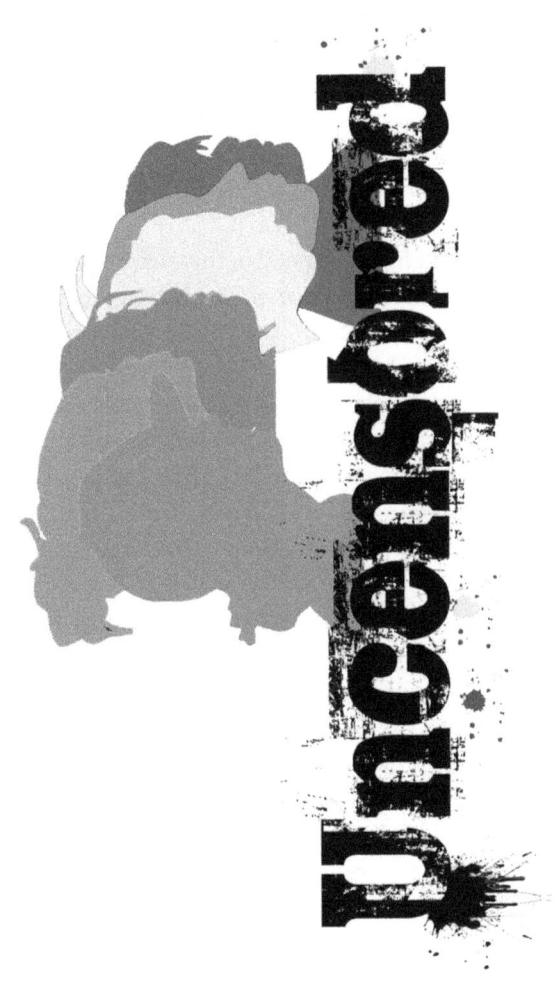

FIGURE 3.4: T-shirt design from the Uncensored project, 2011. © D. Conrad & iHuman Youth Society. Design support from Naureen Mumtaz.

to listening to and learning from them it would be a really exciting discussion. So, I don't know what you guys are doing, but I hope you can pull it off. (00:25:57–00:26:16)

Critical reflection can take many forms – from individual journal writing, to creative responses, to group discussion. In applied theatre, as reflection is inherent to many of the processes involved, it most often occurs through enacted, embodied responses and collective analyses of the emergent discoveries, as part of the shared meaning-making endeavour.

Concluding Thoughts on Applied Theatre Processes

The applied theatre processes I have outlined in this chapter describe some common approaches used by both drama education practitioners and applied theatre facilitators. The need to build a sense of cohesion in order to work together, to develop or hone some basic theatrical skills, and to lay the groundwork for exploration is consistent across groups and contexts. Through twenty-plus years of applied theatre facilitation, I've learned that even the simplest of drama games can be exploited to elicit insights and develop content. The strategies I have employed for devising work, specifically, Boal's (1974/1979) image theatre and forum theatre are common approaches in applied theatre that I have found productive and adaptable for working with systemically marginalized youth. Image theatre is a low-risk way into an applied theatre process with participants who may have limited theatre experience or are hesitant to engage. Forum theatre's problem posing approach is a brilliant avenue for opening up dialogue.

I offer these processes here as practical starting points for those interested in developing an applied theatre practice. Applied theatre, however, is not learned from books. I took formal training sessions with experienced applied theatre facilitators – Augusto Boal, David Diamond, and others, joined many applied theatre workshops as a participant, and practiced applied theatre facilitation over the course of many years before I felt somewhat comfortable in the role of facilitator. Above all, facilitating applied theatre requires close listening, learning to attune to the needs of the group, and a willingness to adapt activities to meet those needs.

While the processes described in this chapter are applicable to most groups, my applied theatre projects within the context of incarceration presented some constraints and considerations which demanded adjustments to the process, which I discuss in the following chapter.

4

Applied Theatre in the Context of Incarceration

The applied theatre processes that we engaged in within the youth jail were somewhat different from the processes described in Chapter 3. The context of the jail setting necessitated different framing with regard to intentions and expectations. Both the six-month pilot project and the longer three-year funded study were ostensibly designed to be more focused on youths' personal growth and social development (or so-called 'rehabilitation') as we needed to be seen to be complying with the expectations of the corrections system, with our underlying youth justice aims being more subtle or covert. I use the term *rehabilitation* in scare quotes above because, although Canada's Youth Criminal Justice Act (Department of Justice Canada, 2013; Doob & Cesaroni, 2004) declares rehabilitation, not punishment, as the primary goal of youth incarceration, I saw limited opportunity for real rehabilitation in the jail. Instead, as I've already mentioned, priority seemed to be given to containment for the purposes of security. Others who have facilitated applied theatre projects with incarcerated youth (Kaplan, 2022; Lamparter, 2022; Tate, 2022) concur that the setting presents particular challenges for the work because of the highly punitive nature of the environment.

While it may be true that conditions of basic security must be met before any rehabilitation can occur within the context of incarceration, if the scant resources allotted are only enough to accomplish the bare minimum: security – along with some well-intentioned, but tokenistic attempts at rehabilitative programming – real change is unlikely to occur. I saw relatively little attention given to appropriate programming for the youth; nor was the jail environment conducive to it. Some of the psycho-educational programs offered at the jail, going by names such as High Risk; What are you thinking?; Anger Management; as well as a Substance Abuse program offered at a local hospital, were derided by the youth. In any case, the notion of *rehabilitation* is itself problematic in being deficit focused (Adler & Adler,

2003; Blanchet-Cohen & Salazar, 2009; Lavie-Ajayi & Krumer-Nevo, 2013; Sapiro & Ward, 2020) – constructing individuals as having deficiencies in need of fixing, rather than considering the social context of the offending behaviour.

Regarding the context of incarceration, it is also worth noting that with the youth constantly coming and going (Kaplan, 2022) – whether unexpectedly released or banned from participating due to behaviour considered inappropriate and new youth joining – we had highly inconsistent groups of participants across sessions. The youth we worked with in the jail were mostly boys, involved with the centre's Community Transitions Program for the pilot study and the Native Program for the longer study. The number of girls in the jail was relatively fewer; only on a couple of occasions were the girls allowed to join the boys for our applied theatre sessions. While the introductory aspects of our processes began with trust-building and skill development, applied theatre in the youth jail required considerable innovation.

The Context of Incarceration

I remember how nervous I was entering the young offender centre for the first time for our applied theatre pilot project. The jail setting is quite unique – a sort of microcosm of society that is hard to describe to those who haven't experienced it. Applied theatre practitioner Baz Kershaw (1999), who spent time working with inmates in the United Kingdom, captured some of the poignancy of the setting when he suggested, the prison is

> inherently dramatic, because it is built on a context between a supposed immutable rigour of rule and the infinite suppleness of the human soul ... [and] also quintessentially *theatrical* because it stages the absolute separation thatsociety seeks to impose between good and evil. (p. 131)

His description of the prison setting, in terms of drama and theatre, offers a sense of the macro power dynamics at play in that locale in which those who are incarcerated are caught, shaping all interactions in such places. Similar to Lamparter's (2022) orientation to the setting for her work, we were cautioned to be wary of the youth described as untrustworthy and manipulative.

As a maximum-security facility, the extremely heightened sense of security in the youth jail we attended made me immediately uneasy. Approaching the outer door of the facility under camera surveillance we were buzzed in, required to identify ourselves, state our purpose for being there and were reminded of the rules. Our personal items such as purse, keys, money, pens, phone, jacket, etc., had to be left in a locker in the lobby. We were then buzzed through another set of locked doors, made to sign in at the 24-hour surveillance desk, given our identity badges which had to be visible on our persons at all times, and then told to wait for our escort. When the corrections officer we'd be working with arrived we would be buzzed through another door, walked down a long, barren corridor of drably painted cinder block to the location where our sessions would take place. The corrections officer would alert the 24-hour desk by walkie-talkie that we'd arrived at the unit and we'd be buzzed in yet again. We waited there while the youth were collected and escorted, single file, down other long, barren corridors to us. A similar procedure was repeated each time we visited and it never got any less uncomfortable. Leaving the facility always came with a sense of relief as the ominous atmosphere lifted. Even though we knew we'd be leaving at the end of each session, we couldn't help feel a rush of freedom at shedding that palpable sense of confinement ever present on the inside. The experience gave us a glimmer into how the youth must be experiencing their incarceration.

Processes of Applied Theatre with Incarcerated Youth

What we were able to do within the context of the jail was highly constrained due to the unique circumstances. In working with the youth, we were prohibited from eliciting personal stories from them as the basis for our dramatizations – particularly details related to the reasons for their incarceration. Youth in jail are often still embroiled in the justice process with court cases and legal actions pending, and with decision-making about their ultimate fates still in progress. Youth are advised by their legal counsel not to divulge any details about their current cases or details from their pasts that may be incriminating and the jail administration insisted that our work could not have youth sharing their experiences about present or past illegal activities involving gangs, drugs, violence, etc. Their fear was that discussing or enacting such activities would somehow validate or glorify the behaviour (Lamparter, 2002), or, as I mentioned previously, cause disturbances that would prevent the administration from being able to maintain control. Conversely, we were really just trying to help the youth make sense of the circumstances that led to their incarceration.

While non-incriminating elements of the youths' personal experiences did at times surface through our work together, we dared not focus on these in our theatre devising. We had to find ways for youth to intuitively draw on their experiences and understandings in our explorations without the content of our drama work requiring any explicit disclosures from them. Moreover, our work was constrained by the fact that there were limited performance opportunities within the jail setting.

Opportunities to gather a group of youth together inside the jail as an audience were precarious at best and we could not invite outside audiences into the jail as the process for being granted admission was onerous (criminal record checks, etc.) and youths' identities strictly protected. We had to conceive of audiences for our work in unconventional ways. For several of the projects we undertook, technology became a way to document and share the work back to the youth, with the technology, in effect, becoming our audience.

Over the course of the six months we spent working with youth for the pilot project and the three years for the larger funded project, we developed a series of activities and projects that were more process than product focused (Kaplan, 2022), which involved imagined/fictional scenarios to avoid drawing too directly on youths' actual personal stories. For the pilot project, we focused on exploring the youths' experiences of incarceration including their arrival at the facility, their experiences of navigating interpersonal relationships within that setting and their affective responses to being isolated and confined. The following short poem written by one of our youth participants (n.d.) captured the sorts of the sentiments the youth expressed:

> I'm looking up at the stars
> the starlight behind metal bars
> watching the car lights pass by
> wondering if I could ever be free
> this jail has me trapped
> has me praying on my knees.

Although we were not so naïve as to assume the youth were all entirely innocent, we could not help but empathize with their predicament – especially since they were always so friendly towards us and appreciative of our willingness to come to the jail to spend time with them. In our work with the Native Program for the longer project, each of our sessions ended with a smudge (an Indigenous cleansing ritual involving the burning if sacred medicines, in this case prairie sage) and a Cree prayer. Each week the youth thanked us for coming, wished us a safe drive home and a good week ahead. The strong sense of comradery we managed to develop within the jail setting was unexpected for me – I've found it hard to capture those feelings in words. The sincere warmth and affection that circulated amongst us during our group sessions were no doubt in large part due to the attentiveness of the Native Program coordinator and perhaps precisely because of the highly constrained nature of that context. The youth were always enthusiastic to participate in any activities we had planned for them. Below, I describe some of the projects we undertook with the youth and how they responded.

Adapting 'Blagg!'

Due to the extended three-year duration of the funded study, rather than facilitating one continuous project, we initiated a number of smaller activities. In considering how to begin, I recalled an exercise developed by the University of Manchester's Theatre in Prisons and Probation program, which also worked with incarcerated youth. The exercise, which they called 'Blagg!' (Centre for Applied Theatre Research, 2003), used a life-sized cut out of a young person, whom they named Joe Blagg, which participants were invited to imbue with personal details. They would explicate the character's life situation and detail a story of his involvement in criminal activity and incarceration to analyse the situation via the fictionalized scenario.

We successfully explored a version of Blagg! for one of our projects. The group collectively devised the details of the character and his life. The youth named their cardboard cut-out character Fox Fernando, a 17-year-old youth. He was a lady's man and a talented athlete – characteristics the youth admired, but he was also someone who was involved with drugs and sometimes got into fights. He had a broken nose and a scar on his face because he had fallen on a barbed wire fence .... Together we explored Fox Fernando's life choices and their consequences which ultimately led to his incarceration.

When a newspaper reporter came to the youth jail one week to write a story about the research, one youth expressed: 'It's all about decisions. One measly little decision will change your life totally, completely turn it right around, turn it upside down'. Another youth said that the theatre process 'helps me to come out of my shoes, so I can look at myself'. Their comments implied that the youth had gained insights from the activity that they could apply to their lives. I found it interesting how the youths' comments, directed to the journalist, who was writing a story about them for public consumption, seemed to indicate a sophisticated understanding of what the public might have wanted to hear from them: that they were deeply engaged in the process of *rehabilitation*. Whatever prompted the youth to respond to the journalist in the ways they did, whether they sincerely felt the work was assisting in their personal development or whether they were telling the journalist what they thought he wanted to hear (see Chapter 6 for more on youths' performative resistance), their comments went some way towards validating the work we were doing together, which the youth clearly valued for their own reasons.

We used approaches similar to the Blagg! exercise for other projects we developed, for creating fictionalized scenarios that resonated with youths' realities, sometimes evoking peripheral details from their personal experiences and always speaking to their understandings and desires. These projects primarily focused on analysing circumstances and envisioning alternatives.

Re-Storying Self Through Transformed Magazine Images

One project we undertook utilizing magazine images was initiated by one of my graduate research assistants; her interest was in visual literacy and gender identity. It involved the group of boys in meaning-making from images and storytelling around values and life choices.

We began by bringing in a wide selection of images cut from popular magazines of males of various ages and racial-cultural backgrounds engaged in a wide range of activities. We asked each boy to choose an image of a man whom he thought he might like to be and another of a man whom he would not like to be. We asked the boys to say something to describe each of the characters in the images they chose and provide a sentence or two of explanation for each of their choices. Discussion amongst the group regarding their choices elicited a lively exchange of ideas regarding the portrayals of the men in the images. For example, one popular choice of a man they wanted to be was a skateboarder, whom they were attracted to because they thought skateboarding was cool; they liked the sport and exercise involved. A man some chose as someone they would not want to be was a young man asleep on a bus. They identified him as homeless and in danger of being pick-pocketed. An image of an old man in a soldier uniform was selected by one youth as someone they didn't want to be, as he didn't want to be old, and by another as a man he wanted to be; he said he would be proud to be a veteran.

With the images of the men that the boys wanted to be, at one of the boy's suggestion, we cut out the faces of the men in the magazine pictures and replaced them with the boys' faces, cut and pasted from digital photos we took, for which the boys astutely posed in positions that exactly matched the positions of the men in the images. The boys were thrilled to see their faces superimposed on the bodies of the men in the images – giving them an opportunity to see themselves differently. This visual activity greatly enhanced the drama work that followed.

We engaged in various activities to help the youth bring their characters to life, including an activity that had them imagining the kind of shoes their character might wear and imagining themselves walking in those shoes. We had them interview one another in character, role play conversations with persons close to them, tell stories of key events in their characters' lives, and identify significant life choices they imagined their characters had made. Finally, we had them devise three alternative endings for their characters' life stories to emphasize the existence of multiple possibilities, rather than focusing on only a single outcome.

The work was insightful in the choices the youth made, in the contrast between the images different youth selected and in the language they used to describe or explain them. The work provided new understandings of the life-worlds of the youth, presenting their perspectives as both quite ordinary – what we might expect from boys of their age, and quite distinctive – for example, in their specific sub-cultural referents.

Selecting images, creating characters, and telling stories involved a process of examining and articulating youths' ways of being, becoming aware of the nuances of their values and choices. The images spoke to the participants in unique and varied ways. Through character development and story-telling the boys had opportunities to speak through their characters' voices, using *I* statements, internalizing and making connections to their own lives. The storytelling and multiple endings to their stories explored choices, actions, and consequences. We moved from the stereotypical to a more relational level through developing nuanced life histories, exploring key life events and possibilities for their characters' futures. We examined how a life story can unfold in various different ways based on one's choices. The boys considered how their characters' stories could end. Through the drama, through enacting the characters, through imaginative interactions between self and other, the youth had opportunities, in reflecting on their own identities, to also imagine themselves as otherwise – as potentially other than *offender* or *criminal*, to help them make sense of their own life experiences and look for alternatives.

Envisioning Incarcerated Youths' Wildest Dreams

Another project we facilitated was an adaptation of Diamond's (2007) 'Your Wildest Dream', which employs Boal's (1974/1979) image theatre techniques. We integrated image theatre and digital photography with the aim of exploring possible future goals, and for assisting the youth in developing self-understandings about how to make positive change in their lives possible. The exercise drew on Freire's (1994) suggestion that 'you never get there by starting from there, you get there by starting from some here' (p. 57). The process helped participants envision paths from *here* (a current reality) to *there* (an ideal reality).

The activity involved creating a series of *now* or *real* images symbolizing how the youth perceived their then present realities. For each real image, we created a number of different *ideal* future images. All the images were digitally photographed. For each pairing of real to ideal, we then created and photographed a series of images tracing the steps needed to achieve the ideal. The photos were all printed and laid out on the floor. Participants negotiated placement of each image on a continuum for each scenario representing the choices and decisions the characters needed to make to get from the present real to the desired future ideal. We gave images titles and articulated the thoughts and wishes of the characters in the images. The youth then had opportunities to each present their version of a story for any of the sequences of photos, in the process elucidating their narrations of self, relationships, community, culture, values, beliefs, and desires. The activity provided a structured space for the youth to make sense of their lives, their circumstances and to generate new meanings about their futures through inter-acting with peers, images, and a creative process. The youth thoroughly enjoyed making images and telling stories.

Here I share details of two image series that emerged as examples. The first series began with a real image which they titled *In Line*. It showed a number of youth walking in single file formation as they were required to do in the corridors of the jail. One corresponding ideal image, which they titled *Role Models*, showed a group of youth proudly posing and flexing their muscles for a photo. One story that was told about this sequence was about a group of youth in jail committing themselves to weight lifting (which was an activity the youth participated in and enjoyed at the facility) and achieving their goal of becoming *ripped*. The ideal image showed them posing for a photo for a weight-lifting calendar. This story elicited discussion around: What is a role model? How does one become a role model? Why is being a role model important to you? The responses, seriously considered and sincere, involved the need for giving and receiving respect, good decision-making, and caring for oneself in terms of eating well, working out, and not smoking weed. These were all positive goals the youth could imagine for themselves.

Another interesting image sequence began with a real image of a group of youth sitting in a circle around a drum – an image of a traditional Cree drumming group, which they titled *Spiritual Gathering*. The corresponding ideal image showed the youth in a pose of celebration, which they titled *Indigenous Champions*. One iter-ation of the corresponding story involved the drum group entering a drumming competition and having to overcome a series of challenges to ultimately emerge as the winners. This story was understood as a positive metaphor for the youths' lives – the need to overcome challenges in order to succeed and also drew on their Indigenous cultural pride (more on this in the following chapter).

Recurring themes that we identified throughout all the images, both real and ideal, and the corresponding stories included aspects of Indigenous culture, friend-ship, competition, sports, food, sexuality, and street-life. Not surprisingly, many of the images and the stories elicited related closely to the youths' then current lived experiences in the jail. We noted that the images and stories, in fact, never ventured very far from that reality – i.e., into the realm of fantasy, which could also have been an option. Even the ideal images they created were still quite realistic, set in the not-too-distant future and in familiar venues. The *Role Models* ideal image, still set within the jail, was not a far stretch from their then present reality, but was clearly very significant for them. The *Indigenous Champions* ideal image was perhaps a bit more distant, with a more challenging goal, but still set within the realm of their experiences.

As Diamond (2007) related in working with this exercise, he had witnessed communities that had extreme difficulty imagining an ideal, as they were so deeply entrenched in their present reality. Castell and Jenson (2006), in working with street-involved, queer, and otherwise marginalized youth, also noted that youth in difficult circumstances were challenged to set realistic goals. Dominant or mainstream 'discourses of power', they claimed, 'of "self-realization" and "careers", of education and lifestyles and "planning for one's future" – [were] superimposed on, but too often discontinuous with, the identities, positions and conditions of [those] and many other marginalized youth' (p. 239). This seemed to have been the case for our project and in the pilot project with incarcerated youth as well. In an activity exploring the youths' future goals for the pilot project, we were struck by how challenging it seemed to be for them to set positive long-term goals. Their responses were most often focused on short-term gratification. When we asked what they would do when they got out. Their answers included: have a cigarette, get stoned, and get laid. When pressed to think longer-term, one scenario they created, involved getting married, which, however, ended in tragedy with the man getting drunk and beating up the woman. On the up-side, this scenario did initiate an intense discussion amongst the youth about how men should treat women, during which multiple sides of the issue were debated.

Castell and Jenson (2006) suggested, we need to offer youth discourses that make sense for them. We did notice, in the 'Your Wildest Dream' activity that we undertook for the longer project, that the work overall displayed very positive relationships amongst the youth and much support for one another, a sense of community – in itself suggesting a hopeful future. At the very least, the project was an opportunity for the youth to reflect on their real circumstances and consider choices – to dialogue with and consider the multiple perspectives presented by their peers and to imagine possible futures on their own terms.

Exploring Issues of 'Citizenship' through Newspaper Theatre

Newspaper theatre, one of Boal's (1974/1979) earliest Theatre of the Oppressed forms, allows topics raised by newspaper articles to be re-examined from multiple alternative perspectives through theatre. Newspaper theatre's aims, as outlined by Boal, were to popularize the means of making theatre, to demonstrate that theatre can be practiced by anyone to show and defend their ideas and to demystify the pretended objectivity of journalism, allowing people to read newspapers differently.

A newspaper theatre project, which we undertook, began from the youths' response to a newspaper article, from which we devised a forum theatre type scene. To work within the centre's demand that we not talk explicitly about criminal activity, I looked for material that would raise challenging issues, and be relevant to the life experiences of the youth, without addressing crime or criminality directly. The *Edmonton Journal* (Kent, 2007) newspaper article we drew upon discussed our then mayor's suggestion to adopt a bylaw that threatened fines up to $10,000 for coercive panhandling. (In 2008, such a bylaw was passed in Edmonton, but with fines only up to $250.) The issue of panhandling in Edmonton, as raised in the article, met the criteria for appropriate and provocative content with which to work. It pushed the limits of what is and is not considered *criminal* and engaged with a meaningful local current event with broad social implications.

When I first read the news article, I was struck by its absurdity which I suspected would not be lost on the youth. I was particularly incensed by the article's claim that, 'while [the mayor] isn't concerned about someone quietly seeking a handout ...' (Kent, 2007, para. 4). I reflected that perhaps if our mayor *were* more concerned over the need for citizens of our city to seek handouts there would be no need for concern over coercive panhandling.

To justify the project to the centre's administration, I drew on Alberta Education's rationale and philosophy for their K-12 Social Studies program:

> Social studies provides opportunities for students to develop the attitudes, skills and knowledge that will enable them to become engaged, active, informed and responsible citizens ... Social studies helps students develop their sense of self and community, encouraging them to affirm their place as citizens in an inclusive, democratic society ... It promotes a sense of belonging and acceptance in students as they engage in active and responsible citizenship at the local, community, provincial, national and global level. (2005, p. 1)

The language of the Social Studies curriculum around *responsible citizenship*, which read as benign neo-liberalism, full of vague platitudes and empty rhetoric, was easily reinterpreted by us in more radical terms.

As I had, the youth responded to the article with fervour. We began our process with discussion of the article and the issues it raised. As I anticipated, the youth too perceived the proposed bylaw as absurd. They wondered how someone who needed to panhandle could be expected to pay a $10,000 fine. They saw the tactic for what it was – the criminalization of the poor, a way for the municipal government to control undesirable behaviours. The youth saw panhandling as a measure of desperation and they all agreed they would never want to be in a position to have to panhandle to survive. They identified poverty and addictions as factors that led to panhandling and described a vicious cycle that was difficult to escape once caught up in it. They felt that rather than create bylaws against panhandling, the government had a responsibility to address the needs of the poor, the homeless and citizens with addictions. They linked the criminalization of the poor with the similar criminalization of youth (Giroux, 2003) by police and *citizens*, claiming that in their experiences, any group of two or more youth gathered together in public were treated as a threat. They spoke at length about their experiences of police harassment and, in fact, wanted to create a scene about police harassment of youth. When I responded that the administration would never allow such a scene, they were incensed that they were not allowed to say what they wanted. This led to a lengthy discussion about censorship and how to get around it within the context of the jail. In devising our scene, we practiced ways of saying what the youth wanted to say without overstepping the boundaries of what was permitted.

To elucidate our discussion, we created images and scenarios about panhandling, addictions, loitering, conflict between citizens, and police harassment that built towards our forum theatre style scene – presenting a problem with no resolution. We entitled it '*Need Change?*' The setting for our scene was a store owned by a local businessman – a presumably *good citizen*. The storekeeper's character was established as he complained to his employee about the employee's laziness. Next, a group of three youth arrived outside the store, their pre-arranged meeting place, to purchase what they needed for the eighteenth birthday party that evening for one of their cousins. A panhandler approached the friends asking them for money for food. They gave the panhandler five dollars just as another customer approached the store. The panhandler also asked the newly arrived customer for money and got a bit pushy with the reluctant customer. The customer became angry shooing the panhandler away before proceeding into the store where he immediately complained to the storekeeper about being *harassed* at the door. Meanwhile, the panhandler returned to the group of friends asking them for a cigarette which they gave him. Just then the storekeeper stepped outside, saw the group of friends and accused them of loitering and harassing his customers. The friends tried to explain that they were customers too, but the storekeeper refused to listen. A heated argument ensued with the youth trying to defend themselves all the while sheltering the panhandler from the wrath of the storekeeper. When the storekeeper threatened to call the police, frustrated, the friends left saying they'd do their shopping elsewhere. After the friends had left the storekeeper noticed the panhandler still standing where the youth had been and realized his confusion. Angry, the storekeeper knocked loose change from the panhandler's hands and returned into the store to call the police. The scene ended with the panhandler picking up his coins from the ground.

While circumstances in the jail did not unfold in a way that allowed us to present our scene as a forum theatre performance to an audience of other inmates as we'd hoped to, we did talk with the youth about the intentions of forum theatre in posing a problem and seeking solutions. The group was very aware that we had created a problem scene and we even practiced a few interventions looking for more positive outcomes for the three youth and the panhandler. We did perform the scene once for a small audience of staff and administrators (sans interventions), to give them an opportunity to vet the scene. The youth were very excited to perform – nervous beforehand, but very willing, and afterwards elated by the performance rush, their achievement, and the opportunity to have spoken out. Our small audience was thoroughly impressed at the youths' performance skills and the emotional reality they were able to portray. The level of emotional reality achieved was, of course, precisely because the content was based on the youths' analysis of the issues relevant to their actual lived experiences. The audience also commented on the compassion the youth characters showed towards the panhandler. In a small way, the performance at least gave the administrators and staff in attendance an opportunity to see the youth differently – as active, productive, and empathetic individuals. It gave the youth an opportunity to express their ideas, gaining agency and empowerment through the process.

Comics Creation: An Anti-violence Message Pre-empted

On one occasion we began a project that we were forced to abandon; when the administration learned about the nature of the work we were undertaking, they deemed it overstepping the bounds. I was censored and reprimanded, putting the entire applied theatre research program at-risk.

I should have known better since the fictionalized collaborative story we were in the process of creating, which we planned to turn into a comic book, involved two fictional rival gangs. The message of the story that emerged, though, was so positive that I was excited to proceed. The title we gave the story was *Violence Effects Everyone*; it was intended as an anti-violence message. As the story unfolded, week-by-week, we took photographs of the youth in positions to tell the story, to which we planned to apply a comic creation filter and then add dialogue bubbles and text to narrate the story.

The story began with two rival gangs with long-standing disputes. Through twists and turns of the storyline, it was revealed that one gang leader's daughter was in love with a member of the other gang. After the boys had devised this aspect of the story, upon reflection, it dawned on me that we were, inadvertently, creating a Romeo and Juliet story. True to Shakespeare's (1597/2014) tragedy, the rivalry in our story came to a head when first the boyfriend and then the daughter were both killed in the crossfire between the two gangs. At the funeral, the two gang leaders came to their senses and decided to make peace.

I was so excited by this story that I shared it with the head administrator, at which point she immediately shut our comic creation project down. It was disappointing for the group that their positive intentions were not received as such.

Concluding Thoughts on Applied Theatre
in the Context of Incarceration

Foucault (1979) described incarceration as an apparatus of power and punishment governed by a mentality which more effectively re-inscribed criminality than it deterred crime or reformed offenders. Indeed, in the youth jail, I witnessed a mentality that gave priority to security – justified as being for the protection of youth from themselves, from other youth, and for the protection of society from them. Security was accomplished through containment and control – close surveillance and segregation; a fixed schedule and a set of strictly defined rules and procedures; a daily point system for behaviour that awarded or revoked privileges; regular pat downs; the risk of punishment, dorm confinement or isolation for bad behaviour; and the ever-present threat of strip-search (Figure 4.1). Within such a context, engagement with youth which resists the taken-for-granted view of youth as a threat (Giroux, 2022) might be deemed radical.

Kershaw (1999) believed that if the *radical* (by which he meant politically subversive) can exist in performance, it is not in mainstream theatres, but in alternative sites, such as in prison contexts. He described radical performance as performance that invokes

> not just freedom *from* oppression, repression, exploitation – the resistant sense of the radical, but also freedom *to reach beyond* existing systems of formalized power, freedom to create currently unimaginable forms of association and action – the transgressive and transcendent sense of the radical. (p. 18)

It was, perhaps, the very constraints imposed by the institution of incarceration that compelled moments of performance in our projects with incarcerated youth that had radical potential.

What we achieved through our applied theatre projects in terms of knowledge generation and interpretation was, in my opinion, profound, despite the constrained environment of the youth jail, or perhaps precisely because of it. I offer here the following as a final example of recurring moments of performance within the context our work with the incarcerated youth, which, I believe, showed radical potential. These micro-performances did not occur during our drama work, but in random, spontaneous moments in between the formal activities. In our passing interactions with the youth; if ever I commented on the way they wore their standard-issue, faded and stretched-out, navy-blue sweat pants low on their hips almost to the point of falling down, a youth might spontaneously pull his pants all the way up to his chest, tight around the crotch, and posture in mocking imitation of some despised authority figure. This always

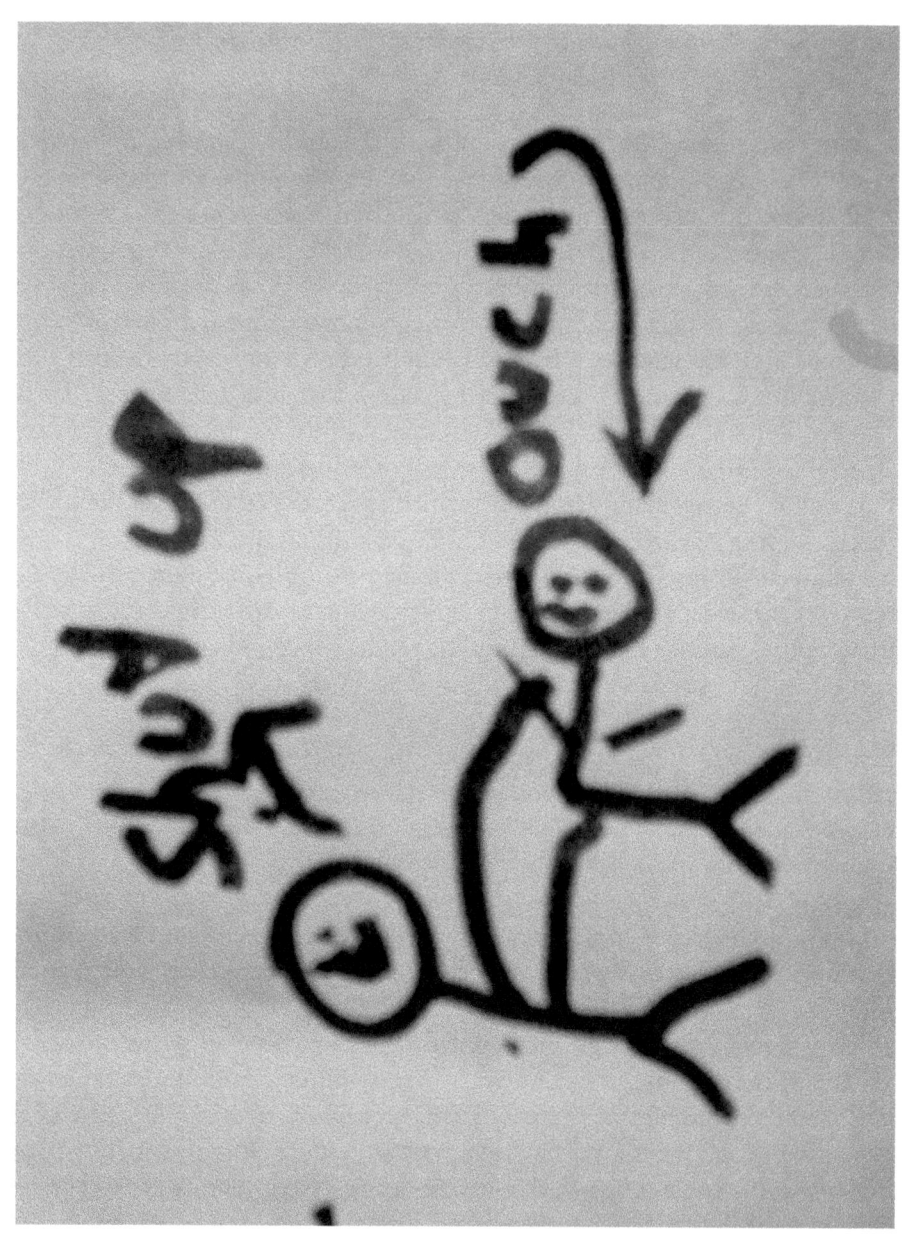

FIGURE 4.1: Strip-search image from graffiti wall for pilot project with incarcerated youth, 2004. © D. Conrad. Project co-investigator Gail Campbell.

raised a raucous round of laughter amongst the youth. The counter-cultural fashion style of wearing one's pants low on the hips like that, known as *sagging* (Wikipedia, 2022), had been described as a symbol of freedom and rejection of mainstream values, which possibly even originated in prison settings. (I found this antic of the youths' so compelling, that it even found its way into a scene in the play I wrote about my research experience [Conrad, 2012]). Kershaw (1999) proclaimed, and I agree, 'if radicalism can flourish through performance as part of *those* social processes [in jail], then it may potentially prosper in many others' (p. 20).

Referring again to the play I wrote about my research experience in the youth jail, *Athabasca's Going Unmanned* (Conrad, 2012), as in forum theatre style, the forward movement of my play's plot ended at a high point of action without resolution. I left the ending to the narrative deliberately ambiguous to evoke the complex realities of the youths' lives, the search for solutions to the broad social challenges they faced and alternatives for enacting youth justice. Interspersed throughout the play, disrupting the plots linearity, were several alternative endings to the play, written as short video scripts, from the perspectives of various characters in relation to an escape plan which was the plot's driving force. The alternative video endings were offered as possible outcomes to the potential choices the characters made. Audiences were called upon to make sense of the alternative endings for themselves, imagining how they think the story might have resolved. Whether the escape plan was actually executed, successful or failed, performed or imagined, also remained ambiguous. This deliberate ambiguity drew attention to the multiple performative possibilities of any situation (de Certeau, 1984; Schechner, 2003) – to highlight the fact that the endings to the incarcerated youths' stories had yet to be written, that opportunities for doing things differently existed, which was a focus of much of our applied theatre work with the youth.

I share other details of the work achieved with youth in the jail in the next chapter where I specifically discuss Indigenous themes addressed throughout all the applied theatre projects. I also touch on an example of storytelling with incarcerated youth in Chapter 6, which focuses on the potential for empowerment through applied theatre with systemically marginalized youth.

5

Engaging with Indigenous
Youth through Applied Theatre

This chapter draws on details from the projects previously discussed in all of which many Indigenous youth were involved, to specifically explore the potential for Indigenous youths' *survivance* and *resurgence*. To do so, I draw on relevant literature by Indigenous scholars, theatre artists, and applied theatre facilitators. As I mentioned in Chapter 1, while I did not specifically seek to work with Indigenous youth in my applied theatre research engagements with systemically marginalized youth, I realized that I could not evade the reality that Indigenous youth were so widely over-represented amongst the youth most marginalized in the region where I worked, and therefore over-represented within the youth projects that I facilitated. As a non-Indigenous scholar, I undertook this work with care, as best I could, already deeply immersed in a journey towards educating myself about Indigenous histories, cultures, issues and perspectives, and with some experience living and working in a Dene community.

I use the term *Indigenous* to be inclusive in speaking about the youth with whom I researched as the youth identified as members of various First Nations, including the Cree, Dene, Blackfoot, and Anishinaabe nations, as well as Métis and Inuit and often as some combinations of these Indigenous groups and other racial-cultural groups. I want to emphasize that what I share here regarding my engagement with Indigenous youth is based on my limited experiences which were always learning opportunities for me; I claim no expertise in working with Indigenous youth. Also, I have to acknowledge that while our work together, across all of the projects, did address issues of marginalization, which included the marginalization of Indigenous peoples, we never explicitly addressed/critiqued settler-colonialism. I see this now, especially following the Truth and Reconciliation Commission's Calls to Action (Government of Canada, 2015), as a serious omission that would need to be addressed in any such future work.

Prior to beginning my graduate studies in Alberta, I had worked in two vastly different contexts in which people Indigenous to the lands on which I was then situated had suffered and continued to suffer from colonial rule. My first experience was in the small southern African country of Lesotho which had been a British *protectorate* during the Boer Wars. While Lesotho maintained its political independence as a country, it was entirely surrounded by South Africa and so was economically and politically under the thumb of the then Apartheid regime. I lived there for five years working as a volunteer teacher in two different schools – one run by the Catholic Church, and in both of which English was the language of instruction. Then, upon my return to Canada, I lived and taught high school for three years in two different Northwest Territories Dene communities in which the influences of settler colonialism – via, for example, the mandated use of the Alberta curriculum and the schools' dependence on employing teachers from the *south* (including me) – were evident. In both of these contexts I was tasked with teaching Indigenous youth (Basotho and Dene). My experiences of living and working as a white, outsider to the Indigenous cultures and the education I gained from these experiences, informed my understandings of appropriate approaches for facilitating applied theatre and researching with Indigenous youth.

In relation to the research projects I discuss in this text, my social location as an adult, white settler, university-based researcher, who was living and working on stolen Indigenous lands, researching with Indigenous youth, requires ongoing interrogation. I acknowledge that while my self-reflexivity is important for bringing structural power relations of colonization in which my subjectivity and research are enmeshed into view, it can never mitigate, neutralize, or transcend those relations (D'Arcangelis, 2018). Rather, I must inhabit the discomfort and complexity of my positionality (Ahmed, 2006) and remain implicated in the incommensurable critique of ongoing colonization (Tuck & Yang, 2012). As a scholar, I sought and found methods – namely applied theatre and participatory research (which I discussed in Chapter 1) – that aligned with my personal political commitments to social justice, anti-racism, and decolonization. I sought and continue to seek to make use of the power and privilege that come with my location in ethical ways and hope that the work I describe in this chapter and elsewhere in this text made at least a small, positive contribution towards counteracting ongoing structural violence in the lives of Indigenous youth.

As we know, sadly, Indigenous youth are the inheritors of a colonial legacy characterized by ongoing economic and social injustices perpetrated against Indigenous peoples. Their marginalization involves systemic injustices within our institutions including, for example, in our schools, in the justice system and in the social/child welfare systems. Indigenous youth in Canada are twice as likely as non-Indigenous children to live in poverty (Citizens for Public Justice, 2015;

McDonald & Wilson, 2013); they have been taken from their families by child services at a rate eight times higher than that of their non-Indigenous counterparts (Anaya, 2014). They are disproportionately incarcerated (Chalverley et al., 2010) with approximately two-thirds of inmates in jails (for youth and adults) in Alberta and across Canada identifying as Indigenous due to a systemically racist justice system (Neugebaur, 2000; Office of the Correctional Investigator Canada, 2006). Indigenous youth have high rates of high-school incompletion (Canadian Council on Learning, 2009) and are over-represented amongst youth identified as at-risk in schools (Alberta Learning, 2001). Indigenous youth disproportionately find themselves under-housed and on the streets (Public Health Agency of Canada, 2006), are amongst the numbers of Indigenous women and girls missing and murdered (see e.g. Laboucan-Massimo & Big Canoe, 2015), and are more likely than non-Indigenous youth to die by suicide (Health Canada, 2014). Moreover, services for Indigenous children and families such as infrastructure on reserves (e.g. clean drinking water, housing), education, and healthcare continue to be underfunded (French, 2021; Hyslop, 2019).

Others who have facilitated applied theatre projects with Indigenous youth in Canada (Ansloos & Wager, 2020; Linds et al., 2013) noted an obligation to address the dire circumstances as described above. Any research undertaken with Indigenous youth must avoid furthering colonial violence and damage-centred narratives (Tuck, 2009; Donald & Krahn, 2014) and assist, in any ways possible, in supporting their survivance (Vizenor, 1994, 2008) and resurgence (Alfred, 2004; Simpson, 2016). I believe applied theatre research with Indigenous youth can respond to ongoing settler-colonial injustices through opening space to allow Indigenous youths' voices and perspectives to be heard, their desires to be acknowledged, and for others to see their wisdom and hope.

Survivance and Resurgence in the Lives of Indigenous Youth

I realize it may be presumptuous of me, as a non-Indigenous scholar, to invoke the terms *survivance* and *resurgence* in relation to my work with Indigenous youth; I do so to draw attention to these vital concepts. While I did not begin the applied theatre research I facilitated with explicit reference to *survivance* and *resurgence*, I contend that these are powerful concepts that may offer appropriate, decolonial ways of understanding the potential value applied theatre engagement can have for Indigenous youth (Donald et al., 2012; Korteweg & Bissell, 2016; Tuck & Wang, 2011).

The concepts of survivance and resurgence are critical analytic tools utilized in Indigenous studies. *Survivance*, as introduced by Anishinaabe scholar Vizenor

(1994), is 'more than survival, more than endurance and mere response' (p. 15). It indicates Indigenous presence as active, vibrant, and alive and survival as resistance to dominant discourses of disappearance. Michi Saagiig scholar Simpson described (2016) Indigenous *resurgence* as a generative process of nation-building and mobilization for land reclamation and 'regeneration of Indigenous political, educational and knowledge systems' (2016, p. 21). Tsalagi Cherokee scholar Corntassel (2012) saw resurgence in everyday acts that challenge the destructive forces of ongoing colonialism.

The significance of applied theatre with Indigenous youth is in the potential of these methods for revitalizing or regenerating youths' ways of being and for amplifying their voices. As Kanien'kehá:ka scholar Alfred insisted, stories, ritual, and ceremony are essential for 'the regeneration of authentic indigenous existences' (2005, p. 249). Likewise, Choctaw scholar Kenny (1998) described the arts as fundamental to life for First Nations peoples, as ways of experiencing and expressing qualities of life and Tewa scholar Cajete (1994) noted that engagement with the arts for Indigenous education and development is 'an integral part of learning, being, and becoming complete' (p. 141). In these ways, arts processes offer youth spaces for expression of their identities and for sustaining and revitalizing their cultures – for examining who they are, how they understand their cultures and communities and their place in the world. Cajete claimed that as processes of re-creation and celebration of self, the arts offer possibilities for healing – 'for developing and perpetuating a process of life-enhancing relationships' (p. 150), to work against the effects of colonization (Battiste, 2013) and to envision possible alternative futures and ethical spaces of possibility (Ermine, 2007). As L'nu Mi'kmaq scholar Battiste noted, there is promise in youths' 'self-reflective narratives that help them to understand their own situation ... and refram[e] what has been cast as negative into more positive ways' (p. 71).

As my recounting of our experiences below will attest, the Indigenous youth involved in the applied theatre research I facilitated displayed sophisticated understandings of their circumstances; our work reflected youths' vitality and insights. My discussion in this chapter seeks to acknowledge the youths' agency, to respect their complex personhood (Tuck, 2009), and to highlight the ways in which the research supported processes that offered youth opportunities to be seen and heard.

From Life in the Sticks to Agency and Choice

As I mentioned previously, my doctoral research was set in a rural Alberta high school with a large Indigenous population, the public school being in close proximity to several Cree reserves. In this setting, although a majority of the youth were Indigenous, reference to Indigenous culture and identity was only made occasionally. I wondered to what extent the systemic conditions of the school context with its unequal power relations, overlaid by race – as all of the teachers including me were white – shaped the content of our research. Perhaps youth self-censored as a defensive strategy to keep their most sensitive stories, those related to their Indigenous identities, well out of the reach of the institutional grasp. Or perhaps, as our theme Life in the Sticks suggested, at least within the context our work together, they collectively identified more with or were more willing to engage with the theme of their rural environment as the source of their oppression.

Risky Choices on 'The Bus Trip'

The example of 'The Bus Trip' scene, which I discussed in some detail in Chapter 3, perhaps addressed Unangax̂ scholar Tuck's (2009) call for research that captures youths' desires, which is generative and engaged. In our work around that scene, youth explored the motivations for their risk-taking behaviours: drinking on the bus trip was for *the rush*; they shared their perspectives on rule-breaking, and positioned themselves at odds with the authority of the school in insisting that the punishment of expulsion imposed on the instigator of the illicit activity was unjust since no harm had come from it, articulating their shared sense of justice.

When I asked the youth at the end of the study what they thought about the label *at-risk*, they claimed that their *risky* behaviours, examples of which were depicted in 'The Bus Trip' scene and other scenes we devised together, were a matter of personal choice. In our discussion, when asked why youth engaged in risky behaviours, the student who called herself Lady said, 'just because you want to', and Lucky responded 'because it's your own choice'. This reversal of their claim at the outset of the project that their behaviours were due to the boredom of living in a rural environment gave them back a sense of agency and control over their lives. Yet, their risky choices may still have led to negative consequences, perhaps meted out by authorities over whom the youth had no control.

As 'The Bus Trip' example perhaps illustrates, desire-based research (Tuck, 2009) shifts the theory of change away from the oversimplifying binary of repro-duction *or* resistance towards a synthesis of oppression *and* agency – which in this case manifest as an understanding between youth being objects of their rural environment *and* being subjects with free choice. Applied theatre created an alter-native space (Gallagher & Rodricks, 2017b; Hughes, 2013) for exploring the complexity of the youths' personhood including the contradictions, complicities, and interdependencies that characterized their lived realities. It did not ignore the challenges they experienced, but emphasized hope, vision, their wisdom as individuals and communities, and celebrated *survivance*. For Visenor, 'stories of survivance [indicate] an active presence ... an active repudiation of dominance, tragedy, and victimry' (1994, p. 15). In this sense, the scenarios that the youth devised and their analyses of them may perhaps be seen as acts of survivance.

Anishinaabe/Ashkenazi theatre scholar Carter (2016) spoke of the significance of stories in Indigenous knowledge systems and the power of re-creation stories, the re-creative act, as 'survivance-intervention' (p. 61). These are expressions of Indigenous presence and what Carter refers to as *sovereignty* in terms of the individual rather than the nation – as self-recognition of strength in one's way of being. For Indigenous youth, a sense of individual sovereignty/survivance is vital. The stories youth created for our project perhaps offered the youth 'a new way of seeing and recreating themselves as sovereign human beings' (Carter, 2016, p. 35).

Radical Performance with Incarcerated Youth

My applied theatre research with youth in jail confirmed the statistics across Canada at the time (Chalverley et al., 2010) that approximately 60% of incarcerated youth were youth of Indigenous descent. The Native Program in the youth jail was a concession, on the part of the facility's administration, to this disproportionate incarceration rate of Indigenous youth. I credit the Métis corrections officer who invited my applied theatre research to join her afterschool, extracurricular program and who worked alongside me throughout the study for much of the success of the project. For the Native Program, she offered the youth Indigenous cultural activities and arts activities – often inviting Elders and guest artists in to work with the youth, which they appreciated and enjoyed. In her dedicated program space, she posted the youths' artworks (Figure 5.1) and photos of the youth engaged in positive activities making it a welcoming home-space in which the youth knew they were valued and respected – so counter to the suspicious and punitive climate in the jail overall. She provided a safe, nurturing, culturally appropriate, and creative environment for the youth. The Native Program offered youth interludes of humanity and agency in a setting otherwise constrained and dispassionate.

The Native Program coordinator believed in the value that my proposed engagement with the youth through applied theatre might offer and therefore invited me to work with her program. It is also significant to acknowledge that any youth interested in participating in the Native Program, whether they were Indigenous or not, were welcomed to participate. While the majority of the youth were Indigenous, some non-Indigenous youth also joined in. As the study was part of the Native Program, we often intentionally introduced Indigenous themes and/ or left space for the youth to introduce such themes.

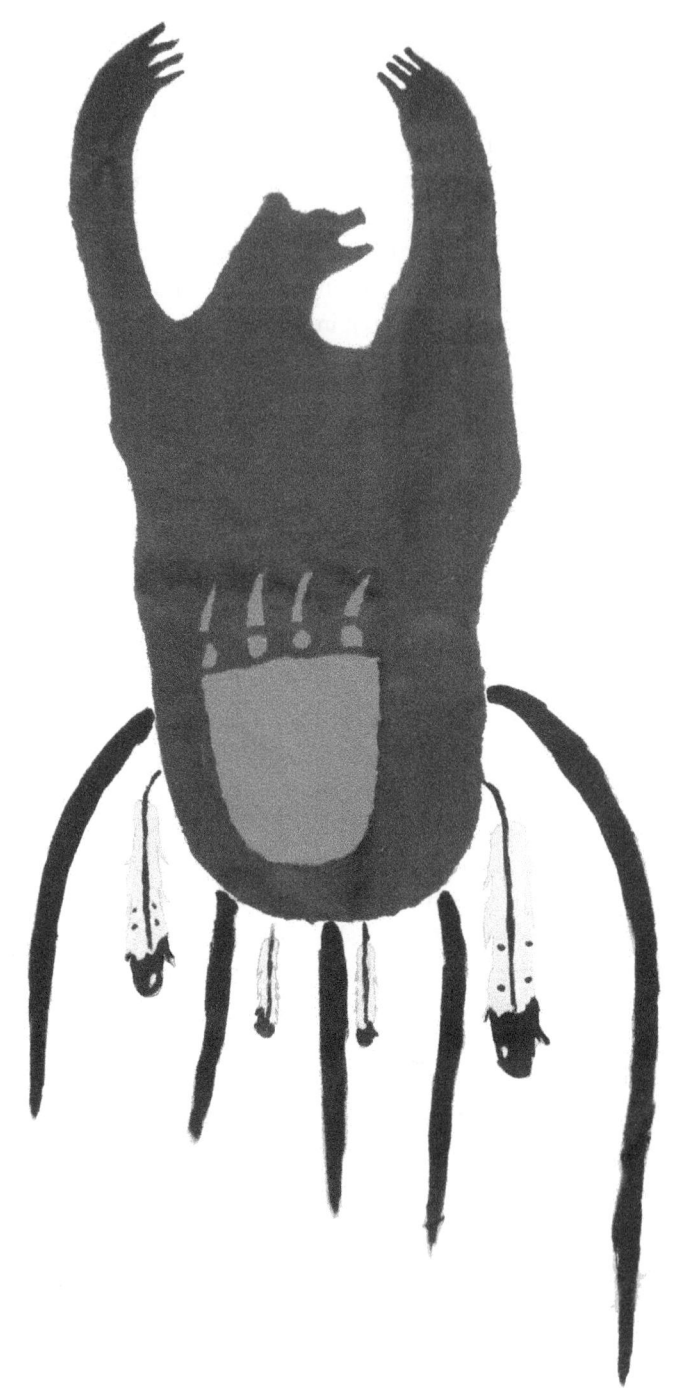

FIGURE 5.1: Artwork by one of the incarcerated youth, gifted to the author, 2007. © D. Conrad.

In my reflection on the work we undertook in the jail with these youth, I found moments of what Kershaw described as the freedom invoked by *radical performance* 'to reach beyond existing systems of formalized power … to create currently unimaginable forms of association and action' (p. 18). Kershaw's radical performance perhaps spoke to Corntassel's (2012) understanding of Indigenous resurgence as involving 'the courage and imagination to envision life beyond the state' (p. 89) as the examples below attempt to illustrate.

Symbolic Escape through Digital Storytelling

A digital storytelling project (Alrutz, 2013; see StoryCentre https://www.storycenter.org/ for examples of digital stories) we undertook began with the group of youth choosing one of the Cree cultural teachings represented on posters that the Native Program coordinator had hung on the walls of the unit. From amongst *humility*, *faith*, *kindness*, etc., the group chose *respect* as the theme for a story. The story they devised, which they entitled 'Bobby Learns Respect', involved a young man learning respect from his Kohkum (grandmother in Cree) and then enacting the teaching within his community. The story began with a group of friends hanging out in front of the band office with nothing to do. They went to Kohkum's house to play video games, but when a fight broke out amongst the friends, Kohkum chased them outside and told Bobby to *show some respect*. The friends went outside to enjoy barbequed bannock burgers and soda in Mosom's (grandfather in Cree) backyard. Later that day they went to the community hall for a round dance. When a group of rowdy youth arrived at the dance with alcohol, Bobby told them to *show some respect*. He let them know that they were welcomed at the round dance, but not with alcohol.

For this project, we collectively devised and storyboarded the narrative with the youth drawing on their cultural backgrounds and experiences to elucidate the story details. We then took digital photos of the youth posed in positions that represented each scene from the story. We took the photos to the facility's computer lab where we edited them onto various digital backgrounds appropriate to the events of the story. Then we strung the edited photos together with video editing software and added visual effects, transitions, background music, and audio narration of the story in the youths' voices.

The result was a five-minute video/digital story with which the youth were quite pleased. The story helped them express their understandings of respect and showed how they understood learning and change as ongoing processes. What most delighted the youth was how the digital medium allowed the youth to see themselves on the *outs* (a term they used to describe the world outside of the jail) – to symbolically escape the constraints of the jail, to move them into other times and places, engaged in everyday situations and relationships other than those in which they found themselves at the time.

Similarly, in other projects with the incarcerated youth, as described in Chapter 4, youth had opportunities to symbolically imagine themselves otherwise. Through altering magazine images of men the youth said they might like to be – including an image of an attractive Indigenous man that several of the youth chose and whom they described as a horse whisperer and chick magnet – they devised individuals' life stories, considering key life events, significant choices, and possible alternative outcomes of their life choices. In the 'Your Wildest Dream' activity, youth imagined the goal of becoming Indigenous drumming champions and the possible steps needed to get from the *real* to the *ideal* of their imagined scenario. In the Newspaper Theatre project, in response to the article proposing fines for aggressive panhandling, the youth expressed their sense of justice in resistance to what they saw as the criminalization of the poor and of youth. For a traditional storytelling project, which I describe in further detail in Chapter 6, youth devised an alternative ending for the story entitled 'The Ghost Stallion'. They imagined a way for the story's protagonist, an offending Chief condemned for cruelty to his weak and sick horses, to redeem himself through becoming a coyote and committing to caring for his coyote pups. For each of these projects, the youth envisioned life beyond the constraints of the jail and the broader unjust social structures that impacted their lives.

The potential for *radical freedom* that Kershaw (1999) described, for creative expressions of autonomy and agency, was apparent throughout our performance work with the Indigenous youth in jail. Our applied theatre processes perhaps allowed the youth opportunities for survivance and resurgence through resistance and renewal, through envisioning their lives beyond the context of incarceration.

Street-involved Youth Uncensored

For the project with street-involved youth which we called Uncensored, over three years we presented a total of 26 workshops for a range of service provider groups, for university students, for academic and practitioner conferences, and for community arts events. The service provider audiences with whom we conducted an evaluation (E&RS, 2011) commented that the theatrical process initiated embodied dialogue with youth like none they had had with youth previously. They indicated that for the most part they appreciated the opportunity to converse with the youth. Our most challenging audience, however, included several municipal police officers who were quite resistant to critiquing their own behaviours (see also Brendel Horn, 2017; Gallagher, 2016; Lamparter, 2022).

In the evaluation video the youth created for the project (YUEV, 2012), one young Indigenous man who was one of our most active performers began by recounting his prior negative experiences with police:

> I remember when I first moved to this city about five years ago … every time I'd, like, go to work or something, I'd be in my hoody getting ready for work, I'd go and wait at the bus stop and a cop would stop me … You feel degraded when you get stopped by a cop … They tell you put your hands on the wall and they, just, feeling you up and shit … I was mad all the time. That's one thing that got me mad. I hate the cops. They always try to do the good cop, bad cop shit … I remember when I got stopped this other time … I was walking home from playing ball … This cop stopped right in front of me … on the road and I was walking on the sidewalk. He walked up to me. He was holding his gun … Fuck. I'm like, "what's the matter?" He said, put your hands on the hood … His partner, he got out. He's like "What's your street name? What's your nickname?" I go, "I don't got a street name." "Bullshit." And a bunch of, like, five other cop cars come out of nowhere. And I was asking: "Why did you stop me?" They didn't tell me why, until way later when they gave my ID back. But every time they checked my ID, and my record was clean, they check it five times more. They check it again, and again, and again to see if I got any … got anything wrong … It's because I'm Native, I guess. (00:18:53–00:20:21)

This young man expressed his anger at being frequently profiled and stopped by police whom he identified as racist. Our workshops gave him opportunities to air his grievances to those he saw as his oppressors.

Revealing Recalcitrant Attitudes of Peace Officers

A scene that we presented which we entitled 'Peace Officer' for that audience which included some police officers depicted a highly contentious issue in the city: transit security officers' treatment of youth when caught on public transportation without proof of payment. As we learned, street-involved youth were often charged and fined although clearly unable to pay, leading to further charges, failed court appearances, and ongoing legal barriers sometimes ensnaring youth within the justice system for years. Our argument against such charges was that the ensuing public legal costs far outweighed the few dollars youth had not paid to access public transportation. The partner organization's outreach worker had advocated several times on behalf of youth in court regarding this issue.

Our scene was set in a transit station. A security officer approached two youth aggressively from the outset. One of the youth's transfer was 10-minutes expired. The officer asked for identification, but the youth claimed not to have it and refused to provide their name. The officer decided to charge the youth. His attempt to handcuff the youth escalated into an argumentative verbal exchange and ended in a physical altercation. When an officer from the audience came onto stage to replace the transit officer character for a forum theatre intervention – which was meant to resolve the conflict, he attempted to convince the youth that their behaviour was the problem rather than considering how his own behaviour might be changed to interact more positively with the youth. In the youths' improvised response to the intervention, they held firm to their conviction that the officer's expectations were unjust; the police intervenor also refused to re-consider his perspective. The performed scenario was highly unsettling for youth and for the officer, forcing us to stop the performance to talk through everyone's concerns. Following this performance, the Indigenous youth quoted above had an interaction with the police in attendance which, he commented, felt as though they were still interrogating him:

> Uncensored gives me an outlet to speak my voice, to, like, cops. I get to talk to them about what they do to me. Some of them take and listen, but other cops, no … I remember one time we did a show for cops. Those cops still seemed like they were on duty while they were at our workshop. They were like interrogating me on the side while I was there, but I still got to speak a little bit. At the graffiti [workshop], I was talking to those cops. It was good because they took and listened. The cops from [another city], they were nice. They went back to [city] and did a workshop on attitude adjustment [with police]. I felt good about those cops. [The cops in the workshop mentioned above] felt like they have to follow their guidelines instead of taking our advice … like, okay, we have to gain a little respect for these kids and build a relationship. (YUEV, 2012, 00:28:56–00:34:59)

Although the youth expressed frustration at the police officers' responses to the 'Peace Officer' scene, he nevertheless appreciated opportunities for such dialogue with police. He was able to compare the negative encounter in that workshop and his previous negative encounters with police with some more positive responses from police during other workshops.

Through their participation in the Uncensored workshops for service providers, the youth were able to see themselves as activists and educators, speaking up to make a difference in their lives and the lives of other youth. Alfred (2005) described resurgence as involving 'a dynamic of power generated by creative energy flowing from [Indigenous peoples'] heritage through their courageous and unwavering determination to recreate themselves and act together to meet the challenges of their day' (p. 22). In this sense, the Uncensored project offered opportunities for the Indigenous youth to speak back to the powers that constrained their lives and envision alternative futures for themselves on their own terms.

Concluding Thoughts on Engaging with Indigenous Youth

My experiences working with Indigenous youth were echoed by Ansloos and Wager (2020). While they acknowledged their study with Indigenous youth on homelessness and applied theatre 'did not achieve the rematriation of Indigenous homelands ... [it did] precipitate decolonization ... by supporting and enlivening youths' own sense of power, agency, and knowledge of collective action to garner material changes and redistributions' (p. 62).

The United Nations Declaration on the Rights of Indigenous Peoples (United Nations, 2007), the Truth and Reconciliation Commission of Canada (Government of Canada, 2015), and the National Inquiry into Missing and Murdered Indigenous Women and Girls (2016) have been major steps forward in our efforts towards decolonization in Canada, but there is still a long way to go. As Anaya suggested (2014), the greatest challenge we still face in implementing the principles we espouse is the imperative for changing attitudes. Alfred (2017) insisted that decolonization will not be achieved without 'a resurgence of authentic land-based Indigeneity' and that 'support for Indigenous youth to reclaim, rename and reoccupy their homelands' (p. 13) is needed to ensure that reconciliation is not just recolonization.

Robinson and Martin (2016) asserted that,

> almost nothing [scholars] can do will lead immediately or directly to the return of land or to the unsettling or dissolution of Canada's claim over Indigenous territory ... [but] that even small, symbolic, and everyday actions are significant. While focusing on small actions puts us in danger of feeling that we have "done enough" (thereby avoiding the larger decolonizing actions that need to take place), discounting them not only risks creating a sense of powerlessness and despair, but also misses the potential of micro-actions to ripple, to erode, and to subtly shift. (pp. 1–2)

As Ojibwe author Wagamese learned:

> 'This is how you change the world ... the smallest circles first' ... That humble energy, the kind that says, 'I will do what I can do right now in my own small way,' creates a ripple effect on the world. (2019, pp. 80–81)

While it is not my role as a non-Indigenous scholar to lead the way forward in facilitating Indigenous survivance and resurgence, I can, as an educator, applied theatre practitioner, and researcher, support processes that in some small ways allow Indigenous youth to be seen and heard, to exercise agency, display their strength, and that foster more constructive attitudes about them. Applied theatre research offers opportunities for Indigenous youth to tell their stories about the personal and systemic struggles they face, about their understandings of their life experiences, and their desires for the future. These are small steps forward in our collective efforts at dismantling colonial structures. Ultimately, it is not for me but for Indigenous youth and Indigenous scholars to determine what, if any, relevance the work described here had for Indigenous youths' survivance and resurgence.

6

The Potential for Youth Empowerment and Advocacy

This chapter at the heart of the book will share what I have come to see as the overarching goals and potential benefits of applied theatre for systemically marginalized youth participants, namely, youth empowerment and advocacy. In Chapter 1, I offered a critique of the notion of *empowerment*. Based in western colonial logics (Donald et al., 2012; Korteweg & Bissell, 2016; Tuck & Wang, 2011), discourses of empowerment are often erroneously read as narratives of linear progress from marginalization to empowerment with a powerful leader graciously bestowing power upon the disempowered. I acknowledge that the term is not without contention, so I use it cautiously. As I also expressed in Chapter 1, I cannot definitively claim that youth empowerment (or advocacy) occurred through our work together as empowerment is an elusive and disparate quality. While youth empowerment and advocacy may be something I aimed for, their achievement is not for me but for the youth themselves, with whom I have allied, to assess. I acknowledge that what may have seemed empowering to me may not have been empowering for the youth, or what may have been empowering for one youth may have been disempowering for another, or that any sense of empowerment or advocacy they experienced may have only been fleeting. I do want to offer hope that the potential for empowerment and advocacy existed for the youth through participation in our applied theatre projects and that this potential exists in engaging systemically marginalized youth in applied theatre generally.

Empowerment seen as 'creative and life-affirming' (hooks, 1984, p. 84) is a strength-based, relational concept linking individual well-being and agency to social justice or systemic change. Kohfeldt et al. (2011) defined empowerment as 'a process through which individuals and groups gain increased control over access to the conditions and resources that affect their lives' (p. 29). Other definitions claimed empowerment interventions enhanced individual wellness and included: mutual respect and caring, democratic participation with others towards common goals, opportunities to develop knowledge and skills, and a critical understanding of one's environment (Perkins & Zimmerman, 1995). Rappaport (1995) claimed that the capacity to tell one's story is a powerful resource, that 'the metacommunications that follow from listening to and giving respect to the stories of peoples' lives' (p. 801) towards creating positive, shared community narratives are consistent with empowerment goals. Likewise, many other applied theatre facilitators working with marginalized youth suggested youth empowerment and/or agency as outcomes of their processes through giving youth opportunities to tell their stories on their own terms (Ansloos & Wager, 2020; Barton-Farcas, 2022; Brendel Horn, 2017; Lamparter, 2022; Linds et al., 2013; Rhoades, 2018; Santiago-Jirau, 2022; Tate, 2022).

In this chapter, I explore some ways of understanding how and why applied theatre processes might have the potential to offer systemically marginalized youth, who may often experience powerlessness, a sense of empowerment. Through providing opportunities for youth to express their truths and share their stories – through speaking truth to power, applied theatre can perhaps advocate by, with, and for marginalized youth. I know from my own experiences as a youth that drama can be a powerful medium for offering youth (as it did me) a sense of belonging and well-being. As a youth, I didn't know what it was about drama that achieved this, but I knew it was significant. I have dedicated my academic career to trying to understand not only the processes involved in drama for empowerment but also how and why this potential for empowerment may exist. What is it about drama, or applied theatre processes specifically, that capture youths' imaginations for envisioning possibilities and increasing their sense of agency?

I've come to believe that a number of aspects inherent to the processes of drama or applied theatre may set the stage for youth to claim power for themselves or acknowledge the power that they hold in their own lives. Though I don't make any claims to certainty, the remainder of this chapter explores a number of the dynamics present in applied theatre that individually or together may play a role in unleashing the potential for youth empowerment and advocacy.

Collaborative Engagement and Analysis

Firstly, I believe that the collaborative, relational, or communal nature of applied theatre creates a context in which youth can flourish (see also Ansloos & Wager, 2020; Gallagher, 2016; Gallagher & Rodricks, 2017b; Linds et al., 2013; Wager, 2015). Adolescence is a time in life when peer group interaction and socialization are particularly valued (Newman et al., 2007). As we saw during the early days of the COVID-19 pandemic, when lockdown and quarantine were mandated, mental health, especially amongst young people, was negatively affected by the social isolation they experienced (Goldberg, 2020).

While peer groupings on their own can be fraught with conflict around inclusion and exclusion, within an applied theatre context, which creates a supportive, non-judgemental space and in which youth are working together towards a common goal, productive peer relations can emerge. The same could be said for other supportive peer group activities such as participating in sports (Howie et al., 2020) or outdoor adventure programs (Mutz & Müller, 2016). What is unique about drama or applied theatre that differentiates it from sports or adventure programs, I would argue, are the means by which it explicitly and intentionally engages youth in holistic ways, drawing on all of youths' physical, mental, as well as their emotional and imaginative capacities, to elicit a deep level of engagement. My drama education students often comment on the strong bonds they developed with their teachers and classmates in their high school drama classes prompting them to pursue teaching drama as a career to create similar experiences for their future students. I believe it is the engagement of the whole self, inherent in drama processes within a supportive environment – which encourages participants to allow themselves to take creative risks, to open up, and to become vulnerable – that encourages such bonding to occur. For marginalized youth for whom close relationships are sometimes absent, applied theatre can create vital opportunities for youth to develop feelings of solidarity, comradery, and belonging (Arteaga & Chavez-Arteaga, 2022; Hughes, 2013; Iwasaki et al., 2014) as I suggest was the case for our projects, at least to some extent.

For the research with street-involved youth, in the evaluation video which youth created to examine the outcomes of the project for them, the youth were able to comment on the benefits they gained through the positive relationships they developed with both the adult facilitators and with other participating youth. For example, in one youth's words:

> I went to Uncensored and met a lot of good people, friends that I still talk to outside of Uncensored … Everyone was really nice to me. I've never been so freely accepted in my life … When I came here [racism] didn't exist. I didn't feel like I was judged … They gave me a lot of support, I guess, the whole community – taught me a lot of resilience-ness. Getting introduced to Uncensored … got me involved with good people. (YUEV, 2012, 00:07:59–00:08:04, 00:13:58–00:15:28, 00:33:55–00:34:05)

In drama processes, participants bring their whole selves to the experience; as unique individual qualities are seen as assets, youth find acceptance for who they are.

The applied theatre processes in which we engaged – for all the projects discussed in this book involving drawing on youths' experiences and perspectives – allowed youth to listen to one another's expressions of their life experiences, offering them opportunities to feel heard and listened to (Barton-Farcas, 2022; Kaplan, 2022; Lamparter, 2022; McCreery, 2001). When one youth's experiences resonated with other youth in the group and elicited stories in a similar vein, the youth's experiences were valued and validated, as was their willingness to open up and share those experiences. Bringing fictionalized versions of youths' experiences to life through theatre, perhaps for presentation to others on stage, validated those experiences further.

In my experiences of working with youth for almost 40 years, first as an educator and later as a researcher, I have found that youth are most productive when engaged in working alongside others in group settings (versus working alone) and actively involved in decision-making towards meeting achievable goals (DeCarlo & Hockman, 2003). As Granger (2006) suggested, youths' strengths are most 'meaningfully manifest only in the transaction between the person and the environment' (p. 153). Within supportive group settings, youths' problem-solving and analysis skills flourish in that they can encourage, question, and build upon one another's thinking. Applied theatre further enhances youths' capacities by drawing on their multiple ways of knowing for meaning-making, including their personal experiences, imagination, emotion, and reason.

For my doctoral research in the rural Alberta high school, for example, youth demonstrated their powers of collaborative analysis. Via the applied theatre process, their thinking shifted from their initial superficial understanding of their behaviours as determined by their rural environment – Life in the Sticks, to re-claiming their agency by the end of the project through re-thinking their risky behaviours as matters of personal choice. The research made space for youth to act as co-researchers in collaboratively generating knowledge about and interpreting their lived experiences and in sharing their new understandings with other youth through performance.

Similarly, in the Newspaper Theatre project with the youth in jail, the youth showed an ability for sophisticated analysis of the issues raised in the newspaper article which claimed the mayor was considering a bylaw imposing a $10,000 fine for coercive panhandling (Kent, 2007). Collectively, the youth had no difficulty articulating the absurdity of the mayor's proposition, identifying it as criminaliza-tion of poverty, linking it to the criminalization of youth based on their own life experiences, and devising a scenario to illustrate their understandings to others.

Edgework

In the applied theatre project in the rural Alberta high school, the youths' belief underlying our theme Life in the Sticks was that 'kids get into all kinds of trouble because they are bored'. In our work with 'The Bus Trip' scene, as described in Chapter 3, one of the reasons that youth gave for engaging in the behaviour of drinking alcohol on the school bus trip, although well aware of the illicit nature of the activity and its associated risks, was in their words *for the rush*. As I pondered over the motivations for youths' risky choices in my research interpretation, I came across Lyng's (1990) social-psychological theory of voluntary risk-taking which he called *edgework* (p. 864) described as 'experiential anarchy' (p. 875) – self-created opportunities for spontaneous, authentic actions in response to overwhelming social constraints. Lyng's theory was based on his study of skydivers which he later also applied to high-risk activities such as motorcycle racing and base jumping (Lyng, 1993), and which Ferrell (1995) applied to illicit activities such as graffiti writing and crime. I would suggest that substance use may also fall within the category of high-risk activities understood as edgework. I wondered if youths' behaviours which deem them at-risk could be seen as voluntary risk-taking in some cases. Youths' substance use, for example, might serve an aesthetic function (Buck-Morss, 1992) – to fulfil a desire for an experience of the sublime through an altered or non-ordinary state of consciousness. The youth in my study did describe *the rush* they sought through the illicit activity of drinking alcohol on the bus in the same terms as Lyng's edgeworkers who skydived and raced motorcycles *for the rush*, highlighting the seductive appeal and enjoyment of engagement in risky activities. Ferrell (1995) too described the young graffiti writers whom he encountered as driven by the 'incandescent excitement, the adrenalin *rush*, that result[ed] from creating their art in a dangerous and illegal environment' (p. 82). The youths' alcohol use perhaps provided an escape from the shared anti-climax, the boredom of that long bus ride home from the class trip.

I recently had the opportunity to speak with the recreation coordinator of a small community where I sojourned briefly. She had spent years advocating for a skate park in the community, understanding that the youth would benefit from access to the risky sport of skateboarding within a positive, structured environment. From the same perspective, she welcomed the applied theatre workshops for youth that I was proposing at the time. Drama and theatre, I would argue, again similar to activities such as sports or outdoor adventure programs, provide youth with some of that feeling of the rush that they seek (Lamparter, 2022; Linds et al., 2013; Wager, 2015). I know from my own performance experience, as others I'm sure would attest, that performing, whether engaged in improvising a scenario or performing for an audience, involves an element of risk-taking giving rise to feelings of nervousness followed by elation. Prior to performing, a sense of anxiousness is common; during performance the performer is in a heightened state of awareness and after a performance the release of endorphins creates a pleasurable feeling – a performance high. Along with that pleasure comes a sense of accomplishment and increased self-confidence. One youth in the project with street-involved youth (YUEV, 2012) described her first performance experience thus: 'I thought it was good, but it was very stressful and I was very nervous. After that I felt I could do anything. I was on top of the world' (00:28:29–00:28:36). Another youth commented: 'Being able to go on a stage helps me ... it gives me a lot of confidence ... I could never do this before' (00:08:04–00:08:23).

Role Theory in Action

Role theory originated in the psycho-dramatic work of Moreno (1977) in the 1920s–1930s. In discussing the significance of the roles we play in everyday life, Moreno claimed 'role playing is prior to the emergence of the self. Roles do not emerge from the self, but the self emerges from roles' (p. ii). This echoes contemporary post-structuralist conceptions of identity and identity performance/performativity (Britzman, 1992; Butler, 1999). Contrary to our common understandings of identity as singular and unified, these theories suggest that our sense of self comes through repetition of behaviours in our performances of the roles we play within various contexts in our day-to-day lives. These roles might include the roles of friend, employee, son or daughter, mother or father, teacher, student, or how we perform gender roles, race, social class, etc. In our presentation of ourselves through these roles, we are engaged in a continuous process of defining, constructing, and enacting our identities based on our inner desires as well as on the external expectations of others or society at large.

The numerous roles in our everyday role repertoires help us to meet our basic needs and function successfully by offering various performative strategies from which to choose in various situations. The imitative nature of identity opens space for questioning how we live in the world – space for both critical self-reflexivity and resistance. Agency is gained through understanding the possibility of variations in performing our self. Performance, then, is a means to 'problematize how we categorize who is "us" and who is "them", and how we see ourselves with "other" and different eyes' (Madison, 1998, p. 282). An understanding of role theory is valuable in heightening our level of awareness of the processes involved in our presentations of self. Role-play activities in drama and theatre draw on our everyday performative capacities, so applied theatre with inherent opportunities for role-play can be a means for nurturing and strategizing a sense of one's self – developing agency through identity negotiation (Ansloos & Wager, 2020; Brendel Horn, 2017; Eichas et al., 2021; Lavie-Ajayi & Krumer-Nevo, 2013).

In his drama therapy work with prison inmates, Baim (2004) believed that 'we can use the concept of roles and the language of drama to help us understand the factors influencing [offending behaviours and] help the offenders to re-write the script and the roles that they choose to play in it' (p. 142–145). Experimenting with *re-writing the script* or telling *counter-narratives* (Brendel Horn, 2017; Gallagher & Rodricks, 2017b; Lavie-Ajayi & Krumer-Nevo, 2013) was the basis for much of the work we undertook with youth in the jail. Several of our projects focused on the youth inventing characters with whom they identified, imagining themselves in those roles and elucidating their life stories and/or developing stories that resonated with their experiences, exploring alternative choices and consequences. This allowed the youth opportunities to take on various roles and consider alternatives for their own lives.

Engaging youth in applied theatre research encourages youth to see themselves in new roles. For the project in the rural Alberta school, as I've mentioned, by the end of the project the youth were able to see themselves as agents in making their own life choices, rather than as victims of their rural environment. In the project with the street-involved youth, through participating in the examination of their life experiences and in devising and performing scenes for service provider audiences, youth were able to see themselves and be seen otherwise. Youth embodied the roles of researcher, educator, artist, and performer (Rhoades, 2018) through which they felt seen and heard, as the following comments from their evaluation video (YUEV, 2012) illustrated:

> When we went to [city] ... I liked how they brought us down there and we were honourary guests. They made us feel really important ... The best part was when we got a standing ovation ... I was like, damn, people are actually learning from us. I felt like they really respected what we had to say. Ya, I felt, like, really important at that moment. (00:14:33–00:14:54)

> Uncensored does empower me. It gives me a voice. Before I was completely voiceless and alone and now I'm actually able to say what's going on and actually have people hear me. (00:32:29–00:32:50)

Metaxis or Role Distance

Related to role theory within a theatrical context is the notion of *role distance* or what Boal (1974/1979) referred to as *metaxis*. The act of consciously embodying a role through taking on a character in theatre generates role distance allowing a performer to exist in two realities simultaneously – in the performer's real world and in the world of the role and situation being performed – in the *as if* world. As Shaughnessy (2015) described, 'performance is a medium that is in between states of being and representation as a form that is both real (as experienced) and not real (as fictive/pretence/constructed and performed)' (pp. 121–122). In this *in-betweeness* or position of *estrangement* (Brecht, 1957/1964), the performer can imaginatively step back and witness their own performances – or as the youth in jail astutely commented to the newspaper journalist, the theatre activities allowed him 'to come out of [his] shoes, so [he could] look at [him]self'. Such aesthetic distance (Lamparter, 2022) evokes the capacity for critical self-reflection and insight.

The space created in theatre when an actor takes on a role that is not them is a liminal, in-between or threshold space (Linds, 2006; Schechner, 1985). Such a space is opened up because a performer necessarily brings aspects of themselves to any role – physically, as well as experientially and emotionally as they work to understand and connect with the character who is both similar and different from themselves, to bring authenticity to the character and situation. What evolves within the liminal space is a dance between performative proximity and distance, what Schechner calls an encounter between the 'not me' and the 'not not me' (p. 123). This is a powerful space for learning where a performer can reflect upon their own perspectives and behaviours in relation to the given dramatic situation at a safe distance (Gallagher & Rodricks, 2017b; Hughes, 2013) while fully engaging their critical, emotional, and embodied ways of knowing. As Linds suggested, 'through metaxic action, our bodies become generative sites of knowing; learning is tangible and available for future exploration' (2006, p. 115).

Psychotherapist Blatner (1997) described the power of role distance in the integration of cognitive analysis with experiential, emotional, and participatory engagement. He recommended the application of psychodramatic techniques to help youth explore their feelings and attitudes, complex life issues, or interpersonal conflicts. The meta-cognitive level of awareness created through role distance encourages reflection on behaviours and assumptions that may motivate future actions. It gives youth insights into the various complex parts of themselves – their identity, values, etc. It validates their sense of who they are, increases their sense of having choice in their lives, develops empathy, and helps youth expand their role repertoires – their capacities to perform a variety of roles that balance and complement each other, giving them more flexibility in playing out these roles in their real lives.

Mimetic Excess

Mimesis, understood as the capacity to mimic, imitate, reproduce, or represent similarities in life and/or in art, has been theorized since ancient Greek times (Aristotle, ca. 335 B.C.E./1997; Plato, ca. 375 B.C.E./2003). The word mimesis comes from the ancient Greek word mimos, a theatrical reference, denoting an imitator, actor, or mime (*Online Etymology Dictionary*, 2019). Humans have a high capacity for mimesis, the mimetic faculty being considered an essential component of humans' higher intellect (Benjamin, 1933/1999). As an innate human capacity, mimesis was at the heart of ancient peoples' ritual practices as they honoured the animals they hunted through imitation, for example. It is at the heart of children's play, also of language and learning and, of course, of theatre. Taussig (2020) insisted that 'mimesis is always creative' (p. 9) as reproduction or imitation can never be complete or precise. *Mimetic excess*, for Taussig, involved a reflexive awareness of the mimetic faculty, a mimicry of mimesis. This is manifest through, humour, exaggeration, and parody as examples of mimetic excess. Taussig believed mimetic excess had subversive and transformative potential.

Alluding to the function of mimetic exaggeration in theatre, Eisner (2008) suggested 'the individuals portrayed by actors are often larger than life … It is in the very exaggeration of the features of the situation through which we come to grasp its significance. Put another way, exaggeration can promote understanding' (pp. 21–22). Moreover, Bloustien (2002) argued that mimetic excess is often called upon 'when the seriousness or danger underlying the issues explored becomes too acute to accept full on' (p. 444). She believed that mimesis 'facilitate[s] the safe exposure, exploration and negotiation of the contradictions and complexities of everyday life' (p. 445). Taussig (1993) too believed that 'mimetic excess provides access to understanding the unbearable truths of make-believe as the foundation of an all-too-seriously serious reality, manipulated but also manipulatable … [permitting] the freedom to live reality as really made-up' (p. 255). He spoke of mimesis as a kind of sympathetic magic (e.g. as the basis for ancient ritual) in that, through the process of copying the original, one assumes its power. Taussig claimed, 'to mime is to get the power of what is mimed and power over it' (2020, p. 8).

The functions of mimetic excess, then, are three-fold. Firstly, it serves as a self-defensive strategy, as a sort of filter or buffer when confronted with harsh realities, to lighten their burden, to lessen their disturbing impacts. Secondly, mimetic manipulation of the truths being confronted, through humour or exaggeration for instance, involves engagement that promotes a deeper understanding of those complex and contradictory truths. Finally, the mimetic capacity allows for the gaining of a sense of power or control over those challenging realities. Thus, mimetic excess can counter the domesticating effects of oppressive situations.

Mimesis through raucous humour, laughter, satire and exaggeration was a characteristic feature of the work with the youth through all of the applied theatre projects I facilitated (Arteaga & Chavez-Arteaga, 2022; Lamparter, 2022; Wager, 2015). As I mentioned in Chapter 3, the fun and enjoyment participants experience through applied theatre is a valued aspect of the work (Thompson, 2003). Much of the enjoyment for the youth with whom I worked was self-created by the youth themselves through humour and exaggeration. The improvisational and devised nature of our theatrical explorations allowed ample room for youths' expressions of mimetic excess. The example I shared in the previous chapter, of the incarcerated youth pulling up their sweat pants tight around their crotch in mocking imitation of an authority figure whenever I commented on the way they wore their pants low around their hips, showed an astute manipulation of the mimetic faculty by the youth. The great enjoyment they always gained from this gesture was evident through their exuberant laughter. Both the youths' running, inside joke, and the sa*gging* style itself are perfect examples of subversive mimetic excess in action. The youths' mockery symbolically disinvested the despised authority figures of their power in the youths' imagination.

Another example of mimetic excess which I share here to illustrate the pervasive humour that characterized the youths' applied theatre engagement comes from the project at the rural Alberta high school. We devised a scene, which we entitled Friends, based on a story students told about conflict in a friendship relationship. (The pseudonyms the youth adopted were themselves examples of mimetic excess.) The scene was set in Lucky's truck and involved an argument between Lucky and his girlfriend, Flower. Flower wanted to party with her male friend Smokey, who was in town visiting and whom they'd just picked up, rather than spend the Friday evening with her boyfriend as usual. In a forum theatre performance of the scene for a neighbouring school, in search of an alternative strategy for resolving the conflict, Frootloop replaced the boyfriend character, Lucky, to try out his idea. To distract Smokey from spending the evening with Flower, Frootloop (as Lucky) offered Smokey a date with his younger sister. The suggestion was met with enthusiasm from Smokey and an uproarious response from the audience. His intervention had the potential to resolve the conflict in a perverse sort of way, but after addressing Flower's discomfort with the plan the group ultimately rejected the solution as unrealistic on the grounds that brothers are usually more protective of their little sisters. They agreed that Frootloop should introduce one of his female friends to Smokey instead. Whether or not it was Frootloop's intention to be funny (though I'm quite sure it was), his intervention certainly got a laugh. But his mimetic excess also had broader implications through opening up the space for serious dialogue about relationships between friends and siblings.

As I was writing the play about my research with incarcerated youth (Conrad, 2012), I sought to better understand the astute humour I'd witnessed from the Indigenous youth I'd interacted with over the years, which my play was attempting to capture. Anishinaabe playwright and humourist Hayden Taylor's (2005) explanation of humour amongst First Nations people was consistent with the descriptions of mimetic excess shared above. As he commented, 'Native humour comes from five hundred years of colonization, of oppression, of being kept prisoners in our own country … Native humour was a little bit of home tucked away for when we needed it. Sort of spiritual pemmican' (p. 69). Hayden Taylor's explanation too suggested humour as a seriously serious response to unbearable truths. I expect that humour, parody, and exaggeration offered the youth involved in our projects some escape, however temporary, from the struggles they faced in their lives, gave them insight into those struggles, and thereby allowed them to assert a measure of power over them. Mimetic excess or humour, then, far from being merely pleasurable, plays a serious role in achieving the empowerment, advocacy, and justice goals of applied theatre.

Affective Engagement

Broadening out from the above discussion touching on the emotion of joy, *affect* refers to subjectively felt sensations, bodily experiences, and inner emotional states or flows of energy in the body (Sloan, 2018) – or as Thompson described, 'moments that make the heart beat faster' (2011, p. 56). Affect theory posits that our human ways of being and acting in the world revolve around our capacity to affect and be affected through our interactions or intra-actions (Barad, 2007) with others and encounters with the world around us. Affect is a part of aesthetic experience (Shaughnessy, 2015) in our responses to sensory stimuli.

The sense of *aesthetics* I refer to here is not the modernist sense of aesthetics related to taste or judgment of fine arts based on notions of beauty (Kant, 1790/2007), but what might be more aligned with the classical Greek sense of aesthetics (Aristotle, ca. 350 B.C.E./1998). The origin of *aesthetic* comes from the Greek word *aisthanesthai* which means to sense, perceive, or feel (*Online Etymology Dictionary*, 2014). This is an understanding of aesthetics as a sensory, perceptual, and emotional way of knowing that occurs prior to cognitive-linguistic knowing (Whitfield, 2005). Aesthetic experiences leave affective imprints or traces on the body. For example, we say a beautiful landscape is breathtaking. The awe we experience in perceiving the view has an embodied effect of breathlessness. Both the visual image and the sense of breathlessness can stay with us as we recall the experience. Similarly, the shock of hearing bad news, such as the sudden death of a loved one, we might say feels like a punch in the gut. The emotional distress along with that feeling in our body lingers.

Thompson (2003) argued that participating in applied theatre activities leaves affective imprints on the body too. In applied theatre, affects encountered by participants range from the exuberant joy experienced through playful abandon and deep belly laughter to the empathy felt when witnessing another's expression of sincere emotion – of love, sadness, pain, or anger (Tate, 2022). These affective expressions are especially poignant when shared amongst youth whose challenging life circumstances may have robbed them of the simple joys of childhood and/or forced them to present a stoic demeanour in the face of struggle after struggle.

Thompson (2003) claimed, 'however small, any physical/mental engagement in a theatre process will have developed phrases and traces that will be interventions in the embodied lives of participants' (p. 169). These imprints form points of connection (e.g. to embodied emotions, sensations, memories) that remain available to be accessed in the future to re-form those connections. In this way, Sloan (2018) saw applied theatre-making as an affective performance ecology, which creates spaces of potentiality. Shared affective encounters, Nicholson (2014) claimed, are life-affirming, creating a sense of aliveness, with the potential for shifting patterns of power. When humans work together in expressions of affect, this in itself opens space for creative potential, for re-imagining experience, for unsettling engrained attitudes and habits, for making visible a better world, all of which count as positive change.

An Affective Encounter through Traditional Storytelling

I'll share here, as an example of the power of affect, my experience of a project we undertook with youth in jail which I feel illustrates how affect lives on in the body. Not only were the youth participants presumably affected by the work we did together (Hughes, 2013), but I, as facilitator, was also deeply affected (Lamparter, 2022). (I draw on my own experience here as it is only my own affective encounters that I have full access to.) Whenever I share details of this traditional storytelling project during scholarly presentations, for instance, it always brings tears to my eyes, even more than a decade later. This project was inspired by an interest in exploring aspects of environmental education through drama with the incarcerated youth. We began by sharing stories of our experiences with nature. Based on the stories youth shared, many of which were about hunting animals, animal attacks, fighting animals for sport and the like, we decided that relationships with animals might be a fruitful area for further exploration and chose to do so through traditional storytelling. I found a traditional Indigenous story online, which, it happened, one of the boys told us, his Cree grandfather had also told to him. The story, entitled *The Ghost Stallion* (First People, n.d.), was about a wealthy Chief who loved his horses, but was cruel to any that were weak or sick. In retribution for his cruelty, he was visited by a supernatural power in the form of a Ghost Stallion who took away his prized horses and cursed him to spend the rest of his days travelling the land in search of them.

We decided, as a relevant approach with the youth, to devise an alternate ending to the story in which the Chief, seen as an offender in relation to his cruelty to his horses, would have an opportunity to redeem himself. As the alternate ending unfolded, as told collectively by the youth, two opportunities for the Chief's redemption arose, but both times he failed to change his offending attitude. When asked about this, one youth explained that the Chief ought to be given at least three opportunities to fail before he could be expected to make meaningful change in his life. This was a performative reversal of the popular *three strikes and you're out policy* (Galloway, 2006) common in both criminal justice and school discipline procedures. The youths' understandings of human nature and the challenges involved in making life changes proved much more realistic, charitable, and compassionate than the intolerant three strikes policy.

In the youths' conclusion to the story, the Chief made an arrangement with the Ghost Stallion to transform him into a coyote in order for him to learn to empathize with animals. As a coyote, the Chief fell in love with a female coyote and had a litter of pups. When his new family came under attack by a bear, the Chief-turned-coyote fought to protect them, but unfortunately the coyote mother was killed. The Chief's bravery in the face of danger and his loyalty to his coyote family earned his redemption. When the Ghost Stallion offered to return him to his life as a man, however, in an unexpected final twist to the youths' ending, the Chief chose to remain a coyote in order to look after his vulnerable pups. (This is where I always choke up with tears.) The episodic alternate ending to the story, as collectively devised by the youth, took a turn that I could never have imagined and was absolutely heart-wrenching. It revealed insights into the youths' understandings of offending behaviour, of discipline and punishment, of the process of making meaningful life changes, and of the empathy needed to truly know the Other.

For me, this experience which occurred towards the end of the three-year project left a powerful affective imprint on me that I find difficult to fully articulate in words, but which reveals itself, again and again, through my emotional, embodied, tearful response in my re-telling. It was not only the surprisingly moving alternate ending that the youth devised that always brings tears to my eyes but also the entire context of its telling. I have a vivid memory of the group of burly 16–18-year-old incarcerated boys lounging on the floor together, comfortable and relaxed, deeply invested in the storytelling process with the playful innocence of children. I'm flooded with feelings of warmth and affection for the youth in this memory – feelings that contradicted how I may have anticipated feeling about incarcerated youth given how they are commonly perceived, and perhaps precisely because of this incongruity. I hope and trust that the youth had similar affective responses, that their memories of the work we did together remain life-affirming and that the experiences we shared left positive affective imprints that they can still access to re-connect to the imaginative play, the emotional meaning-making, and the warmth and comradery fostered within the group.

Claiming Agency and Paying It Forward

As Baim described, 'at the root of all theatre, and indeed all storytelling, is the human need to make meaning of the world and to communicate this meaning to other people in the form of stories' (2017, p. 86). Indigenous author King (2003) would concur with the significance of stories in our lives in claiming 'the truth about stories is that that's all we are' (p. 92). The stories we tell help us make sense of who we are and our place in the world; through sharing our stories we construct and reconstruct ourselves and our realities. Storytelling is a powerful medium for taking ownership of our lives, for exercising agency (Ansloos & Wager, 2020; Barton-Farcas, 2022; Lamparter, 2022).

In all of the applied theatre projects I facilitated with youth, most often youth were willing and eager to share their stories. Given the opportunity, I have found, youth are more than happy to talk about their life experiences and have others listen. In school contexts, where the curriculum too often neglects to make personal connections to youths' lives, such opportunities are welcomed. For marginalized youth who often do not feel listened to, such opportunities are particularly valuable. Applied theatre scholars (Salverson, 1996; Stuart Fisher, 2008) contended that those who have suffered trauma are compelled to tell about their experiences, that there is a necessity to be heard. In our projects, youths' authentic desires to tell their stories drew us all into ethical encounter as listeners.

While the applied theatre I undertook was never intended as therapy, it sometimes did have therapeutic effects (Barton-Farcas, 2022). While for some applied theatre practitioners (see Baim, 2017; Cohen-Cruz & Shutzman, 1994; Jennings, 2009), as for Boal (1995) himself, the connections between theatre and therapy were fundamental, as an educator and researcher but not a trained therapist, I always do make a clear distinction. As for Rohd (1998), the applied theatre processes I facilitated were not meant to directly address individuals' problems, but rather they utilized individuals' stories to identify shared, systemic struggles. So, while our work with youth was never aimed at eliciting youths' testimony for their personal healing, we recognized for some of the youth our work had this effect. The applied theatre process itself held space for youth to express their vulnerabilities and offered support for their mental health from individuals trained to offer such support if they needed it. I discuss the ethics related to working with personal stories further in Chapter 7.

Some youth participants expressed how opportunities to tell their stories, opening space for their voices and experiences to be heard, helped them. The words of two youth involved in the project with street-involved youth, which they shared in the evaluation video they created (YUEV, 2012), described the significance telling their stories had for them:

> Being able to tell my story, Uncensored helped me in that way ... I didn't really have the motivation to go out and tell people what I've been through, but it helps me too, I guess. (00:07:37–00:08:34)

> I was asked by [name of social worker] to come to this project where I could share my past experiences. I could also have a positive outlet to express myself ... And together the group that we made has supported me. (00:27:14–00:27:34)

For these youth, telling their stories – creating opportunities to be heard and engage in dialogue (Lamparter, 2022) – were first steps towards making change in their lives. Anderson and Wilkinson (2007) confirmed that agency and self-respect are assets offered through personal storytelling and promotion of these qualities was consistent with the goals of the projects I facilitated: to benefit and advocate by with and for the youth.

The desire to share stories of their struggles was an authentic response from the youth which sustained their participation in our applied theatre processes. Beyond benefiting themselves, some of the youth in the project with street-involved youth said they wanted to tell their stories to educate service providers in order to help other youth in similar circumstances (Ansloos & Wager, 2020; Gallagher, 2016; Ottaway et al., 2009; Sapiro & Ward, 2020). Some said they wished to and ultimately did pursue careers to help other youth. Again, in the evaluation video (YUEV, 2012), two youth commented:

> If I can impact somebody, or one person, that's even what I want to do as a social worker, just improve the lives of other people ... So, doing Uncensored helps me do that. (00:34:10–00:34:59)

> In hopes that I could benefit someone else's life, I have stayed with Uncensored ever since. (00:27:25–00:27:29)

These youth felt their own life stories, their experiences of struggle, would benefit their work in helping other youth. Their empowering applied theatre experiences contributed towards motivating them want to reach out to support other youth with similar experiences of struggle.

Dialogical Performance

Performance ethnographer Conquergood (1985), whose research worked with refugees in the United States, saw the potential in performance through creating space for being 'vulnerable and open to dialogue with the world' (p. 1). Conquergood described performance as an embodied, empathic and ethical act, 'as a way of knowing and deeply sensing the other' (p. 4). His dialogical performance stance sought to bring different voices, beliefs, value systems, and world views, together in conversation with each other. Bringing self and other together in this way, he declared, opens space for debate, for questioning and challenging of one another. Such an approach is committed to keeping dialogue open and ongoing, resisting conclusions. As such, ethical performance requires dialogue, care, and responsibility.

Dialogical performance was inherent to the applied theatre processes we undertook. As youth shared their stories and listened to one another, analysed circumstances, and worked together to devise scenarios that resonated with their experiences, and shared those scenarios with others – sometimes performing for and engaging audiences in interrogating the issues raised, they created space for dialogue. Our applied theatre work provided opportunities for youth to come to better understand their own life experiences and aspects of the lives and struggles of other youth in deeper ways. Some of the projects gave audience members opportunities to come to know aspects of the youths' life experiences and also gave the youth opportunities to encounter the perspectives of those audience members regarding the incidents they presented.

For the media studies project in the alternative inner-city high school, dialogical performance took the form of youths' mediated responses – through the print and video ads they created, speaking back to the world of mainstream advertising. For the research in the rural Alberta high school, the youth had opportunities, through applied theatre, to dialogue amongst themselves regarding the risky youth experiences we were exploring and through forum theatre we extended that dialogue to other youth in their school and to youth at a high school in a neighbouring community.

In the youth jail, dialogue occurred amongst the youth through engaging in applied theatre activities exploring their perspectives, listening to the perspectives of their peers, and at times capturing those perspectives in creative applications of technologies for their further consideration. While having the incarcerated youth perform for outside audiences was not an option, upon completing the three years of workshops with the youth for the funded project, as a culmination of the study, as I mentioned, I wrote a full-length play – a performance ethnography, entitled *Athabasca's Going Unmanned* – to disseminate my experiences of doing applied theatre research with incarcerated youth (see Conrad, 2012). While the play was entirely fictionalized, it presented truths about youths' experiences of incarceration and advocated on their behalf. As *Alberta Native News* (Copley, 2010) reported in their article promoting the production of the play, '*Athabasca's Going Unmanned* is about society's responsibility to stand up and take an active role in ensuring that young offenders have the opportunity to overcome their dilemmas and take advantage of that second chance that everyone is entitled to' (p. 14).

The 2010 production of the play, with assistance from the University of Alberta's Canadian Centre for Theatre Creation, reached audiences of inner-city youth, Indigenous community members, corrections workers, educators, university faculty and students, and included talk-back sessions after each performance with me (the playwright) and the professional actors hired to perform. One Indigenous woman who told me her son had spent time in a youth offender facility attended three of the four performances of the play, bringing different family members along with her each time. A young Indigenous woman who attended a matinee performance with her high school class (from the same alternative inner-city high school where I conducted my master's research) and who had also briefly participated with us in the youth jail expressed to me after the performance how one of the fictionalized inciting incidents in the play had actually happened to her: In the play, an incarcerated youth creates a comic depicting an escape plan (Figure 6.1), which he is forced to conceal for fear of punishment from the jail's administration. His comic inspires another youth to plan a real escape, which becomes the central driver of the play's plot. The young woman audience member, after seeing the play, told me she had been dorm confined for daring to write about her desire to escape the jail. Similarly, the corrections workers who attended the play shared that my depiction of the jail environment also resonated with their experiences of working there. The play, it seemed, successfully communicated the experiences of incarcerated youth opening space for dialogue.

Likewise, our workshops with street-involved youth opened space for youth to confront, converse with, and/or educate service providers. Those service providers who attended our workshops generally wanted to do better at serving youths' needs and were open to conversation. These were 'integral audience[s] … already interested and engaged' (Prendergast & Saxton, 2009, p. 192), committed to exploring this content even if it was critical of service providers' actions. For some, it was the first time they had ever had candid dialogue with youth about youths' experiences.

Based on the evaluation of service providers' experiences (E&RS, 2011), the dialogic workshop space offered productive exploration of the sorts of power dynamics common amongst youth and service providers in order to promote deeper understandings of youth. Youths' performances allowed audience members to see the youth in a new light, as indicated by some of their comments in the

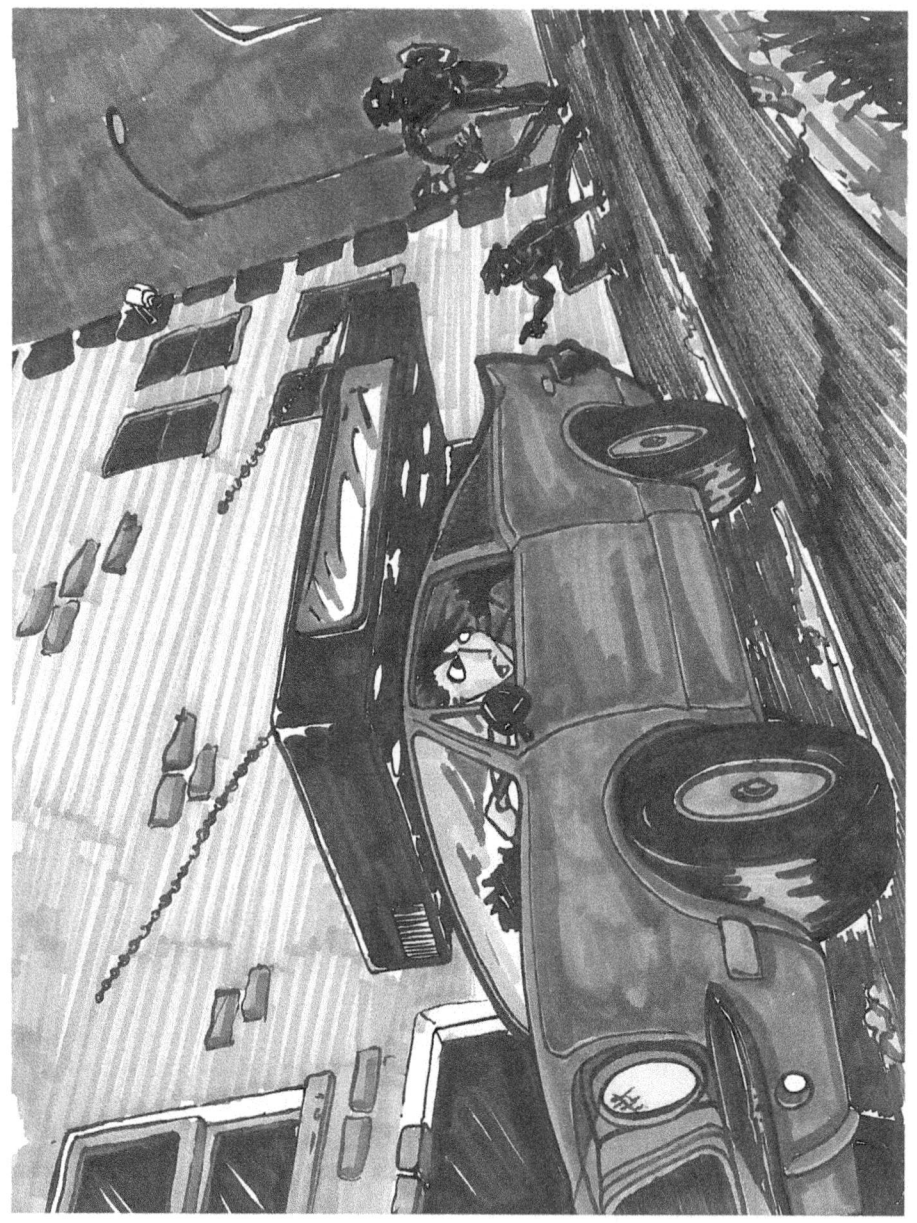

FIGURE 6.1: Comic depicting an escape from the play *Athabasca's Going Unmanned*, 2009.
© D. Conrad. Artwork by Mark Jenkins.

evaluation of service provider outcomes. They said, the workshop: 'helped me to understand these youth as articulate individuals who have well-founded opinions and expectations'; 'opened my eyes to not only the challenges and hardships [youth] have faced, but more importantly their strengths and talents'; 'really made me think about who [youth] are and what they might need' (E&RS, 2011, pp. 16–17). Through witnessing the performances, service providers were able to see beyond the challenges, deficits and damage by which they had previously defined the youth, highlighting instead their strengths. Opportunities for dialogical performance allowed the youth to feel seen and heard by service providers.

Youth Cultural Production

In his groundbreaking essay, Gaztambide-Fernández (2013) proposed a new vision and new language for arts education that are relevant in thinking about the empowerment and advocacy potential of applied theatre in the lives of systemically marginalized youth. He argued that the *rhetoric of effects* is pervasive in advocating for arts education in schools – those common arguments that claim the arts have either instrumentalist benefits for those participating in arts experiences (e.g. arts engagement leads to improved academic achievement), and/or for society in general (e.g. for cultivating social cohesion) or that claim benefits intrinsic to engagement in the arts (e.g. enhanced sensory perception, imagination, empathy, etc.) (see, for example, Jindal-Snape, 2012; Jindal-Snape et al., 2014; Marsh, 2012). Arts educators have found the need to deploy such advocacy strategies to sustain a place for the arts in education within an environment that demands measurable outcomes. Gaztambide-Fernández, however, argued for the need to move away from the rhetoric of effects to instead consider what we commonly refer to as *the arts* as an inherently educational process – a process of meaning-making through symbolic, creative work, which is a natural extension of our everyday engagement in cultural practices. Culture, Gaztambide-Fernández claimed, is 'something people do ... [and] symbolic creativity is fundamental to cultural life' (p. 226). The arts are not valuable because of what they do, but are vital and integral to our way of being.

Similarly, in Indigenous understandings, a sense of art is life-enriching and life-sustaining related to coherence, authenticity, health, and spirituality; as Kenny stated, 'art is not a separate language, but rather the way we live' (1998, p. 77). Likewise, in all cultures and through time, prior to modernist conceptualizations of the arts as elitist practices carried out by special individuals known as *artists*, the creation and embellishment of everyday objects and processes were intrinsic aspects of life. In her anthropological study of art, Dissanayake (1992) expressed her belief that such aesthetic activity must have had a biologically adaptive purpose in its own right for it to have been so pervasive across cultures and to have endured through time. She suggested *artification* or *making-special* felt good and so contributed towards individual and communal well-being. What we now call *art* was integral to identity and survival (Whitfield, 2005) for sharing meaning and value. In this vein, alternative to the rhetoric of effects, Gaztambide-Fernández (2013) claimed 'the rhetoric of *cultural production* focuses on rethinking the very terms of engagement around which education [and/or the arts] happens; it focuses on the conditions that shape experience rather than the outcomes' (p. 216).

Explicit in my master's research at the alternative inner-city high school, for example, students were engaged in cultural production. The media studies project repositioned students from being consumers of advertising to being media producers. Students critically analysed a range of mainstream advertisements and then, based on their applied theatre explorations, created their own print and/or video ads in response – to talk back to mainstream media. One youth, through his analysis of fashion advertisements, realized that he may have missed an opportunity to have a meaningful relationship with a girl because his views regarding what sort of girl might make an appropriate girlfriend was influenced by the images of women in ads. The ad he created asked: Who's the perfect girl? This student used this media production opportunity to gain a deeper understanding of cultural influences in his life – the effects of the romantic-industrial complex (Mukhopadhyay, 2012), to make sense of his previous experiences, to potentially inform his future actions and share his understandings with others.

Engaging youth in applied theatre, understood as cultural production, then, is one way of ushering youth towards claiming their rightful place as meaning-makers and recognizing their capacity for making meaningful contributions in our shared social and cultural contexts. As I hope this book illustrates, the applied theatre research projects undertaken with the youth as described throughout have shown youth to be active producers of culture and the products of their work as significant acts of cultural production.

Performing Resistance and Hope

In my doctoral research, part of my interpretation of our work considered how youths' engagement in at-risk or risky behaviours might been seen as acts of resistance. Above, I described such behaviour as edgework (Lyng, 1990) – as a response to the overwhelming social constraints youth experience. Other critical education scholars (Giroux, 1992; Apple, 1995; McLaren, 1998) have also suggested that youth behaviour deemed at-risk may be enacting resistance to schooling directed at the schools' authority and the alienating and repressive education system. Such resistance, however, is also understood as merely reproducing the status quo leaving youth marginalized (Willis, 1977). Alternately, I look for ways of understanding youth resistance that do not adhere to the common progress-oriented theory of change based on western colonial logics (Tuck & Wang, 2011) – resistance that ultimately works to reproduce existing structures, but creative, agential, socially transformative forms of resistance. As Tuck and Wang suggest, we need resistance theories that 'do not fetishize progress, but understand that change happens in ways that make new, old-but-returned, and previously unseen possibilities available at each juncture' (p. 522).

Perhaps youths' at-risk behaviours are mimetic appropriations – performative portrayals of the deficiency and deviancy so often attributed to them by the powers that be. As anthropologist Scott (1990) showed, subordinated peoples throughout history have resisted incorporation by the dominant ideology through their seemingly insignificant performative acts. Through documented examples from peasant uprisings, slave rebellions, working-class culture, gender relations, prisons, and classrooms – wherever relations of domination and subordination have traditionally existed, he described the subversive potential of their acts to protest their oppression against the odds. Scott recognized the undermining of mainstream perspectives through covert or low-profile forms of performative resistance as the *infrapolitics* of the powerless, those who do not have the luxury of direct confrontation and insisted that infrapolitics are real politics aimed at a re-structuring power relations. Fabian (1990) too saw the performances of subordination of oppressed groups as part of their means for survival, including their engagements in popular arts 'for asserting creativity, independence and critique' (p. 56). In studying young graffiti writers, criminologist Ferrell (1995) agreed that there is potential in resistant youth behaviour to undermine existing social arrangements and create new ones in the lives of youth.

Representation of youths' life experiences through applied theatre performance can be seen as a form of *poiesis* (Turner, 1982) – a creative re-making of culture and identity, or *kinesis* (Tyler, 1987) emphasizing its capacity for the transformation of reality. Boal (1974/1979) too regarded performance as a means to change and re-create social reality, and Bhabha (1994) also saw the potential in performance for *breaking and re-making*, referring to discursive acts that interrupt or undermine master-discourses. Applied theatre, then, in giving youth opportunities to speak truth to power (American Friends Service Committee, 1955/2020) – even if only in covert or low-profile ways, might be seen as a form of performative, infrapolitical resistance (Rhoades, 2018; Wager, 2015).

Thompson (2003) believed that in giving youth space to voice their perspectives through applied theatre research, their position might be altered in their own eyes or in the eyes of the community. The act of telling or listening to a story is not only research into problems that are revealed but an affirmation that the story is important. Telling and witnessing that telling is transformative in the moment, as well as providing inspiration or research information for the future. (p. 170)

In the ways Thompson described, which I have already alluded to throughout my discussion, applied theatre with systemically marginalized youth has the potential to resist and subtlety shift power dynamics – to change the story from one of deficit to one of strength (Blanchet-Cohen & Salazar, 2009). This shift allows youth to see themselves as active participants in their lives and in society. The inherently political dimension of applied theatre, which critically questions relations of power, endows youth with a sense of agency and control to speak back to the authorities or the authoritative structures that govern their lives and challenge hegemonic knowledges about them.

Along with calling out or disavowing the oppressive structures in youths' lives – enacting resistance towards the way things are – applied theatre as resistance can also offer hope for positive change. Hope is a vital ingredient in applied theatre with marginalized youth (Ansloos & Wager, 2020; Rohd, 1998; te Riele, 2010). Through enacting alternatives to challenging conditions or struggles portrayed in stories or scenarios, through imagining other possibilities for the future, youth are rehearsing radical hope – hope despite the odds (Gallagher & Rodricks, 2017a; Lear, 2006). Through practicing hope, it is brought to life in the imaginary.

Applied theatre as performance of both resistance and hope offers opportunities to break through entrenched feelings of powerlessness and hopelessness that may pervade youths' struggle-filled lives, towards something more productive. While applied theatre may not have the capacity in itself to bring about tangible, lasting changes in youths' lives (e.g. housing security, release from incarceration, etc.), it can allow youth space to question existing social structures, to re-imagine self, to offer counter-narratives to how they are usually seen, and to envision how the conditions of their lives might be otherwise (Hughes, 2013; Gallagher & Rodricks, 2017b), which might contain the seeds that lead to action and to real, material change (O'Connor & Anderson, 2015).

Concluding Thoughts on Youth Empowerment and Advocacy through Applied Theatre

It is my contention, based on my experiences of doing applied theatre with youth over the past twenty-plus years, that applied theatre does have the potential to do some good in the lives of systemically marginalized youth. While applied theatre may not be able to intervene directly in material realities, the qualities and processes inherent to the aesthetics of applied theatre – through the form or structures as well as the content of the work – create spaces of possibility for youth empowerment and advocacy. Through engaging collaboratively to explore and analyse their life circumstances, through self-created opportunities for spontaneous action and productive risk-taking, through exploration of the various roles youth can perform in life – by taking on different attitudes and perspectives that allow them to reflect on their own, through asserting power over challenging life issues via mimetic excess, through deeply affecting and being affected by others engaged with them in the undertaking, through claiming their voices and using their life experiences to help others, through opportunities for dialogue with others through theatrical means, through using the tools of cultural production for meaning-making, and through performing resistance and hope, youth can come to see themselves as active players and agents of change. As Rappaport (1995) concluded,

> much of the work of social change, organizational and community development in the direction of greater personal and collective empowerment, may be about understanding and creating settings where people participate in the discovery, creation, and enhancement of their own community narratives and personal stories. (p. 804)

Applied theatre research can be such a setting, allowing youth opportunities to reconstruct narratives for their lives.

7

Tensions and Ethical Considerations in Doing Applied Theatre with Systemically Marginalized Youth

This chapter will discuss some of the tensions and ethical considerations that warrant contemplation when engaging systemically marginalized youth in applied theatre research, beyond the requirements of institutional ethics review boards that regulate our engagement with research participants. To do so, I draw on my experiences with all of the projects previously discussed. While there are often no easy answers or definitive solutions to the messy conundrums that sometimes arise when working with groups of vulnerable individuals around sensitive issues, careful attention and ongoing reflection are needed to navigate this terrain. Scholarship on an ethics of care (Edwards & Mauthner, 2002; Noddings, 1984), relational ethics (Lévinas, 1989), and situated ethics (Nicholson, 2005; Simons & Usher, 2000) offers insights for negotiating ethical practice.

An ethics of caring begins from an innate feeling of care for the Other, followed by a corresponding ethical obligation – as Noddings suggested, a response to the call 'I must if I wish' (1994, p. 88). Similarly, Assante asserted, 'if you make an observation, you have an obligation' (2008, p. xi). Relational ethics emphasizes responsibility to and respect for those with whom we are in relationship and situated ethics considers how ethical practices must attend to the particularities of concrete situations and specific individuals. Together these approaches call for sensitive, respectful, and flexible engagement.

Situated Ethical Practice

What I have learned through doing applied theatre research in community contexts is that ethical dilemmas can arise unpredictably at any time during the research process, both in relation to the particular research activities and tangentially to the research itself, within the broader context in which the research is set. In Chapter 2, I already shared an incident that occurred in the youth jail when I overheard the youth talk about the many injuries they had sustained during their sports programming, implicating the sports coordinator. My reporting of this to the jail authorities, out of a sense of care and responsibility for the youth, however, got me into hot water with the youth when an investigation into the matter put the youths' valued sports programs in jeopardy. In this case, my sense of ethical obligation came into tension with the youths' desires. Such messy ethical dilemmas inevitably arise, sometimes with no clear path forward, no immediately apparent right or wrong solutions, suggesting the painstaking situatedness of ethical decision-making. Below, I share details of two other such incidents that left behind a moral residue (Hardingham, 2004) – those lingering feelings of less-than-complete satisfaction with the outcomes of the incidents that continue to haunt me.

Two School Dance Stories

The following incident, which occurred while I was doing research at the rural Alberta high school with drama students (see Conrad, 2004c), illustrates some tension I encountered in navigating ethical space within the context of my research on youths' risky experiences. During my time in the community, I volunteered one evening to serve as chaperone for a school dance. At one point that evening, while I was outside in front of the school building, I saw a suspicious looking dark object tucked under a bush along the fence that enclosed the school grounds that I hadn't noticed before. I looked closer and saw that it was a backpack. This was the first point at which I wondered what to do. Part of me wanted to pretend I had never seen the backpack and leave it be, but my misgivings got the best of me. I groped under the bush to recover the backpack; I could immediately hear the clinking of glass. Inside the backpack, I found a six-pack of fruity, alcoholic coolers, and a skimpy, colourful tank top. I wondered what the backpack's owner, probably female based on its contents and perhaps one of the young women who was participating in my research, had in mind: a few drinks with friends after the dance, perhaps a tryst with a boyfriend. I remember thinking that this was something I might have done as a teenager. Just a bit of harmless teenage fun, right? This was just the sort of risky youth experience that my research was interested in exploring too. I still wasn't sure what to do. I felt an obligation of care for the youth, who were so generously sharing aspects of their experiences with me. Would turning the backpack in be a betrayal to them?

As I was considering what I should do with the backpack, I recalled an incident that occurred before a school dance while I was in high school: One evening, before attending the dance with my boyfriend, we went to a friend's house for some socializing and a few drinks. A little later, on our way to the dance – my boyfriend was driving, he veered out of his lane and partially up the embankment on the wrong side of the road. We must have been travelling fairly slowly – my memory here is a blur, because the car ever-so-gently flipped over onto its roof and landed in the middle of the roadway. It was on a particularly treacherous stretch of the road, curving through a valley, with a very, very steep gully down the other side. If he'd veered a few feet in the other direction, things could have ended badly for us. As it turned out, neither of us was hurt. We both crawled out of the up-side-down car. The police and emergency vehicles showed up in moments with sirens blaring. They took my boyfriend away to the drunk tank for the night, while my other friends whisked me away to the school dance. The police later caught up with me at the dance and called my parents, who were relieved I was alive.

Thinking back to my risky school dance experience, the backpack with the coolers suddenly seemed less benign. What was intended as *just a bit of harmless fun* before the school dance when I was a teenager could very well have ended in my death, in a crashed car at the bottom of a ravine. I wondered what might happen if I returned the backpack to its hiding place under the bush where I had found it. What if the young woman got into a car with her drunk boyfriend or drove a car after drinking the alcohol? I wondered if I could live with myself if something terrible happened to the youth, not having done anything to prevent it. While I didn't want to get the youth in trouble and I thoroughly understood the youth's desire for a little self-created, spontaneous excitement, I also couldn't just leave the backpack there.

I eventually decided to take the backpack to the school's vice-principal, who was also supervising the dance. I remember he chuckled at my find and put the back-pack on top of a bookshelf in his office in clear view of anyone who entered. Not surprisingly, no one ever claimed the backpack. I was left feeling ambivalent. I had robbed the youth of their backpack, its contents and the fun it represented. I was left feeling, in part, disloyal to the students who were sharing stories of their risky experiences with me. I had turned in the backpack to prevent some potential harm to the youth – out of ethical caring, but also to avoid my having to live with the guilt should anything bad have come of it. In this instance, my ethical decision-making was informed by the specific context of the research site as well as by my personal history with the topic of inquiry. No solution to this particular dilemma would have been fully satisfactory, as was the case with the next example too.

Struggling with Issues of Race

The following is an incident that I have not previously written about, but which I recall now as I think further about situated ethical practice. Towards the end of the Uncensored project with street-involved youth, we were invited to present at an Indigenous storytelling conference in Yellowknife, Northwest Territories. I made travel arrangements for a small group of us – those who were willing and available to travel, including some Indigenous, Black and white youth. I mention individuals' racial identifications because, unexpectedly, race became a point of tension. An Indigenous outreach worker from the organization also accompanied us. None of the participants had ever before been to Yellowknife which has a large Indigenous population.

The small conference we attended, which was focused on Indigenous storytelling and took place in a Dene community just outside of Yellowknife, involved a majority of local Dene community members as well as some invited Indigenous and non-Indigenous scholars from across Canada. Non-Indigenous participants were in the minority. The conference proceedings naturally included much discussion about Indigenous lived experiences in which the effects of colonization, residential schools, cultural genocide, etc., featured prominently. In such discussion, white settlers are of course negatively implicated. I didn't see any of this as an issue, since the youth organization and our project worked with a majority of Indigenous and racialized youth. All the youth involved with the project were familiar with working alongside diversely racialized others, although, within the broader urban locale where the youth organization was set, non-white youth would still have been in the minority overall. The work of organization and our project also regularly addressed issues of race and racism.

During our stay in Yellowknife, towards the end of the conference, I happened upon one of our participant's Facebook posts. Facebook was, at the time, the means by which we all kept in touch. The post featured a selfie by one of the white youth alongside another of the white youth and declared pride in being white. I was taken aback, not sure at first how seriously to take this pronouncement. Was it a case of blatant racism, a display of white supremacy or something more innocent? It seemed to me that the participant's reaction was likely in response to their experience of culture shock, being in the minority as a white person for the first time, or white fragility (DiAngelo, 2011), feeling implicated in settler wrong-doing perhaps for the first time. I had not anticipated that our excursion to Yellowknife would have caused this level of discomfort for this young, white participant. I was also surprised to see the other white youth in the photo, but unsure of the level of their involvement in the declaration of white pride. This second youth, I knew was racially aware as they had previously talked openly with the group about their prior negative encounters with skinheads.

I wasn't sure how to proceed, but I knew I had to address the Facebook post somehow. The attitude the youth seemed to be expressing was unacceptable in relation to our social justice focused work for the project and not something I was willing to just let slide. I was uncomfortable confronting the youth directly, though, based on my own uncertainly about how to broach the issue, fearful of furthering the distress they were likely already experiencing. Nor did I want to single them out within their peer group and cause a scene. In consultation with the Indigenous outreach worker who knew both youth well, I decided to take a more oblique approach. (Perhaps as a way of evading my own discomfort around the situation?) I contacted one of the other members of our team who had stayed back in Edmonton, but also regularly connected with the youth on Facebook. I felt that any intervention in this matter might be most effective coming from them. They contacted the second youth to discuss the dynamics of the incident, to get a feeling for what the other youth was experiencing and perhaps provide some support with their racial discomfort.

The discrete approach we took to address the issue perhaps pre-empted any escalation of negative sentiments in the short term – we were scheduled to return home the very next day, but I'm not sure it really resolved anything. Our intervention may have evaded any further entanglement of the second youth in their friend's racially offensive expressions. It may have made the youth who posted the declaration on Facebook reflect upon their action, but the outcome remains uncertain. On the way home, I briefly questioned the youth about their experiences at the conference. They mentioned preferring Edmonton to Yellowknife and quickly re-directed the conversation. The youth dropped out of our project – which was already winding down, and we never heard from them again.

In this case, I struggled with how to enact an ethical response, caught between a marginalized individual's seeming distress and a social justice imperative. Similar dilemmas have arisen in my teaching when addressing issues of racial injustice, Indigenous rights, and even whiteness with groups of mostly white students. White individuals' fragility (DiAngelo, 2011) in discussing issues of race, I have found, as others have, more often than not creates extreme discomfort and yet we know it is essential to address such difficult knowledge (Britzman, 1998), to destabilize white students' comfortable identity positions and beliefs about the world (Felman, 1991) within educational contexts that aim to promote social equity. In education, as in research, there are no easy solutions to resolving deeply ingrained ideological conflicts. Situated ethical decision-making is never a straightforward undertaking; even our actions that come from a position of care and responsibility can leave uncomfortable moral residue (Hardingham, 2004).

I turn now to discussion about ethical considerations in relation to the various contexts in which my applied theatre research was conducted.

Applied Theatre Research in Institutional Contexts

As applied theatre scholar Thompson (2008) noted, however altruistic the intentions of an applied theatre project, it still always exists within the bounds of historically structured power dynamics. Wilkinson and Kitzinger (2008) concurred there is no possibility of ever completely evading the grasp of dominating power structures as they are deeply implicated in all the work we undertake. It is prudent then to reflect upon how our applied theatre research with systemically marginalized youth performed within the specific contexts of our research and within larger socio-political contexts with their inherent power dynamics, to explore the tensions of ethical practice. This line of inquiry raises many questions for which I do not have definitive answers; nevertheless, such questions must be asked as we continue to interrogate our practice as applied theatre researchers in an effort to produce ethical outcomes.

I begin here by discussing the limitations imposed on the research by each specific context in which the various applied theatre research projects I undertook were set. I understand that these contexts shaped the outcomes of the research; the expectations and histories of the institutions/organizations, the places, the people, the timelines involved, along with the larger socio-political environments in which they were set all played a role in what was achieved, for better or worse. Moreover, when participants are vulnerable youth, and given that youth in our society – particularly within institutions in which youth are considered under the legal age of consent – are largely under the control of adults, we do also have to consider the limitations of youths' authentic participation.

University-based Research

For all of the applied theatre research discussed in this text, the fact that as a researcher I was embedded within a university context undoubtedly shaped the possibilities afforded through these projects. As a university-based researcher – a graduate student during the earlier projects, and later as a professor, I brought a level of power and authority to the work that could not be evaded (D'Arcangelis, 2018). Neither my motivations for doing the work, nor the benefits I gained in relation to doing it, such as research grants, publications, promotion, etc., can be taken for granted. Also, my role as an adult researching youth experiences undoubtedly added a level of disjuncture to the overall dynamics of the processes undertaken that need to be scrutinized.

Well aware that power differentials influence research relationships, I sought research methodologies and methods that strove to alleviate these power differentials to the extent that this was possible. Both participatory research and applied theatre research seek to collapse the divide between researcher and researched, to instead create subject/subject relationships (Park et al., 1993), focusing on research for, by, and with participants. Realistically, though, I knew I could never, through any conceivable efforts, divest myself of the power inherent in my role as adult and university-based researcher. Reflexively considering the implications of this impossibility helps at least to mitigate some of the presumptions that I may have brought to the research.

My position as university researcher in the field of Education made possible the space and time needed for me to conduct the research. The university mandated research as part of my faculty workload; I was privileged to be able to set my own research agenda and to have access to funding opportunities and other resources to make applied theatre research with youth possible. My research was never subject to any specific expectations or outcomes determined by external interests (e.g. expectations imposed by funders). The university context allowed me to initiate and carry out my work with youth across various contexts (schools, jail, community organization) – to compare and contrast settings, intentions, practices, etc., which may otherwise not have been possible.

The university context did come with some expectations and requirements which may have limited possibilities for fully authentic youth engagement. In order to gain university ethics board approval for conducting research involving youth participants, much of the detail of each research process needed to be set out by me in advance. Likewise, my applications for funding required finely tuned proposals. In participatory research, however, ideally the community has input into shaping the research from the outset and is involved in decision-making through all stages of the research process. In this sense, the expectations of the university conflicted with the tenets of the research methodology. The youth participants, while they did give shape to the knowledge generated, had no input into determining the overarching research agendas limiting their sense of ownership of the work.

Over the years, I did learn how to frame research proposals with enough detail to satisfy expectations, while leaving room for participant input. (That is not to say that all the funding applications I submitted were successful. Some funders simply did not comprehend applied theatre as research.) More recently, via considerations regarding ethical research practices with Indigenous communities amongst the federal guidelines (Panel on Research Ethics, 2022), allowances have been made by research ethics boards and funding bodies to permit some pre-research engagement with potential participants in developing research protocols. Our project with street-involved youth adhered more integrally to the tenets of participatory research since the community organization initiated the research agenda: to educate service providers about the youths' experiences. Also, for the first two years of the project, we successfully argued that youth were not research *subjects* – we were not researching the youths' experiences, but rather, youth were co-researchers and together we were researching service providers' responses to our workshops. In the project's final year, for which we did an evaluation of youth outcomes, the youth were framed as both researchers and the subjects of the evaluation. As I mentioned in Chapter 2, we also advocated for youth to receive honoraria as co-researchers.

Time is another factor that always influences research processes within university and community contexts. As funding is usually tied to timelines, funding plays a role in determining the length and progress of a project, but funding timelines do not always correspond to the timeframes needed for working within other institutional or community settings. Schools, for example, are incredibly busy places with teachers' time always at a premium. Similarly, community organizations are often underfunded and understaffed. Scarcity of time limits what school and community collaborators can realistically contribute to research, limiting their participatory engagement.

My attempts at using my power as a university-based researcher to open space for youths' perspectives did lead to some productive engagement. I feel that the relationships I was able to develop with the youth through all our work together led to some valuable insights, which spoke to the research questions being addressed, as discussed throughout this book. I could not assume, however, that the youth were always fully open to authentically sharing every detail of their experiences. As Scott (1990) suggested, we cannot take the public behaviour of those over whom we have power at face value. As such, I expect that the youths' responses were always only ever partial, guarded by what they were willing to share based on their readings of the context and me. I was always wary to configure my questions or prompts to youth to elicit their stories in such ways that they would have been less likely to just tell me/us what they thought I/we wanted to hear, which is a common problem when garnering participants' stories for research purposes (Nunkoosing, 2005). Moreover, the applied theatre process does lend itself to more open and diverse expression than perhaps the common research method of interviews may. Nevertheless, I always assumed that there were other youth stories that would not or could not be told within the context of the research. This being the case, I applaud the youth for their sophisticated negotiation of the research terrain on their own terms and thank them for what they were willing to share.

Applied Theatre Research in Schools

As a professor of drama/theatre education, having been a high-school drama teacher myself, and through my instruction of pre-service drama teachers over many years, I have become acutely aware of how drama is often taken up in secondary schools. I've been disappointed to see that drama in schools too often focuses on large-scale theatrical productions – putting on scripted plays or musicals, mimicking a professional theatre training model. Drama teachers are also often pressured by their schools' administration to put on *the school play* for the purpose of public relations. While I have no qualms with the desire to showcase students' work and applaud efforts at bringing parents and community members into schools, I take issue with the fact that much of the educational potential that drama offers through more youth-focused methods, such as the applied theatre processes described in this book, is lost via an emphasis on theatrical production. I was disappointed to once hear a drama teacher describe herself as a *traffic cop* when directing the school play – which positions the students as objects of the teacher's direction. The educational potential here is lost, reminiscent of Freire's (1970/2000) critique of the traditional banking model of education, in which the teacher deposits knowledge into the student, which the student is expected to simply memorize and regurgitate as required.

As much as I have tried to instil in my pre-service teacher education students the pedagogical significance of drama that draws on youths' knowledge and experiences – youths' stories to pose problems and inquire into social conditions, which gives youth a forum for their voices to be heard – I have found it challenging to counter dominant trends that value drama/theatre education for its optics, for entertainment appeal, and/or as professionalization. Such trends, I would argue, buy into a neoliberal agenda – seeing the aim of education as developing students' future prospects for supporting the market economy that increasingly governs schooling (Davies & Bansel, 2007; Giroux, 2003).

Another disappointing characteristic of contemporary secondary schooling is the way subject areas have been fragmented or siloed, robbing students of inter-disciplinary learning opportunities. I doubt that much drama pedagogy is taken up in subject areas other than Drama. Applied theatre strategies, particularly image theatre, would have especially rich potential in English Language Arts to explore literary content or initiate creative writing activities and in Social Studies to collaboratively explore social issues. I share this here to emphasize how main-stream schools are embedded within broader socio-political power structures antithetical to the aims of applied theatre.

Hierarchical levels of oversight manage all aspects of what occurs in schools. From teachers setting agendas and expectations in their classrooms, to schools' administration, to school boards, to parent groups and teacher unions, to government departments determining curricula, schools are heavily regulated spaces. Expectations and rules determine all aspects of what occurs in a school: what students wear, how they speak, their movements around the space, the activities they engage in, how they behave towards one another and their teachers.

Such oversight creates schools as sites of conflict and resistance (Foucault, 1991; Giroux, 2003; Rhoades, 2018). While some practitioners have broad definitions of community, which acknowledge the possibility of involuntary community membership (e.g. see Diamond, 2007), it's questionable to me whether schools can be considered communities given that students are required to attend and have such limited input into schools' day-to-day affairs.

Schools are also extremely busy places with mandates to cover curriculum and assess students within limited timeframes alongside the need for controlling throngs of young bodies. Carving out the time and space to allow an outsider like me in to conduct research is always a big ask. Of the two school settings in which I conducted research, the alternative inner-city school which served students who had not met with success in their previous mainstream schools was much less restrictive than the more traditional rural school. Although all students who participated in the research at the rural high school did so willingly (as did the students at the alternative high school), I acknowledge that their attendance at school was not necessarily always by choice.

The limited timeframes within which I conducted my graduate research in schools warrant mentioning. My master's research in the alternative inner-city school was conducted for a total of only 16 hours over 8 days, and my doctoral research for approximately 3 hours per school day over one month – approximately only 60 hours in total. I made efforts in both cases to make the work I was undertaking with students fit with the mandated curricula to maximize the benefit of my imposition to the school. For the media advertising project at the alternative inner-city school, the research was geared towards credit in the communications media stream of the Career and Technology Studies curriculum (Alberta Education, 2009). In the rural school, the project was a unit for their drama classes. As such, I was introduced as a visiting instructor/researcher with some of the power and authority as *leader* or *expert* that came with those roles. I did negotiate, however, in line with university ethics expectations that my power did not extend to assigning grades to students to avoid any potential conflicts of interest.

While these school settings, no doubt, restricted what youth were willing to share, the research did make space for them to generate knowledge about and interpret their lived experiences – bringing aspects of their experiences from both inside and outside the school setting into the work they were asked to undertake as part of their schooling, thereby validating their experiences within that space.

Applied Theatre Research in Jail

Based on what I've already described, it's apparent that the youth jail setting severely restricted the extent to which youth could participate as authentic co-researchers in the studies. Foucault's (1991) notion of *governmentality* suggested that the wielding of institutionalized power is accompanied by an attitude towards those over whom power is exerted, constituting individuals as objects of power, to which individuals often respond with resistance. Such unbalanced distribution of power, which, as Foucault argued, engenders resistance in institutional settings was particularly acute within the context of incarceration. Resistance, however, can be antithetical to education for individual development and social change, so what we could accomplish within that setting was constrained by those inherent dynamics. In this sense, what we did manage to achieve through applied theatre research in the youth jail, I feel, was remarkable.

As well as the requirement for ethics review by the university, an additional ethics review was required from the Alberta Office of the Solicitor General. Plans for the research were necessarily vetted by the administration prior to my entrance into the facility and, as I alluded to earlier, were under ongoing scrutiny throughout. While, according to the Youth Criminal Justice Act (Doob & Cesaroni, 2004), *rehabilitation* not punishment is the primary goal of youth incarceration, as I also mentioned in Chapter 4, I saw priority given to *security* in the jail rather than meaningful programming with the youths' well-being in mind. The only exception to the dearth of appropriate programming seemed to be some sports programming and the Native Program, which with I was involved.

All the youths' movements in and out of jail and around the facility were completely under the control of the system and what they could say or do was heavily curtailed. Youths' participation in the Native Program and in the research was at their choosing, and although the study continued for three years, participation was inconsistent because youth turnover at our sessions was constant. Youth could be denied participation at any time for any number of reasons. I was, for legal and ethical reasons, rightly denied access to the youth outside of jail once they had been released; the fact that the identities of young offenders are so strictly protected, however, limited possibilities for including the youth in any research dissemination. I did get some input for the play I wrote (Conrad, 2012) from one of the incarcerated youth participants, when the youth contacted me upon his release.

To accomplish anything meaningful within the jail, providing the youth with any opportunities for free expression or some small measure of agency required that our applied theatre activities always operate somewhat covertly – which could perhaps be seen as the sort of infrapolitics suggested by Scott (1990). While this slightly furtive attitude may have been ethically questionable in relation to the institution, within that repressive context my loyalties always lay squarely with the youth, my research participants. Our only other options would have been to either create work that was too banal to be meaningful to the youth or to risk being censured by the institution – as was the case for our comics creation project 'Violence Affects Everyone', and ultimately having the research banned entirely.

Applied Theatre Research with a Community Organization

Of all the applied theatre projects that I undertook, the project with the street-involved youth was the best example of applied theatre as youth participatory action research. The fact that the project was initiated by the community organization based on an identified need and was co-facilitated with leaders from the organization, who had established relationships of trust with the youth and understood the youths' needs, supported its success. Moreover, the community organization's values, consistent with mine, were founded on the socially critical belief that systemic barriers, not youths' lifestyles, presented obstacles to youths' well-being. Youth advocacy and non-judgement of youth were central to the shared perspectives we brought to the project. Our aligned intentions and commitments and the processes we undertook created a space where power differentials were minimized – where adults could serve as youths' allies, if not accomplices (Indigenous Action Media, 2014), allowing youth to engage more authentically.

The youth participated because they wanted to and they were free to come and go as they pleased. They were actively involved in all stages of the research as experts: they generated and analysed material for performances based on their life experiences; they prepared and delivered workshop presentations, which included performances and dialogue with service provider audiences; and they conducted an evaluation of the program. While the stories the youth created and performed included stories of pain, hardship, and neglect, the process of telling gave them agency to speak up for themselves and speak back to the challenges they faced in negotiating social systems meant to support them (Arteaga & Chavez-Arteaga, 2022; Barton-Farcas, 2022; Lavie-Ajayi & Krumer-Nevo, 2013).

The conditions necessary to effectively meet the potential of applied theatre for youth existed within this context – in working with a non-profit, community, arts-based organization whose established values and processes were consistent with those of the research project's theoretical and methodological frameworks. Such correlation, I would suggest, goes a long way in supporting a project's success.

I continue now with discussion of other tensions and ethical considerations relevant to facilitating applied theatre research with systemically marginalized youth. Many of these considerations are common for applied theatre projects working with vulnerable populations around sensitive issues.

Representation

Issues related to representation arise in both research and applied theatre in relation to representing others and in relation to representing the so-called *truth*. Representing others through performance always runs the risk of succumbing to multiple ethical pitfalls, as described by Conquergood (1985) such as superficiality, appropriation, voyeurism, exhibitionism, exploitation, sensationalism, and cynicism – which must be avoided. In relation to representing truth, in quantitative research the reliability and validity of the research are said to be based upon its accurate representation of an objective reality. In qualitative and post-qualitative research (St. Pierre, 2011), including applied theatre research and participatory research approaches however, truth is understood to be subjective – determined by individuals' lived experiences and dependant on their socio-cultural milieux (Florczak, 2017).

Representing Truth through Fiction

In applied theatre research, distinctions between fact and fiction become blurred. The scenarios devised and performed for our research were always more or less fictionalized accounts based on youths' experiences – abstracted representations, often compilations of several youths' stories, around common themes. They were self-conscious fabrications and could not have been otherwise.

As Stuart Fisher (2008) insisted, an individual's testimony of their past experiences is never entirely based on facts in any case, but on fragmented recollections 'of emotional, physical and bodily associations, and remembrances' (p. 109). Likewise, Wilkinson and Kitzinger (2008) reasoned that representation of individuals' experiences through storytelling or performance can never provide pure, direct, or true access to reality. Marlin-Curiel (2002) noted, 'memory, though unreliable, nonetheless enables a witness to communicate an embodied reality and solicit an empathic response' (p. 78). Our scenarios were always based on the stories that youth chose to tell, on the selective elements they shared, on the perspectives from which they told them, and on the ways we shaped them for presentation. We always fictionalized youths' stories to provide the aesthetic distance (Barton-Farcas, 2022) needed for the youth to effectively process and perform the scenarios. They were neither real nor not real, neither true nor not true (Shaughnessy, 2005).

As Salverson (1996) claimed, 'the overly literal is a lie' (p. 184). The right distance between facts and their representations, between the intimacy of the real and the distance provided by fiction, is needed for the process to be active, not reductive, to create space to question, to allow for multiple interpretations of an event, to wonder and to contemplate change (Prendergast & Saxton, 2015). For Garde and Mumford (2014), '"inauthentic" performance can paradoxically create a sense of authentic contact with aspects of reality and social truth' (p. 152). They suggested the play between reality and fictionalization is an appropriate strategy for 'engagement with the act of trying to grasp social reality' (p. 164). The fictionalized scenarios created with youth in the applied theatre research projects described in this text told emotional and experiential *truths* of youths' experiences (Ansloos & Wager, 2020) in order for the youth and for audiences to grasp their social realities.

Our scenes were also always influenced by other aesthetic considerations, including my contributions as dramaturge or director. We were selective in choosing which stories to tell, which details to include or exclude in order to best achieve the impact we sought. To amplify youths' storytelling, aspects of the stories were sometimes represented through metaphor or sometimes exaggerated for dramatic effect, as in the case of the 'Labels' scene for the project with street-involved youth, where actual physical labels were clipped onto the youth character for a strong visual effect. Ultimately, the youth and the facilitator(s) informed decisions about what was created and how details were presented. Youth had opportunities to confirm our representations as *true* to what they had to say, thus maintaining their control over the means of our theatrical production.

Representing Youth

In representing youth through performance, we sought balance between representing youth ethically (Preston, 2008) while maintaining their authenticity. Wilkinson and Kitzinger (2008) relayed how feminist practitioners and activists overcame the problem of representing or speaking for others by speaking only for themselves. In our applied theatre research, youth spoke for themselves. The nature of youths' contributions, with a focus on *their* stories, *their* language, and *their* behaviours, served to maintain youths' authentic voices. As Wilkinson and Kitzinger noted however, speaking for one's *identity group* does not entirely evade the problem of assuming all members of that group share similar perspectives – which Diamond (1997) called enacting the violence of the 'we'. Our portrayals required youths' identification with the characters being portrayed, but not facile identification (Conquergood, 1985; Salverson, 1996) as too easy an identification trivializes the differences of the other. While youth spoke for themselves within the collective of each project, undoubtedly nuances of individuals' stories were lost in our compilations. Our collective fictionalized representations, however, avoided implicating specific individuals in behaviours potentially viewed as undesirable.

The nature of our work, our attempts at portraying the truth of youths' experiences, often presented youth characters engaged in risky or self-destructive behaviours, in illicit activities, or as belligerent and uncooperative, and so they were not always presented in the best light. Our work emphasized these behaviours as symptoms of youths' marginalization, as instances for investigation. We had to strike a balance, though, in representing such behaviours as not entirely unproblematic – as we did not want to glorify or promote such behaviours, and in positioning youth neither as villains, nor as powerless victims, both of which would have been disempowering. Throughout all of the projects, we engaged youth in extensive reflection on and analysis of the experiences we were re-presenting to help them gain deeper understandings of their life circumstances.

Regardless of measures taken to represent youth ethically and authentically, when youth experience their stories presented for analysis, objectification or *othering* of their experiences is inevitable and comes with risks (Sinding et al., 2006). Our applied theatre processes mitigated these risks to some extent by allowing for dialogic performance (Conquergood, 1985); authentic dialogue, such as through forum theatre, was strategic for disrupting othering. The line between potential harms and benefits in representing others, however, remains ever blurry.

Representing Others

In advocating for youth through our applied theatre research, we minimized our curtailing of how youth participants depicted youth or other characters. The others represented in our scenes, or implicated in our scenarios, were usually the oppressive authority figures who appeared in their stories. Whether or not those authority figures were actual characters in the scenes we created, we did always work with youth to consider those others' perspectives in our analyses of the issues raised and/or portray fair and realistic representations. In 'The Bus Trip' scene with rural high-school drama students, for example, we considered why the school's administration might have set rules or expectations for youth behaviour such as no drinking on school bus trips, and why they might seek peer informants to enforce those policies.

As another example of our efforts to consider others' perspectives, for a scene we created with the street-involved youth, which we entitled 'Life Line', the scenario began with a youth stranded on the city's outskirts after a party with no money or shoes – someone having stolen them. The youth called their social worker at the end of a workday asking for help, which the social worker was, however, unable to provide – as they needed to attend to other obligations. The social worker suggested the youth call the youth crisis line, but the youth had already burnt that bridge, had no minutes left on their phone, and had also gotten expelled from their residential placement. In devising this scene, we fostered youths' understandings of the professional boundaries that sometimes constrain service providers' actions. In this scenario, the structural circumstances that limit support for youth rather than the individuals' behaviours were depicted as problematic. This despite the call within the literature on working with marginalized youth for the need to sometimes violate boundaries and protocols to meet the needs of youth (Sapiro & Ward, 2020; Smyth & Eaton-Erickson, 2009).

Our scenarios and their ensuing animations/interventions did not suggest simple solutions for overcoming the challenges of conflicting perspectives and expectations between youth, authority figures, and the systems they represent. As our applied theatre work was focused on youth advocacy, we were not overly concerned with making authority figures look good or with sparing their feelings. No doubt our work, sometimes showing negative interactions between youth and authority figures, created uncomfortable spaces that ran the risk of alienating any adult audience members. For the Uncensored project, as one service provider audience member expressed in their response to our evaluation survey: 'Sitting us in opposition to each other didn't foster co-operation. It was "us" vs. "them"!' (E&RS, 2011, p. 13). This service provider obviously experienced tension in considering youths' perspectives. Most of our service provider audiences, however, as professionals committed to improving their engagements with youth, appreciated hearing directly from youth about their experiences. As mentioned previously, our most challenging workshop for the Uncensored project included several police officers. The resistance or defensiveness those officers exhibited, which was antithetical to their meaningful learning, was an example of the sort of tensions our applied theatre work sometimes encountered, which had to be mitigated in seeking productive outcomes.

Although the situation with those resistant police officers was particularly frustrating, the youth did appreciate the opportunities for dialogue with police and other service providers. As one youth commented (YUEV, 2012):

> The most memorable workshop for me that Uncensored put on was because some of [the audience members] were really awesome and really worked with us well and the other half was really resistant. It was interesting to see that balance because usually people are really nice and they're all like, ya, we should work with you that way instead of this way, and these guys [the police officers] were like, no, you have to listen to us because we're right and you don't know what you're talking about, you're just a stupid street kid. It was interesting. (00:10:20–00:10:44)

For this project, the youth indicated our work provided them with opportunities to speak back to authority figures and be heard. They were able to analyse the instances when they had felt unheard and consider the alternative experiences which they felt were more productive. The question remains whether our work had any impact on how authority figures viewed the youth in light of our representations or how they might respond to them in the future based on what they had witnessed.

Mitigating the Risk of Re-traumatizing/Re-victimizing Youth

Applied theatre scholars and practitioners (Blanchet-Cohen & Salazar, 2009; Salverson, 1996; Santiago-Jirau, 2022; Sinding et al., 2006; Stuart Fisher, 2008) have discussed the dangers of re-traumatizing or re-victimizing participants when engaging in the re-telling of difficult or *bad* stories (Fine et al., 2000). The incidents we depicted throughout all the applied theatre projects based on youths' experiences were likely not amongst the most traumatizing experiences in the youths' lives. Youth shared only what they were comfortable sharing within the given contexts, understanding our intentions to investigate what they shared for the critical understandings it could impart. The stories youth shared and our fictionalized portrayals of them nevertheless depicted moments of powerlessness that might have implicated or triggered memories of more traumatic events, heightening youths' vulnerability in their telling and re-telling (Sinding et al., 2008). In portraying youths' experiences, we needed to avoid unjustly appropriating their stories through performance. Characterized by care, responsibility, non-judgement, and efforts at building trusting communities, the applied theatre processes mitigated the potential of re-traumatization/re-victimization to some extent.

Our fictionalizing of youths' stories helped to mitigate risk (Barton-Farcas, 2022) while requiring our attention for maintaining youths' authenticity. As Prendergast and Saxton (2015) argued, when putting personal stories on stage with actors playing themselves, as is the case in some forms of applied theatre, aesthetic distance is disrupted which can be re-traumatizing for participants while also inhibiting audience response. To provide aesthetic distance towards externalizing stories enough to avoid re-traumatization, the youth who performed in our applied theatre projects never played themselves – enacting a protective aesthetic (Hughes, 2013), though characters were often similar to them or the incidents we depicted resonated with theirs. Even if a youth felt strongly that they wanted to portray an incident similar to their story with a character similar to them, we were careful to always create a character and give their character a name. We were clear to always distinguish between the actor and the character they were portraying as we devised, animated, rehearsed, and/or performed scenarios. This also opened space for the fictionalized story to take a turn different from what may have occurred in reality – opening up possibilities for things to be otherwise. In this way, within the liminal performance space youth were simultaneously playing the 'not me' and the 'not not me' (Schechner, 1985, p. 123) which captured the authenticity of their presentations while providing a safety net (Lamparter, 2022).

In negotiating the risk of potentially difficult emotions arising, we also took care to approach every story thoughtfully, seeking to avoid portraying youths' struggles frivolously or romanticizing their struggles for perverse entertainment value or shock value sometimes referred to as *trauma porn* (Hu, 2023) – equivalent to Conquergood's (1985) pitfalls of voyeurism, exhibitionism, or exploitation, which would have been dehumanizing and undignifying (van Fossen & Ndejuru, 2017). Again, the dialogic nature of our performances, which sometimes included interventions from and talk-back with audiences, ensured more meaningful engagement with the issues beyond just passive spectatorship.

The youth involved in the projects described in this text never implied that portraying any of the incidents our scenarios depicted was painful or re-traumatizing for them. Conversely, they described opportunities to tell their stories as personally healing and empowering. Even the one time that a youth with the Uncensored project commented that she felt under-prepared for the forum theatre interventions she experienced the first time she performed, she nevertheless expressed feeling exhilarated by the experience overall. As Nicholson (2005) noted, personal storytelling does not involve a re-living of the actual life events, but a productive and resistant re-writing of those events (Blight, 2015); moreover, the process of disclosure within a supportive community can reduce the self-stigmatization and isolation of holding onto such stories (Sapiro & Ward, 2020).

Certainly, our work elicited frustrations and challenges related to the processes and logistics of the work such as anxieties related to nervousness or feelings of being underprepared for workshops; frustrations related to peers' sometimes lackadaisical attitudes, to audience members' resistances, or to administrators' censorship of our work in the youth jail; or annoyance with me for misunderstanding or forgetting something, for example. I like to think that youth would have let us know had any portrayals been traumatizing for them, but we can never assume that enough trust had been built within a group for completely open and unfettered disclosure.

Avoiding Damage-centred Research

Gubrium et al. (2014) discussed research depictions of difficult stories as potentially 'reify[ing] existing stereotypes about marginalization ... [with] tension over the potential for both emancipatory and oppressive outcomes' (p. 1610).

No doubt, this potential always exists. Unangax̂ scholar Tuck (2009) called for suspension of damage-centred research for Indigenous communities where research narratives by outsiders focusing on damage and deficiency had dominated. I feel Tuck's rejection of damage-centred research should apply to research with any marginalized community, including research with systemically marginalized youth. The alternative research/practice modality that Tuck and others (Hughes, 2013; Gil-Kashiwabara et al., 2007; Santiago-Jirau, 2022) suggested was desire-based, described as a synthesis of oppression and agency, creating space for exploring individuals' full humanity including the complexities and contradictions that characterize life's realities. It does not ignore loss and despair, but emphasizes the hope, vision, and wisdom of individuals, and is generative. Brooks and Kendall (2013) concurred in calling for the need for assets-based approaches – that also celebrate youths' desires, strengths, and talents, to work alongside research initiatives aimed at addressing systemic injustices.

As Baxter (2013) warned, applied theatre in seeking solutions to problems is 'drawn to the presentation of self as tragic … [besought by] the lure of tragedy' (p. 257). While theatrical representations in our work did present youths' struggles and tragic circumstances, they did not blame the youth for their situations, nor depict them as damaged or broken. Rather, our *assets-based* approach (Brooks & Kendall, 2013; Granger, 2002) identified the complex web of circumstances leading to youths' struggles and marginalization while highlighting youths' strengths and capturing their desires.

In the youth jail, for example, our Newspaper Theatre project, 'Need Change?' revealed incarcerated youth as empathetic to the plight of panhandlers, who are criminalized due to poverty and aware of what is needed to make change in one's life. Likewise, in one of our scenes for the Uncensored project, a youth deemed a *problem student* by their teacher was ultimately revealed as a loving care-giver to their infant sibling, which accounted for their persistent lateness and tendency of falling asleep in class. In these ways, our applied theatre work highlighted youths' strengths and resilience in the face of the systemic obstacles they faced; the research showed them actively engaged in working to transform that adversity (Hart et al., 2016). Our projects offered counter-narratives to how marginalized youth are commonly perceived, showing them in new light.

Concluding Thoughts: Unanticipated Repercussions

Thompson (2008) suggested that applied theatre as advocacy can be both therapeutic and political in 'shift[ing] between tactical and strategic performance practice' (p. 121). He referred to *tactics* as those measures enacting private temporary resistance, whereas *strategies* manoeuvred towards public structural change. Based on all the discussion above, it could be argued our projects succeeded in their tactical outcomes in the ways they gave youth opportunities for moments of empowerment. (I'll speak more to the potential our research had for working towards structural change in the next chapter.) Was this enough to justify exposing youths' experiences and perspectives? How might our representations have hindered youth in ways I have not considered, rather than supported them? What was at stake for youth in telling their stories? Thompson suggested the need to carefully weigh 'people's right to speak or not speak ... with the urgent need to challenge society and its marginalising hegemonies' (p. 68). How does one weigh the risks of exposing individual youths' vulnerabilities against potential positive change for marginalized youth generally?

What was at stake for those who listened to youths' stories? Did listening meaningfully change attitudes and behaviours – of the youth participants themselves, of other youth who witnessed the performances and/or of adult audiences? Or did it merely expose youth to the gaze of others, whose listening was sometimes conflicted – such as that of the police officers in our project with street-involved youth? What was at stake for those who facilitated the projects and for the partnering schools, institutions, and organizations? Did our inherent critique of social structures run the risk of reflecting badly on those institutions/organizations? How did this impact their ongoing work with youth? To what extent am I, as a university-based researcher, guilty of appropriating youths' stories to serve my agenda? Did I have most to gain given it served and continues to serve my research agenda through my affiliation with the projects, with the research funding it garnered, and with the publications it produced – this text included? (I return to some of these questions in the following chapter.)

What public acts did our projects perform (Thompson, 2008)? Did exposing youth make them vulnerable to appropriation by the public? Did the projects reinforce the view of systemically marginalized youth as broken and damaged, despite our efforts not to depict them in such ways? Did we run the risk of youths' stories being co-opted (Jordan, 2003) by other, more powerful groups? Did youths' sharing of their experiences serve to prop up initiatives or programs that benefit from youths' vulnerabilities? Did they merely serve to feed the trauma industry (Thompson, 2009)? Though answers to such questions are elusive, they must be asked in relation to any applied theatre project.

8

Applied Theatre Research
as Social Performance

I have been privileged, over my twenty-plus year academic career, to have had rich and diverse opportunities to engage with marginalized youth through applied theatre and it's been my pleasure to share this work here. I began this book in Chapter 1 by introducing the applied theatre work with systemically marginalized youth that I've undertaken within school settings, in a youth jail and with an organization serving street-involved youth. There, I also discussed some key concepts central to my discussion of this work. In Chapter 2, I explored what is needed to meaningfully engage systemically marginalized youth in applied theatre research, and in Chapter 3, described the processes I developed in collaboration with my community partners and youth for doing this work. In Chapter 4, I explored the specific process we developed to work within the context of youth incarceration and in Chapter 5, I spoke to how I have come to believe applied theatre might support the needs of Indigenous youth. In Chapter 6, I attempted to articulate the ways in which applied theatre can be seen to provide the conditions for youth empowerment and for advocacy by and for youth. In Chapter 7, I explored the tensions and ethical considerations involved in my applied theatre research undertakings.

In this concluding chapter, I first raise some questions about the constraints of my academic work and then discuss the potential of applied theatre research for addressing the challenges faced by youth within the broader social context. I begin by reflexively interrogating the value and impact of my academic research and writing.

Questions of Interpretation

Everything I've described and discussed in this text is of course my interpretation of what occurred through my applied theatre research. Based on the previous writing

I have done about each of the projects, as well as my recollections of doing the work (as unreliable as those may be), my interpretations are unavoidably biased and questions regarding the legitimacy of such interpretations should be raised. Does what I have written in this book justly represent the processes in which we engaged and the outcomes that I claim? Does it accurately represent what the youth had to say? Is it *reliable* as research? Does it do justice to the participants? How would the youth respond to all I have written here implicating them? These are among the lingering questions regarding the legitimacy of my writing and research that deserve some response.

All of the youth who participated in the applied theatre projects of course gave their consent as research participants at the outset of the projects. Consistent with university ethical requirements, they were informed as to what our processes might entail and how the understandings I gained would be utilized. Yet, neither they nor I had any way of knowing where our emergent work and my interpretations would lead. The youth participated as co-researchers in the various projects to various extents, but did my final interpretations, the writing of the many journal articles, book chapters and this book, ultimately do justice to my hopeful intentions for our participatory processes? While the youth participants had significant input into our applied theatre work, they were only ever minimally consulted at the culmination of the projects in which they were involved regarding my scholarly writing about our work together. This was due primarily to logistical considerations. Once the applied theatre sessions concluded, since my contacts with youth were via institutions or organizations, I never had access to them outside of those settings. Tracking them down beyond the contexts of our research agreements would have been awkward, if not unethical. In the case of incarcerated youth, attempting to make contact with them on the *outs* was prohibited. I acknowledge that my interpretations would have benefitted greatly from more youth input.

All these years later, although the youth participants are not identifiable in my writing, I wonder if any of them would appreciate being associated with these projects given that they are described as systemically marginalized. Youth move on with their lives and their circumstances change. Would this reminder of a time of struggle in their lives be welcomed or not? I'm reminded of an exchange with the youth in the jail: At the start of the project, as I was reviewing the participant consent forms with them, indicating that their names would not be associated with the research for ethical reasons, some expressed dismay. I mentioned that the youth justice system strictly protected their identities as juvenile offenders, because, I joked, were they to become Prime Minister someday, for example, they would not want their youth incarceration on record. A youth responded to the contrary: As Prime Minister, a juvenile record would help make him relatable to people, he insisted. Perhaps he was correct. Protecting vulnerable youths' identities, though, is a research ethics requirement which is also why none of the many photographs and videos taken of youth throughout the various projects appear in this book.

My research was interested in the knowledge generated with youth through applied theatre about their life experiences and in developing and learning from applied theatre processes aimed at eliciting youths' knowledge. I was also very interested in better understanding theoretically what it was about applied theatre that seemed to offer youth opportunities for empowerment and advocacy and any broader impacts this work could have towards social justice ends. I was never really interested in formally verifying or measuring the impacts of my work as research *interventions* (my affective, embodied experience assured me it was impactful), so my studies did not focus on assessing the impacts of the applied theatre projects on youths' lives (see Barton-Farcas, 2022; Etherton & Prentki, 2006; Taylor, 2002). The arts-based evaluation that the youth conducted for the Uncensored project, once we witnessed how the work was benefitting them – the one time we did do a formal assessment of outcomes for youth, however – did prove very insightful. Other such assessments would be beneficial. My research was never meant to be longitudinal, either. I never sought to research the long-term effects of the applied theatre work, though, I acknowledge a study involving follow-up with youth some-time after their engagement with an applied theatre project might offer valuable insights too. Do the lack of formal evaluations and the passing of time – it has after all been more than twenty years since the first project I undertook – reduce the legitimacy of the work? I hope that the experiences I gained from working through applied theatre over many years with diverse marginalized youth populations give this work some credibility. I can only leave it up to readers to decide for themselves if the work described herein has any relevance for their ongoing efforts.

Now that the research has long concluded, what are my obligations to the research participants and/or to the partnering institutions and organizations regarding all I have written? My allegiances through the research were first and foremost with the youth and my intentions with my writing have always been to advocate for youth. What if my intentions to serve the interests of youth partic-ipants undermined the interests of the partnering institutions/organizations that generously (or begrudgingly, in the case of the youth jail) allowed me to conduct research with the youth under their purview? What are my obligations to them? If I see obstacles to social justice entrenched in schooling practices, in the context of youth incarceration, in the processes of service provision, certainly I am obligated to speak out. In any case, my critique of institutional practices has always been generalized, directed at social-structural conditions, rather than at any particular institution or organization. Do my good intentions mitigate any negative fallout from my research endeavours?

Have my intentions to benefit marginalized youth been achieved? How can I know? As academics, our research *impact* is judged primarily by the number of *outputs* (journal articles, books, etc.) we produce and the number of citations those outputs achieve. Presumably, as academics, our scholarly writing is intended to inform educators, practitioners, researchers, policymakers (if policymakers were inclined to read scholarship on applied theatre research), etc. Such academic writing, however, seems trite in light of the dire circumstances of and ongoing struggles in the lives of systemically marginalized youth and the urgent need to address these issues. Participatory research seeks practical, actionable outcomes to benefit the community with which it engages. The sustainable, tangible outputs resulting from my research, beyond my academic writing, however, have been few. The Uncensored project did develop an innovative workshop model that the youth organization made use of even after the project concluded and can continue to utilize. The comic book created for the Dene community's Youth Leadership conference – though not a research output per se – remains the ownership of the community for community use. Is this enough to validate my academic research? Overall, I'm left wondering now nearing the end of my career what my academic work has really achieved.

My interpretations of our applied theatre work drew on what youth revealed, relevant theory, and my own experiences of doing the research. Based in a post-modern belief that any *truth* can only ever be partial, without however nullifying the possibility that we can know things about reality and act in the world (McLaren, 1994), I cannot claim that anything in this book is *the truth*. In any case, my intentions have not been to provide prescriptive analyses of youth behaviour or youth needs, but only to offer alternative perspectives for consideration. Moreover, given the impossibility of speaking for all marginalized youth as one coherent category, my interpretations can only be partial. I can only hope that my understandings about the topics I have discussed have some resonance with the understandings and experiences of others and that my research and writing has succeeded in amplifying youths' voices and perspectives.

Applied Theatre Is Not a Panacea, but ...

In preceding chapters, I spoke of Kershaw's (1999) notion of *radical performance*, of Lyng's (1990) *edgework*, Scott's (1990) *infrapolitics*, and Gaztambide-Fernández's (2013) understanding of art as *cultural production* to think about how the dynamics inherent to applied theatre processes can benefit youth. If, however, applied theatre is indeed always bounded by historically structured power dynamics (Thompson, 2008) and there is no possibility of evading the grasp of power implicated in our work (Wilkinson & Kitzinger, 2008), within our current social reality, what are the possibilities and limitations of applied theatre research with systemically marginalized youth in achieving broader socio-political impacts? As I mentioned in the previous chapter, Thompson (2008) refers to *strategies* in applied theatre as manoeuvres towards public structural change. Did our research projects succeed at enacting any strategic outcomes? Did they have any lasting structural impacts? What social role can applied theatre research perform? As youth development researcher Granger (2006) conceded, 'given the resources that public and private organizations spend on intervention meant to improve the well-being of young people ... it is discouraging that we know so little about how to create and sustain positive change at any scale' (p. 160). What can applied theatre research offer towards creating and sustaining positive social change to benefit systemically marginalized youth?

The need for addressing the challenges in youths' lives brought on by our unjust social structures is even more urgent now than when I began my research more than twenty years ago. In a recent article, building on what he had been warning us about for decades, Giroux (2022) painted a bleak picture of the current state of relations between youth and United States society – and by extension Canadian society as US-style politics seep across the border via far-right groups and ultra-conservative attitudes, especially in Alberta where my applied research took place. Giroux described *neo-liberalism*, the dominant western political philosophy focused on free-market capitalism, as a *necro-politics* characterized by 'inequality, precarity and moral depravity' (para. 4) aimed largely at racialized and poor, working-class youth. Under this *gangster capitalism* youth are viewed as 'an economic liability and a drain on the resources needed to concentrate wealth in the hands of the ruling classes and financial elite' (para. 2). In response, the ruling powers push 'to privatize public services, deregulate the financial industry, and depoliticize the public realm in order to replace a market economy with a market society' (para. 6). As Giroux describes, neo-liberal fascist politics are evident in the fact that in some US states books on race and sexuality are banned from schools and libraries, medical care for transgender youth is denied, reproductive rights are criminalized, and children as young as fourteen are tried in adult courts.

Giroux (1992, 1997, 2003, 2022) has discussed the war on youth enacted through a slow violence of disinvestment in youth along with policies that treat youth as a threat. 'Already disenfranchised by virtue of their age', he declared, 'young people are under assault today in ways that are entirely new because they now face a world that is far more dangerous than at any other time in recent history' (Giroux, 2022, para. 31). I agree that 'there has never been a more important historical moment for young people to rise up and fight for a notion of agency, justice, and equality that offers them both hope, freedom, and a sense of equality and justice' (para. 4).

In our current precarious times, as we have seen, youth voices can have an impact even on national and international stages; youth activists such as Malala Yousafzai, Greta Thunberg, and Autumn Peltier (Cranley, 2019; Tedford, 2022) have influenced attitudes and policies. While applied theatre research may not be able to intervene directly in transforming social structures, even the small, symbolic actions that applied theatre can enact are significant. As Wagamese avowed, the commitment to '"do what I can do right now in my own small way", creates a ripple effect on the world' (2019, p. 81). Robinson and Martin (2016) also reminded us that discounting the small impacts that our work might have 'not only risks creating a sense of powerlessness and despair, but also misses the potential of micro-actions to ripple, to erode, and to subtly shift' (pp. 1–2). Boal (1974/1979) called his Theatre of the Oppressed rehearsal for revolution. Perhaps this is applied theatre research's contribution within the larger social context – as a means for youth to rehearse their future actions towards seeking social transformation (Santiago-Jirau, 2022; Tate, 2022).

Creating Ripples

In an article I wrote about the study with street-involved youth (Conrad, 2015), I explored the Uncensored project as an example of social innovation. I reiterate and build upon some of those ideas here in relation to the potential impacts of applied theatre research with systemically marginalized youth on a societal scale.

Social Innovation and Complexity Theory

At an international roundtable, the Government of Canada Policy Research Initiative (2010) described *social innovation* as 'responding to [social] challenges that are not being addressed through conventional approaches ... often requiring new forms of collaboration ... including "co-creation" and "co-production" among citizens and institutional actors' (p. 1). In the roundtable summary, it was suggested that social innovation is 'difficult to describe, but you know it when you see it' (p. 4); that social innovation flourishes in an environment that is *risk attractive*, flexible, and yet rigorous, allowing for *safe* and *smart* risk-taking. The impacts of social innovation, the roundtable concluded, are 'difficult to measure with existing evaluation tools' (p. 4) in that measurable outcomes are not necessarily generated. Rather, the outcomes of such iterative and *messy* processes are unpredictable and often take years to fully manifest; they are largely local and place-based, though often leading to 'significant [long-term] society wide changes' (p. 3). While the round table summary does not specifically reference complexity theory, its description of social innovation mirrors complexity theory's understandings of complex systems. The only source that the summary does cite (Murray, et al., 2010) uses the language of systems thinking and feedback loops related to complexity theory as a framework for social innovation.

According to Westley et al. (2007), social innovation is not something we ever entirely arrive at, but something for which we strive. In their book *Getting to Maybe: How the World Is Changed*, the authors also described social innovation through the lens of complexity theory. They saw social innovation as being about an intention to bring about social change, to make things happen within a complex world, without guarantees – hence *getting to maybe*. Social innovation involves a vision for change along with a tolerance for ambiguity and a responsiveness to unpredictable events. Working towards social innovation, they claimed, takes vision, courage, and commitment. It is not without struggles and risk and there is always so much more to do. Westley et al. (2007) described social innovation as 'a juxtaposition of despair and possibility' (p. 189) through its inevitable successes and failures, with despair described as the shadow side of social innovation.

Applied theatre research, I contend, falls well within the Government of Canada Policy Research Initiative's (2010) and Westley et al.'s (2007) descriptions of social innovation. Though I can't confirm that my applied theatre projects led to 'significant [long-term] society wide changes' (Government of Canada Policy Research Initiative, 2010, p. 3), those descriptions of social innovation accurately reflect the applied theatre processes I facilitated in terms of their intentions, complexities, unpredictability, and inherent risks. The Uncensored project even inadvertently followed the Government of Canada Policy Research Initiative's (2010) five steps involved in a co-creative social innovation project, which were:

1) Identifying and resolving to address a given problem;
2) understanding the nature of the problem including its causes and patterns;
3) engaging all relevant stakeholders to develop a prototype for a solution;
4) implementing the solution; and
5) evaluating its impact. (p. 4)

Diamond (2007) also framed his *Theatre for Living* – his adaptation of Boal's work – in terms of complexity theory; he drew on Capra's (1983) understandings of systems thinking to situate his work, seeing a community as a living connected system. He understood that individual and community health is vitally dependent on peoples' capacity to imagine. Applied theatre research seen through the lens of complexity theory shares an understanding of social issues as complex, interrelated, unpredictable, and messy. Ways of working in applied theatre research, as in socially innovative initiatives, are based on imagination and intuition, the recognition of patterns, and emergent, co-evolving processes with transformative potential. Boal (2006) believed that all art is transformative: 'the act of transforming [through creating art] is in itself transformatory' he argued; 'In the act of changing our image, we are changing ourselves, and by changing ourselves in turn we change the world' (p. 62). Likewise, notions of interconnectedness informed my applied theatre research practices with the conviction that engaging groups of youth in expressing and critically analysing their realities could have expansive effects.

If applied theatre processes can, at the very least, subtly shift individuals' perspectives (or ideally, incite them to action), so too perhaps, like a stone thrown into a pool of water creates ever expanding concentric circles on the water's surface, applied theatre research can create ripples in individuals' lives that expand to impact their peer relations, their families and communities, and ultimately our social environment. Or, if my mixing of metaphors can be forgiven, as Scott (1990) suggested, 'the accumulation of petty acts can, rather like snowflakes on a steep mountainside, set off an avalanche' (p. 192).

Applied Theatre as Cultural Democracy

Applied theatre, as a community-based art form, is grounded in what might be understood as an aesthetics of *cultural democracy*, which is about providing access to the means for cultural production and community decision-making (Barndt, 2008; Evrard, 1997; Goldbard, 2009; Graves, 2004). Cultural democracy expresses localized culture, the cultural diversity of a community, through which art becomes a forum for community engagement. Cultural democracy calls for direct public participation in the arts for creating a vibrant, living, and responsive culture and an integration of art and life. This notion of cultural democracy is evident in conceptions of community art as well as in Indigenous perspectives of art (Kenny, 1998; Sheridan & Longboat, 2014) – as integral for recovering a more interconnected worldview and integral to the pursuit of social justice.

The significance of culture and cultural democracy has been emphasized by scholars, artists, and activists. Goldbard (2009) saw cultural democracy as cultural action claiming 'community cultural development projects are laboratories for engaged citizenship' (para. 12). She saw a role for the arts in new paradigm thinking, when she said:

> The old system [i.e., the positivist paradigm] treats everything like so much material that can be weighed, measured, assigned a number and dismissed. The new system is grounded in human stories, recognizing abundant diversity and the power of

relationship. In the old system, art and culture are dismissible as nice, but not necessary; in the emergent system, culture is the crucible for all positive development. (para. 2)

Similarly, Mackey (2010) believed culture is the way human beings create meaning from their experiences and that *vernacular culture* – making culture rather than consuming it – is a dynamic aspect of social life. He said:

Cultural activities form the necessary bridges between aspirations and lasting renewal. Any change must be imagined first. Art stimulates and exercises individual and collective inventiveness, thus promoting the experimentation and adaptation necessary for people to adjust to constantly changing conditions. (p. 241)

Constant change, it may be argued, is a predominant characteristic of our current reality and cultural production, then, is a vital part of social innovation. Indeed, Hawkes (2023) understood *cultural vitality* as a fourth pillar for building a sustainable society along with social justice, economic development, and ecological responsibility. As Matanovic (2002), long-time community arts organizer suggested: 'The idiosyncratic gifts of the artist, with all their uncertainties, may be exactly what we need to create a more humane, sustainable, and beautiful world' (para. 17).

While the individual projects described in this book may have been socially innovative examples of cultural democracy in action, which led to some individual and localized social benefit, the work needed in seeking justice for systemically marginalized youth is far from accomplished. Applied theatre research can play a role in this undertaking.

Final Concluding Thoughts

Facilitating applied theatre research with systemically marginalized youth has not been without its challenges. It demanded flexibility and ongoing negotiation to create the conditions to productively engage the youth whose experiences had understandably left them suspicious of adults and the systems that denied them adequate attention. As an educational researcher and applied theatre facilitator, I was able to support processes that in some small ways allowed youth to be deeply affected, to be seen and heard, to exercise their power, agency, and strength, and that fostered more constructive attitudes towards them.

In Fall 2022, I was honoured to have been granted an artist residency in a small West Coast community where I spent some focused time working on this manuscript. As part of my community engagement for the residency, I offered an initial presentation for the community on the work described in this book, a series of applied theatre workshops for community youth, and a final community dialogue about engaging with the community's youth. My residency highlighted the community-based, applied nature of my theatre practice. Although the workshops for youth that I offered and the youth who attended them were few, I gleaned some interesting insights from both my planning for the workshops and from what youth shared during our work together. Following the residency, the arts council president sent me a blurb they intended to include on their website about the outcomes of my residency:

> Diane Conrad ... professor of drama/theatre education made some amazing connections with [name of community] youth through her applied theatre workshops and by doing so provided those adults who are also working with our youth with new insight on potential programs. (Poschmann, personal communication, January 19, 2023)

What this example illustrates is that even brief engagement through applied theatre can initiate meaningful community dialogue.

Applied theatre research offers opportunities for youth to tell their stories about the systemic challenges they face, about their understandings of their life experiences, and their desires for the future. These are small steps forward in our collective efforts at seeking justice for youth.

Appendix 1:
Five Applied Theatre Projects

Original Project Title	Researcher Status	Funding	Location	Years of Study + Duration of Youth Engagement	Participants	Focus	Publications
Exploring Media Advertising through Drama with Inner-City Students	Master's Research	n/a	Alternative inner-city high school	1999–2001 2 × 4-day orientation sessions	13 grades 10–12 students who had not been successful in traditional high schools	Creating their own ads to talk back to mainstream advertising	Conrad (2002a, 2002b)
Life in the Sticks: Youth Experiences, Risk, & Popular Theatre Process	Doctoral Research	Social Sciences and Humanities Research Council of Canada Doctoral Fellowship	Rural Alberta high school	1999–2004 daily for 1 month	22 grades 10–12 students in two drama classes	Youths' experiences and perceptions of what might deem them 'at-risk'	Conrad (2004a, 2004b, 2005, 2006b)
Arresting Change: Popular Theatre with Young Offenders	Pilot Project	n/a	Young Offender Centre; Community Transitions Program	2003–2004 weekly for 6 months	Approx. 20 incarcerated youth ages 12–18	Youths' experiences of incarceration	Campbell and Conrad (2006), Conrad (2006a)
The Transformative Potential of Drama in the Education of Incarcerated Youth	Faculty Research	Social Sciences and Humanities Research Council of Canada	Young Offender Centre; Native Program	2005–2009 weekly for 3 years	Approx. 50 incarcerated youth ages 14–19	How drama can support incarcerated youth for better outcomes in the future	Conrad (2010, 2012, 2013, 2016)
High Risk Youth Uncensored: An Educational Exchange	Faculty Research	REACH Edmonton Council for Safe Communities; Kule Institute for Advanced Study; University of Alberta	Edmonton non-profit arts-based youth organization	2009–2013 2 years of workshops + 1 year for youth evaluation	50+ street-involved youth ages 12–24	Workshops for service providers to educate them about youths' life experiences and their encounters with service providers	Conrad (2015, 2023); Conrad, Smyth, and Kendal (2015)

Appendix 2:
Guidelines for Drama Ensemble

The following ideas are important for working together as a group in drama:

Trust

☐ willingness to trust others
☐ take care of each other

Confidentiality

☐ respect others privacy
☐ what goes on in the group stays in the group

Commitment

☐ give 100% – give it everything you've got
☐ contribute ideas
☐ use your mind, body, and voice
☐ participate fully

Listening

☐ listen to others and listen to yourself
☐ be sensitive to what others are feeling
☐ listen with your whole being
☐ be aware of what's happening around you

Focus on the Group

- ☐ work with the group
- ☐ avoid cliques or sticking with your friends
- ☐ bring comments to the whole group
- ☐ we're working towards a common goal

Personal Disclosure

- ☐ you will be asked to share your personal experiences with the group
- ☐ stay within your own comfort zone

Willingness to Risk

- ☐ take risks, but don't be reckless
- ☐ try new things
- ☐ don't be shy or afraid
- ☐ don't be afraid to make mistakes or feel silly
- ☐ risk = personal growth

Willingness to Question Your Beliefs

- ☐ recognize that we all have biases
- ☐ respect others' beliefs
- ☐ be open minded
- ☐ be willing to change

All Offers Are Co-owned

- ☐ personal experiences that are shared may be used by the group, anonymously
- ☐ the group may change or adapt ideas

Willingness to Negotiate

- ☐ the process requires give and take
- ☐ state your ideas and listen to others

- there's sometimes a need to reach agreement
- there's sometimes a need to agree to disagree

Give and Accept Critique

- everything is open to critique
- give constructive critique
- don't take critique personally
- learn from critique

Stay Focused on the Task

- concentrate on the activity
- try your best
- don't be distracted or distract others

Accept Offers

- everything can be an offer
- don't block offers
- don't judge ideas
- trust your ideas and the ideas of others

Don't Always Go for the Laugh

- humour is good, but not always the best or most interesting solution
- ideas don't have to be funny or clever

Have Fun

- be positive
- make the most of the experience
- encourage others
- laugh with not at others

Permission to Dissent

- you are encouraged to participate

☐ let us know about any physical limitations
☐ if you are extremely uncomfortable with an activity or issue, you have the right to opt out

Appendix 3:
Index of Applied Theatre Games,
Exercises, and Activities

Here you will find a list of the common drama games, exercises and activities I mention throughout the book. The origins of these are not always known and they may be known by various names. I do not claim proprietary rights to any of them.

Appendix 4:
Image Theatre Example

Setting: On a city bus.

Scenario: A woman's purse has gone missing. She approaches a transit security officer and accuses a racialized young man on the bus of stealing her purse. The security officer questions the young man who claims innocence of the crime. The security officer asks to search the young man's knapsack. The bus driver looks on reluctant to get involved.

The image includes four characters on the bus and four characters representing the social forces influencing the characters on the bus (Figure A4.1).

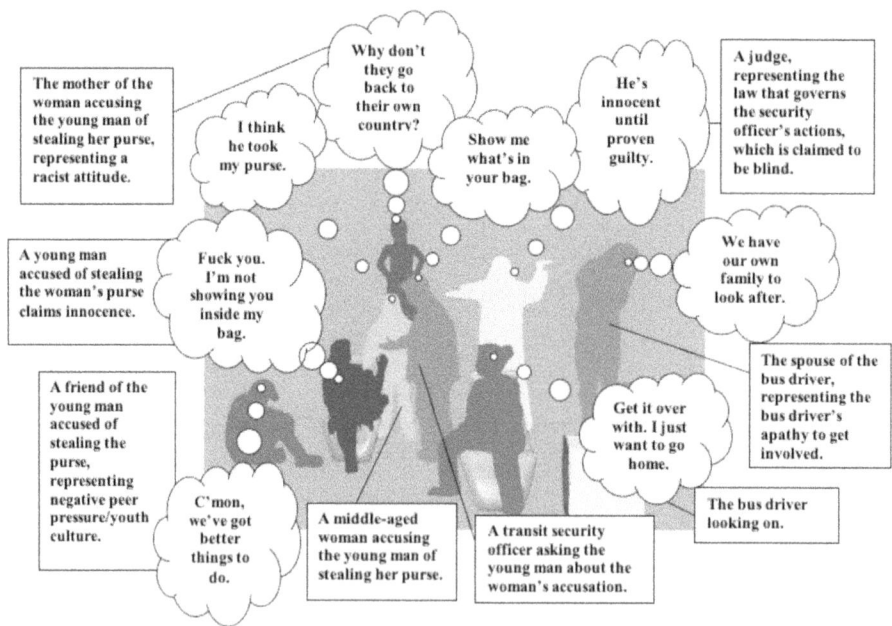

FIGURE A4.1: Example of an image and scenario created through an image theatre process, 2005. © D. Conrad.

References

Absolon, K., & Willett, C. (2005). Putting ourselves forward: Location in Aboriginal research. In L. Brown & S. Strega (Eds.), *Research as resistance: Critical, Indigenous, and anti-oppressive approaches* (pp. 97–126). Canadian Scholars' Press.

Adler, P., & Adler, P. A. (2003). *Constructions of deviance: Social power, context, and interaction*. Wadsworth/Thomson Learning Inc.

Ahmed, S. (2006). The non-performativity of antiracism. *Meridians*, 7(1), 104–126. https://www.jstor.org/stable/40338719

Alberta Education. (2005). Social studies kindergarten to grade 12. https://education.alberta.ca/media/3273004/social-studies-k-6-pos.pdf

Alberta Education. (2009). Career and technology studies. https://education.alberta.ca/media/482254/philosophy.pdf

Alberta Learning. (2001). Removing barriers to high school completion: Final report. https://open.alberta.ca/publications/077851319x

Alfred, T. (2005). *Wasáse: Indigenous pathways of action and freedom*. Broadview.

Alfred, T. (2017). It's all about the land. In P. McFarlane & N. Schabus (Eds.), *Whose land is it anyway? A manual for decolonization* (pp. 10–13). Federation of Postsecondary Teachers of BC.

Alrutz, M. (2013). Sites of possibility: Applied theatre and digital storytelling with youth. *Research in Drama Education: The Journal of Applied Theatre and Performance*, 18(1), 44–57. http://dx.doi.org/10.1080/13569783.2012.756169

American Friends Service Committee. (2020). *Speak truth to power: A Quaker search for an alternative to violence*. Pickle Partners Publishing. (Original work published 1955)

Anaya, J. (2014). Report of the Special Rapporteur on the rights of Indigenous peoples. *The situation of Indigenous peoples in Canada*. United Nations General Assembly. https://www.ohchr.org/sites/default/files/HRBodies/HRC/RegularSessions/Session27/Documents/A_HRC_27_52_Add_2_ENG.doc

Ansloos, J. P., & Wager, A. C. (2020). Surviving in the cracks: A qualitative study with Indigenous youth on homelessness and applied community theatre. *International Journal of Qualitative Studies in Education*, 33(1), 50–65. https://doi.org/10.1080/09518398.2019.1678785

Anzaldúa, G. (2002). (Un)natural bridges, (un)safe spaces. In G. Anzaldúa & A. Keating (Eds.), *This bridge we call home: Radical visions for transformation* (pp. 1–5). Routledge.

Apple, M. (1995). *Education and power*. Routledge.

Arao, B., & Clemens, K. (2013). From safe spaces to brave spaces: A new way to frame dialogue around diversity and social justice. In L. M. Landreman (Ed.), *The art of effective facilitation: Reflections from social justice educators* (pp. 135–150). Stylus Pub.

Aristotle. (1997). *Poetics*. (M. Heath, Trans.). Penguin. (Original work published c. 335 B.C.E.)

Aristotle. (1998). *Metaphysics*. (H. Lawson-Tancred, Trans.). Penguin. (Original work published c. 350 B.C.E.)

Arteaga, M., & Chavez-Arteaga, A. (2022). Laughter, healing, and belonging: Cada quien tiene su lugar. In L. S. Brenner, C. Ceraso, & E. Diaz Cruz (Eds.), *Applied theatre with youth: Education, engagement, activism* (pp. 145–153). Routledge.

Asakura, K., Lundy, J., & Tierney, C. (2019). Art as a transformative practice: A participatory action research project with trans* youth. *Qualitative Social Work, 19*(5–6), 1061–1077. https://doi.org/10.1177/1473325019881226

Assante, M. K. (2008). *It's bigger than hip hop: The rise of the post-hip-hop generation*. St. Martin's Press.

Austin, J. L. (1975). *How to do things with words*. Harvard University Press.

Bailin, S. (1993). Drama as experience: A critical view. *Canadian Journal of Education, 18*(2), 95–105. http://journals.sfu.ca/cje/index.php/cje-rce/article/view/2650/1958

Baim, C. (2004). If all the world's a stage, why did I get the worst parts? In M. Balfour (Ed.), *Theatre in prison: Theory and practice* (pp. 139–160). Intellect.

Baim, C. (2017). The drama spiral: A decision-making model for safe, ethical, and flexible practice when incorporating personal stories in applied theatre and performance. In A. O'Grady (Ed.), *Risk, participation, and performance practice: Critical vulnerabilities in a precarious world* (pp. 79–109). Palgrave.

Baker, D. (1973). Drama and theatre in education. *Journal of Curriculum Studies, 5*(1), 32–45. https://doi.org/10.1080/0022027730050104

Balfour, M. (2010). Developing the capacities of applied theatre students to be critically reflective learner-practitioners. *Australasian Drama Studies,* (57), 54–67. https://search.informit.org/doi/10.3316/ielapa.690520263471654

Barad, K. (2007). *Meeting the universe half-way: Quantum physics and the entanglement of matter and meaning*. Duke University Press.

Barndt, D. (2008). Touching minds and hearts: Community arts as collaborative research. In G. Knowles & A. Cole (Eds.), *Handbook of the arts in qualitative research* (pp. 352–363). Sage.

Barton-Farcas, S. (2022). Our story: How Nicu's Spoon fosters representation, access, inclusion for youth with disabilities. In L. S. Brenner, C. Ceraso, & E. Diaz Cruz (Eds.), *Applied theatre with youth: Education, engagement, activism* (pp. 171–179). Routledge.

Baruth, L., & Manning, M. (1995). *Students at-risk*. Allyn and Bacon.

Battiste, M. A. (2013). *Decolonizing education: Nourishing the learning spirit*. Purich.

Baxter, V. (2013). Postcards on the aesthetic of hope in applied theatre. *Matatu: Journal for African Culture and Society*, 44(1), 257–268. https://doi.org/10.1163/9789401210546_018

Bell, N., & Bell, R. (1993). *Adolescent risk-taking*. Sage.

Benjamin, W. (1999). In M. W. Jennings, H. Eiland, & G. Smith (Eds.), *Walter Benjamin selected writings, vol. 2, part 2, 1931–1934* (pp. 720–722). The Belknap Press of Harvard University Press. (Original work published 1933)

Bhabha, H. (1994). *The location of culture*. Routledge.

Blanchet-Cohen, N., & Salazar, J. (2009). Empowering practices for working with marginalized youth. *Relational Child and Youth Care Practice*, 22(4), 5–15. https://www.mcconnellfoundation.ca/assets/Media%20Library/Youth%20Engagment%20-%20Empowering%20practices.pdf

Blatner, A. (1997). *Acting-in: Practical applications of psychodramatic methods*. Free Association Books.

Blight, R. (2015). Privileging aboriginal voices: Applied theatre as a transformative process for Aboriginal Australian youth. *Applied Theatre Research*, 3(1), 21–35. https://doi.org/10.1386/atr.3.1.21_1

Bloustien, G. (2002). Fans with a lot at stake: Serious plan and mimetic excess in *Buffy the Vampire Slayer*. *European Journal of Cultural Studies*, 5(4), 427–449. https://doi.org/10.1177/1364942002005004429

Boal, A. (1979). *Theatre of the oppressed*. (C. McBride, Trans.). Pluto. (Original work published 1974)

Boal, A. (1992). *Games for actors and non-actors*. (A. Jackson, Trans.). Routledge.

Boal, A. (1995). *The rainbow of desire*. (A. Jackson, Trans.). Routledge.

Boal, A. (2006). *Aesthetics of the oppressed*. Routledge.

Bowers, C. A. (2008). Why a critical pedagogy of place is an oxymoron. *Environmental Education Research*, 14(3), 325–335. http://dx.doi.org/10.1080/13504620802156470

Brecht, B. (1964). *Brecht on theatre: The development of an aesthetic*. (J. Willett, Trans.). Hill and Wang. (Original work published 1957)

Brendel Horn, E. (2017). 'Do you see me?' Power and visibility in applied theatre with Black male youth and the police. *Youth Theatre Journal*, 31(2), 79–91. https://doi.org/10.1080/08929092.2017.1370756

Britzman, D. P. (1992). The terrible problem of knowing thyself: Toward a postructural account of teacher identity. *Journal of Curriculum Theorizing*, 9(3), 23–49.

Britzman, D. P. (1998). *Lost subjects, contested objects: Toward a psychoanalytic inquiry of learning*. State University of New York Press.

Brooks, F., & Kendall, S. (2013). Making sense of assets: What can an assets based approach offer public health? *Critical Public Health*, 23(2), 127–130. https://doi.org/10.1080/09581596.2013.783687

Buck-Morss, S. (1992). Aesthetics and anaesthetics: Walter Benjamin's artwork essay reconsidered. *October*, 62(Fall), 3–41.

Butler, J. (1999). *Gender trouble: Feminism and the subversion of identity*. Routledge.

Cajete, G. (1994). *Look to the mountain: An ecology of Indigenous education*. Kivaki.

Cammarota, J., & Fine, M. (Eds.) (2008). *Revolutionizing education: Youth participatory action research in motion*. Routledge.

Campbell, G., & Conrad, D. (2006). Arresting change: Popular theatre with young offenders. In L. McCammon & D. McLauchlan (Eds.), *The universal mosaic of drama and theatre: The International Drama/Theatre Education Association 2004 Dialogues* (pp. 375–391). IDEA Publications/Soleil.

Canadian AIDS Society (CAS) & Canadian Harm Reduction Network (CHRN). (2008). Learning from each other: Enhancing community-based harm reduction programs and practices in Canada. https://www.cdnaids.ca/wp-content/uploads/Learning-from-Each-Other.pdf

Canadian Council on Learning. (2009). *The state of Aboriginal learning in Canada: A holistic approach to measuring success*. www.afn.ca/uploads/files/education2/state_of_aboriginal_learning_in_canada-final_report,_ccl,_2009.pdf

Capra, F. (1983). *The turning point: Science, society and the rising culture*. Bantam Books.

Carter, J. (2016). Sovereign proclamations of the twenty-first century: Scripting survivance through the language of soft power. In Y. Nolan & R. Knowles (Eds.), *Performing Indigeneity* (pp. 34–65). Playwrights Canada.

Carter, M. (2022). *Smallest circles first: Exploring teacher reconciliatory praxis through drama education*. University of Toronto Press.

CBC Radio. (2020, 29 May). Theatre and film are inherently political, say art critics. *Ideas*. https://www.cbc.ca/radio/ideas/theatre-and-film-are-inherently-political-say-art-critics-1.5590475

Centre for Applied Theatre Research. (2003). The impact of Blagg on challenging and reducing offending by young people. An evaluation of a drama based offending behaviour workshop. Manchester & Bury Youth Offending Teams and TiPP. http://artsevidence.org.uk/media/uploads/evaluation-downloads/tipp-blagg-evaluation-2003.pdf

Chalverley, D., Cotter, A., & Halla, E. (2010). Youth custody and community services in Canada 2008/2009. *Juristat: Canadian Centre for Crime Statistics*, *30*(1). https://www150.statcan.gc.ca/n1/pub/85-002-x/2010001/article/11147-eng.htm

Chatterton, P., Fuller, D., & Routledge, P. (2007). Relating action to activism: Theoretical and methodological reflections. In S. Kindon, R. Pain, & M. Kesby (Eds.), *Participatory action research approaches and methods* (pp. 216–222). Routledge.

Citizens for Public Justice. (2015). On the margins: A glimpse of poverty in Canada. https://www.cpj.ca/on-the-margins

Clarkson, A. (2014). *Belonging: The paradox of citizenship*. House of Anansi Press.

Cobbe, J. H., Legum, C., & Guy, J. J. (2023, October 27). Lesotho. *Encyclopedia Britannica*. https://www.britannica.com/place/Lesotho

Cohen-Cruz, J., & Schutzman, M., (Eds.) (1993). *Playing Boal: Theatre, therapy, activism*. Routledge.

Conquergood, D. (1985). Performing as a moral act: Ethical dimension of the ethnography of performance. *Literature in Performance*, 5(2), 1–13. https://doi.org/10.1080/10462938509391578

Conrad, D. (2002a). Drama, media advertising, and inner-city youth. *Youth Theatre Journal*, 16(1), 71–87. https://doi.org/10.1080/08929092.2002.10012542

Conrad, D. (2002b). Drama as arts-based pedagogy & research: Media advertising and inner-city youth. *The Alberta Journal of Educational Research*, 48(3), 254–268. https://doi.org/10.11575/ajer.v48i3.54932

Conrad, D. (2003). Unearthing personal history: Autoethnography & artifacts inform research on youth risk-taking. *The Journal of Social Theory in Art Education*, (23), 44–58. https://scholarscompass.vcu.edu/jstae/vol23/iss1/5/

Conrad, D. (2004a). Exploring risky youth experiences: Popular theatre as a participatory, performative research method. *International Journal of Qualitative Methods*, 3(1), 12–25. https://doi.org/10.1177/160940690400300102

Conrad, D. (2004b). Popular theatre: Empowering pedagogy for youth. *Youth Theatre Journal*, 18(1), 87–106. https://doi.org/10.1080/08929092.2004.10012566

Conrad, D. (2004c). When autobiography and research topics collide: Two risky school dance stories. *Taboo: The Journal of Culture and Education*, 8(1), 85–95. http://www.eric.ed.gov/PDFS/EJ795528.pdf

Conrad, D. (2005). Rethinking 'at-risk' in drama education: Beyond prescribed roles. *Research in Drama Education: The Journal of Applied Theatre and Performance*, 10(1), 27–41. https://doi.org/10.1080/13569780500053114

Conrad, D. (2006a). Justice for youth versus a curriculum of conformity in schools and prisons. *Journal of the Canadian Association for Curriculum Studies*, 4(2), 1–20. http://pi.library.yorku.ca/ojs/index.php/jcacs/issue/view/725/showToc

Conrad, D. (2006b). Entangled in the sticks: Ethical conundrums of popular theatre as pedagogy and research. *Qualitative Inquiry*, 12(3), 437–458. https://doi.org/10.1177/1077800405284364

Conrad, D. (2010). In search of the radical in performance: Theatre of the Oppressed with incarcerated youth. In P. Duffy & E. Vettraino (Eds.), *Youth and Theatre of the Oppressed* (pp. 125–141). Palgrave.

Conrad, D. (2012). Athabasca's Going Unmanned: *An Ethnodrama about incarcerated youth*. Sense.

Conrad, D. (2013). Lock'em up, but where's the key? Transformative drama with incarcerated youth. *Journal of Contemporary Issues in Education*, 8(3), 4–18. https://doi.org/10.20355/C5S59K

Conrad, D. (2015). Education and social innovation: The Youth Uncensored Project – A case study of youth participatory research and cultural democracy in action. *Canadian Journal of Education*, 38(1), 1–25. https://journals.sfu.ca/cje/index.php/cje-rce/article/view/1774

Conrad, D. (2016). The lives of incarcerated youth in *Athabasca's Going Unmanned*. In G. Belliveau & G. Lea (Eds.), *Research-based theatre: An artistic methodology* (pp. 43–58). Intellect.

Conrad, D. (2020). Youth participatory action research and applied theatre engagement: Support for Indigenous youth survivance and resurgence. *Theatre Research in Canada*, 41(2), 258–277. https://doi.org/10.3138/tric.41.2.a04

Conrad, D. (2023). Engagement, authenticity and advocacy in 'Youth Uncensored': Ethics in applied theatre research with street-involved youth. *Qualitative Inquiry*, 29(2), 365–373. https://doi.org/10.1177/10778004221099567

Conrad, D., Smyth, P., & Kendal, W. (2015). Uncensored: Participatory arts-based research with youth. In D. Conrad & A. Sinner (Eds.), *Creating together: Participatory, community-based and collaborative arts practices and scholarship across Canada* (pp. 21–38). Wilfred Laurier University Press.

Copley, J. (2010, February). New play aims to raise awareness. *Alberta Native News*, p. 14.

Corntassel, J. (2012). Re-envisioning resurgence: Indigenous pathways to decolonization and sustainable self-determination. *Decolonization: Indigeneity, Education & Society*, 1(1), 86–101. https://jps.library.utoronto.ca/index.php/des/article/view/18627

Cranley, E. (2019, 1 October). These 10 young activists are trying to move the needle on climate change, gun control, and other global issues. *Insider*. https://www.insider.com/young-activists-climate-change-guns-greta-thunberg-2019-9

D'Arcangelis, C. L. (2018). Revelations of a white settler woman scholar-activist: The fraught promise of self-reflexivity. *Cultural Studies – Critical Methodologies*, 18(5), 339–353. https://doi.org/10.1177/1532708617750675

Davies, B., & Bansel, P. (2007). Neoliberalism and education. *International Journal of Qualitative Studies in Education*, 20(3), 247–259. https://doi.org/10.1080/09518390701281751

Davis, B., & Sumara, D. (2008). Complexity as a theory of education. *Transnational Curriculum Inquiry*, 5(2), 33–44. https://doi.org/10.14288/tci.v5i2.75

DeCarlo, A., & Hockman, E. (2003). RAP therapy: A group work intervention method for urban adolescents. *Social Work with Groups*, 26(3), 45–59. https://doi.org/10.1300/J009v26n03_06

DeCastell, S., & Jenson, J. (2006). No place like home: Sexuality, community, and identity among street-involved 'queer and questioning' youth. *McGill Journal of Education*, 41(3), 227–247. https://mje.mcgill.ca/article/view/738

DeCastell, S., Jenson, J., Ibanez, F., Lawrence, L., Bennett, D., Jagosh, J., Fink, S., Simon, P. J., Guillion, J., Wright, M., Reed, M., Ruitenberg, C., Salah, T., & Taylor, N. (2002). No place like home: Final research report on the Pridehouse Project. Out/comes: Conclusions from 'interventionist' research. Human Resourced Development Canada and The PrideCare Society. http://www.sfu.ca/pridehouse/

de Certeau, M. (1984). *The practice of everyday life*. The University of California Press.

den Heyer, K., & Conrad, D. (2011). Using Alain Badiou's ethic of truths to support an 'eventful' social justice teacher education program. *Journal of Curriculum Theorizing*, 27(1), 7–19. http://journal.jctonline.org/index.php/jct/article/view/302/95

Department of Justice Canada. (2013). The Youth Criminal Justice Act: Summary and background. https://www.justice.gc.ca/eng/cj-jp/yj-jj/tools-outils/back-hist.html

Developmental Research and Programs Inc. (1995). *Communities that care: Risk-focused prevention using the social development strategy*. US Department of Justice. https://www.ojp.gov/ncjrs/virtual-library/abstracts/communities-care-risk-focused-prevention-using-social-development

Diamond, D. (2007). *Theatre for living: The art and science of community-based dialogue*. Trafford.

Diamond, E. (1997). *Unmaking mimesis: Essays on feminism and theatre*. Routledge.

DiAngelo, R. (2011). White fragility. *International Journal of Critical Pedagogy*, *3*(3), 54–70.

Dissanayake, E. (1992). *Homo aestheticus: Where art comes from and why*. The Free Press.

Donald, D., Glanfield, F., & Sterenberg, G. (2012). Living ethically within conflicts of colonial authority and relationality. *Journal of the Canadian Association for Curriculum Studies*, *10*(1), 53–76. https://jcacs.journals.yorku.ca/index.php/jcacs/article/view/34405/32427

Donald, D., & Krahn, M. (2014). Abandoning pathologization: Conceptualizing Indigenous youth identity as glowing from communitarian understandings. In A. Ibrahim & S. R. Steinberg (Eds.), *Critical youth studies reader* (pp. 114–129). Peter Lang.

Doob, A., & Cesaroni, C. (2004). *Responding to youth crime in Canada*. University of Toronto Press.

Durie, R., & Wyatt, K. (2013). Connecting communities and complexity: A case study in creating the conditions for transformational change. *Critical Public Health*, *23*(2), 174–187. http://dx.doi.org/10.1080/09581596.2013.781266

Edwards, R., & Mauthner, M. (2002). Ethics and feminist research: Theory and practice. In M. Mauthner, M. Birch, J. Jessop, & T. Miller (Eds.), *Ethics in qualitative research* (pp. 14–31). Sage.

Eichas, K., Montgomery, M. J., & Meca, A. (2021). Engaging marginalized youth in positive development: The changing lives program. In R. Dimitrova & N. Wiium (Eds.), *Handbook of positive youth development* (pp. 431–446). Springer Nature. https://doi.org/10.1007/978-3-030-70262-5_29

Eisner, E. (2008). Persistent tensions in arts-based research. In M. Cahnman-Taylor & R. Siegesmund (Eds.), *Arts-based research in education: Foundations for practice* (pp. 16–27). Routledge.

Ellsworth, E. (1989). Why doesn't this feel empowering: Working through the repressive myths of critical pedagogy. *Harvard Educational Review*, *59*(3), 297–324. https://www.hepg.org/her-home/issues/harvard-educational-review-volume-59,-issue-3/herarticle/working-through-the-repressive-myths-of-critical-p

Ermine, W. (2007). The ethical space of engagement. *Indigenous Law Journal*, *6*(1), 193–203. https://jps.library.utoronto.ca/index.php/ilj/article/view/27669/20400

Etherton, M., & Prentki, T. (2006). Drama for change? Prove it! Impact assessment in applied theatre. *Research in Drama Education: The Journal of Applied Theatre and Performance*, *11*(2), 139–155. https://doi.org/10.1080/13569780600670718

Evaluation and Research Services (E&RS). (2011). *High-risk youth uncensored – An educational exchange: Evaluation*. Faculty of Extension, University of Alberta.

Evrard, Y. (1997). Democratizing culture or cultural democracy? *Journal of Arts Management, Law & Society, 27*(3), 167–176. https://doi.org/10.1080/10632929709596961

Fabian, J. (1990). *Power and performance: Ethnographic explorations through proverbial wisdom and theatre in Shaba, Zaire*. The University of Wisconsin Press.

Fals-Borda, O., & Rahman, M. (Eds.) (1991). *Action and knowledge: Breaking the monopoly with participatory action-research*. Apex.

Felman, S. (1991). Education and crisis, or the vicissitudes of teaching. *Psychoanalysis, Culture and Trauma, 48*(1), 13–73. https://www.jstor.org/stable/26304031

Ferrell, J. (1995). Urban graffiti: Crime, control, and resistance. *Youth & Society, 27*(1), 73–92. https://doi.org/10.1177/0044118X95027001005

Fine, M., Weis, L., Weseen, S., & Wong, L. (2000). For whom? Qualitative research, representations, and social responsibilities. In N. K. Denzin & Y. S. Lincoln, (Eds.), *The handbook of qualitative research* (pp. 107–131). Sage.

First People of America and Canada. (n.d.). The ghost stallion: A Yinnuwok legend. American Indian Legends. https://www.firstpeople.us/FP-Html-Legends/Ghost_Stallion-Yinnuwok.html

Flicker, S., Maley, O., Ridgley, A., Biscope, S., Lombardo, C., & Skinner, H. (2008). e-PAR: Using technology and participatory action research to engage youth in health promotion. *Action Research, 6*(3), 285–303. https://doi.org/10.1177/1476750307083711

Florczak, K. L. (2017). Adding to the truth of the matter: The case for qualitative research. *Nursing Science Quarterly, 30*(4), 296–299. https://doi.org/10.1177/0894318417724466

Foucault, M. (1979). *Discipline and punish: The birth of the prison* (A. Sheridan, Trans.). Pantheon.

Foucault, M. (1991). Governmentality. In G. Burchell, C. Gordon, & P. Miller (Eds.), *The Foucault effect: Studies in governmentality* (pp. 87–104). University of Chicago Press.

Foucault, M. (1994). In P. Rabinow & N. Rose (Eds.), *The essential Foucault*. The New Press.

Freebody, K., Balfour, M., Finneran, M., & Anderson, M. (Eds.) (2018). *Applied theatre: Understanding change*. Springer.

Freire, P. (1994). *Pedagogy of hope: Reliving pedagogy of the oppressed*. Continuum.

Freire, P. (2000). *Pedagogy of the oppressed* (M. Bergman Ramos, Trans.). Continuum. (Original work published 1970)

French, C. (2021, 26 April). Indigenous communities face unique challenges in funding infrastructure projects, experts say. *CTV News*. https://www.ctvnews.ca/canada/indigenous-communities-face-unique-challenges-in-funding-infrastructure-projects-experts-say-1.5402799?cache=

Friesen, J., & O'Neill, K. (2008, May 9). Armed posses spreading violence across prairie communities. *The Globe and Mail*, pp. A12–13. https://www.theglobeandmail.com/news/national/armed-posses-spreading-violence-across-prairie-communities/article1055029/

Gallagher, K. (2016). The micro-political and the socio-structural in applied theatre with homeless youth. In J. Hughes & H. Nicholson, (Eds.), *Critical perspectives in applied theatre* (pp. 229–247). Cambridge University Press.

Gallagher, K., & Rodricks, D. J. (2017a). Hope despite hopelessness: Race, gender, and the pedagogies of drama/applied theatre as a relational ethic in neoliberal times. *Youth Theatre Journal*, 31(2), 114–128, http://doi.org/10.1080/08929092.2017.1370625

Gallagher, K., & Rodricks, D. J. (2017b). Performing to understand: Cultural wealth, precarity, and shelter-dwelling youth. *Research in Drama Education: The Journal of Applied Theatre and Performance*, 22(1), 7–21. https://doi.org/10.1080/13569783.2016.1263556

Gallagher, K., Starkman, R., & Rhoades, R. (2017). Performing counter-narratives and mining creative resilience using applied theatre to theorize notions of youth resilience. *Journal of Youth Studies*, 20(2), 216–233. https://doi.org/10.1080/13676261.2016.1206864

Galloway, G. (2006, 13 October). PM targets three-time violent offenders. *The Globe and Mail*. https://www.theglobeandmail.com/news/national/pm-targets-three-time-violent-offenders/article970060/

Garde, U., & Mumford, M. (2014). Postdramatic reality theatre and productive insecurity: Destabilising encounters with the unfamiliar in theatre from Sydney and Berlin. In K. Jürs-Munby, J. Carroll, & S. Giles (Eds.), *Postdramatic theatre and the political* (pp. 147–164). Bloomsbury.

Gascoigne, J., & Kerr, D. (1996). Getting to know generation X: Health education for the thirteenth generation. *Journal of Health Education*, 27(5), 268–273. https://doi.org/10.1080/10556699.1996.10603213

Gaztambide-Fernandez, R. (2013). Why the arts don't *DO* anything: Toward a new vision for cultural production in education. *Harvard Educational Review*, 83(1), 211–236. https://www.hepg.org/her-home/issues/harvard-educational-review-volume-83-number-1/herarticle/toward-a-new-vision-for-cultural-production-in-edu

Gil-Kashiwabara, E., Hogansen, J. M., Geenen, S., Powers, K., & Powers, L. E. (2007). Improving transition outcomes for marginalized youth. *Career Development for Exceptional Individuals*, 30(2), 80–91. https://doi.org/10.1177/088572880703000205

Giroux, H. (1992). *Border crossings: Cultural workers and the politics of education*. Routledge.

Giroux, H. (1997). Youth and the politics of representation: Response to Thomas Hatch's 'If the "kids" are not "alright", I'm "clueless"'. *Educational Researcher*, 26(4), 27–30. https://doi.org/10.3102/0013189X026004027

Giroux, H. (2003). Racial injustice and disposable youth in the age of zero tolerance. *International Journal of Qualitative Studies in Education*, 16(4), 553–565. https://doi.org/10.1080/0951839032000099543

Giroux, H. (2022, May 13). The war on youth in the age of fascist politics. *CounterPunch.org*. https://www.counterpunch.org/2022/05/13/the-war-on-youth-in-the-age-of-fascist-politics/

Goldbard, A. (2009). Arguments for cultural democracy and community cultural development. *GIA Reader*, 20(1). http://www.giarts.org/article/arguments-cultural-democracy-and-community-cultural-development

Goldberg, E. (2020, 12 November). Teens in Covid isolation: 'I felt like I was suffocating'. *The New York Times*. https://www.nytimes.com/2020/11/12/health/covid-teenagers-mental-health.html

Government of Canada. (2013a, 15 February). Upper Canada land surrenders and the Williams Treaties (1764–1862/1923). Crown-Indigenous relations and Norther affairs Canada. https://www.rcaanc-cirnac.gc.ca/eng/1360941656761/1544619778887#uc

Government of Canada. (2013b, 15 February). The numbered treaties (1871–1921). Crown-Indigenous relations and Norther affairs Canada. https://www.rcaanc-cirnac.gc.ca/eng/1360948213124/1544620003549

Government of Canada. (2015). Truth and reconciliation commission of Canada. https://www.rcaanc-cirnac.gc.ca/eng/1450124405592/1529106060525

Government of Canada Policy Research Initiative. (2010). Talking about social innovation: Summary of international roundtable on social innovation. Workshop report. https://publications.gc.ca/site/eng/377815/publication.html

Granger, R. C. (2002). Creating the conditions linked to positive youth development. *New Directions for Youth Development, Fall*(95), 149–164. https://doi.org/10.1002/yd.20

Graveline, F. J. (2000). Circle as methodology: Enacting an Aboriginal paradigm. *International Journal of Qualitative Studies in Education, 13*(4), 361–370. https://doi.org/10.1080/095183900413304

Graves, J. B. (2004). *Cultural democracy: The arts, community and the public purpose.* University of Illinois Press.

Guishard, M., Fine, M., Doyle, C., Jackson, J., Staten, T., & Webb, A. (2005). The Bronx on the move: Participatory consultation with mothers and youth. *Journal of Educational and Psychological Consultation, 16*(1/2), 35–54. https://doi.org/10.1207/s1532768xjepc161&2_3

Hall, B. (2005). In from the cold? Reflections on participatory research from 1970–2005. *Convergence, 38*(1), 5–24.

Hanley, M. (2001, April). Subjects in search of agency: The intersection of performance and critical pedagogy in working with adolescents put 'at-risk'. Paper presented at the Annual Conference of the American Educational Research Association, Seattle, WA.

Hardingham, L. (2004). Integrity and moral residue: Nurses as participants in a moral community. *Nursing Philosophy, 5*(2), 127–134. https://doi.org/10.1111/j.1466-769X.2004.00160.x

Hart, A., Gagnon, E., Eryigit-Madzwamuse, S., Caneron, J., Aranda, K., Rathbone, A., & Heaver, B. (2016). Uniting resilience research and practice with an inequalities approach. *Sage Open, 6*(4), 1–13. https://doi.org/10.1177/2158244016682477

Hawkes, J. (2003). *The fourth pillar of sustainability: Culture's essential role in public planning.* Common Ground.

Haydon Taylor, D. (2005). *Me funny.* Douglas & McIntyre.

Health Canada. (2014). A statistical profile on the health of First Nations in Canada – Vital statistics for Atlantic and Western Canada, 2003–2007. https://publications.gc.ca/collections/collection_2014/sc-hc/H34-193-3-2014-eng.pdf

Heron, J., & Reason, P. (1997). A participatory inquiry paradigm. *Qualitative Inquiry, 3*(3), 274–294. https://doi.org/10.1177/107780049700300302

hooks, b. (1984). *Feminist theory from margin to center.* South End Press.

Howard, H., & Edelman, M. W. (1985). *Barriers to excellence: Our children at risk*. National Coalition of Advocates for Students.

Howie, E. K., Daniels, B. T., & Guagliano, J. M. (2020). Promoting physical activity through youth sports programs: It's social. *American Journal of Lifestyle Medicine*, 14(1), 78–88. https://doi.org/10.1177/1559827618754842

Hu, K. (2023, 30 January). Elaine Hsieh Chou on the ethics of 'trauma porn'. *The Atlantic*. https://www.theatlantic.com/books/archive/2023/01/elaine-hsieh-chou-interview-background-short-story/672851/

Hughes, J. (2013). Queer choreographies of care: A guided tour of an arts and social welfare initiative in Manchester. *Research in Drama Education: The Journal of Applied Theatre and Performance*, 18(2), 144–154. https://doi.org/10.1080/13569783.2013.787256

Hughes, J., Kidd, J., & McNamara, C. (2011). The usefulness of mess: Artistry, improvisation and decomposition in the practice of research in applied theatre. In B. Kershaw & H. Nicholson (Eds.), *Research methods in theatre and performance* (pp. 186–209). Edinburgh University Press.

Hyslop, K. (2019, 4 October). A brief history of Canada's failure to fund Indigenous kids equitably. *The Tyee*. https://thetyee.ca/Analysis/2019/10/04/Indigenous-Kid-Funding-dFailure/

Indigenous Action Media. (2014). Accomplices not allies. http://www.indigenousaction.org/wp-content/uploads/Accomplices-Not-Allies-print.pdf

Institute of Medicine (US) & National Research Council (US) Committee on the Science of Adolescence. (2011). The science of adolescent risk-taking: Workshop report. National Academy Press. https://www.ncbi.nlm.nih.gov/books/NBK53418/

Iwasaki, Y., Springett, J., Dashora, P., McLaughlin, A-M., McHugh, T-L., & Youth 4 YEG Team. (2014). Youth-guided youth engagement: Participatory action research (PAR) with high-risk, marginalized youth. *Child & Youth Services*, 35(4), 316–342. https://doi.org/10.1080/0145935X.2014.962132

Jennings, S. (Ed.) (2009). *Dramatherapy and social theatre: Necessary dialogues*. Routledge.

Jindal-Snape, D. (2012). Portraying children's voices through creative approaches to enhance their transition experience and improve the transition practice. *Learning Landscapes*, 6(1), 223–240. https://www.learninglandscapes.ca/index.php/learnland/issue/view/Creativity-Insights-Directions-and-Possibilities

Jindal-Snape, D., Scott, R., & Davies, D. (2014). 'Arts and smarts': Assessing the impact of arts participation on academic performance during school years. Systematic literature review. Glasgow Centre for Population Health. https://discovery.dundee.ac.uk/en/publications/arts-and-smarts-assessing-the-impact-of-arts-participation-on-aca

Jordan, S. (2003). Who stole my methodology? Co-opting PAR. *Globalisation, Societies and Education*, 1(2), 185–200. https://doi.org/10.1080/14767720303913

Journal for Education of Students Placed at Risk. (2022). Taylor & Francis. https://www.tandfonline.com/toc/hjsp20/current

Juvenile Justice Comprehensive Strategy Task Force. (2000). 2000 annual report: Juvenile justice comprehensive strategy. Office of Juvenile Justice and Delinquency Prevention. https://www.ojp.gov/ncjrs/virtual-library/abstracts/juvenile-justice-comprehensive-strategy-2000-annual-report

Kant, I. (2007). *Critique of judgment* (J. Creed Meredith, Trans.). Oxford University Press. (Original work published 1790)

Kaplan, E. R. (2022). The value of process: Creating theatre with incarcerated youth. In L. S. Brenner, C. Ceraso, & E. Diaz Cruz (Eds.), *Applied theatre with youth: Education, engagement, activism* (pp. 206–209). Routledge.

Kenny, C. B. (1998). The sense of art: A First Nations view. *Canadian Journal of Native Education*, 22(1), 77–84. https://doi.org/10.14288/cjne.v22i1.195796

Kent, G. (2007, June 20). Mayor says Saskatoon's approach worth exploring: Saskatchewan city's bylaw calls for fines of up to $10,000 for coercive begging. *Edmonton Journal*. Retrieved 12 February 2009.

Kershaw, B. (1999). *The radical in performance: Between Brecht and Baudrillard*. Routledge.

Kershaw, B. (2007). Pathologies of hope: Interview with Performance Paradigm. *Performance Paradigm: A Journal of Performance and Contemporary Culture*, 3, 113–124. http://performanceparadigm.net/index.php/journal/article/viewFile/37/38

Kershaw, B. (2009). Practice as research through performance. In H. Smith & R. T. Dean (Eds.), *Practice-led research, research-led practice in creative arts* (pp. 104–125). Edinburgh University Press.

Kidd, R. (1984). *Popular theatre and political action in Canada*. Participatory Research Group.

Kidd, R., & Byram, M. (1978). Popular theatre: Technique for participatory research. Participatory Research Project (working paper no. 5). International Council for Adult Education. https://eric.ed.gov/?id=ED178740

King, T. (2003). *The truth about stories: A Native narrative*. Anansi.

Kohfeldt, D., Chhun, L. Grace, S., & Langhout, R. D. (2011). Youth empowerment in context: Exploring tensions in school-based yPAR. *American Journal of Community Psychology*, 47(1–2), 28–45. https://doi.org/10.1007/s10464-010-9376-z

Korteweg, L., & Bissell, A. (2016). The complexities of researching youth civic engagement in Canada with/by Indigenous youth: Settler-colonial challenges for Tikkun Olam – Pedagogies of repair and reconciliation. *Citizenship Education Research Journal*, 5(1), 14–26. https://ojs-o.library.ubc.ca/index.php/CERJ/article/view/14

Kuppers, P. (2007). *Community performance: An introduction*. Routledge.

Laboucan-Massimo, M., & Big Canoe, C. (2015, 18 March). Missing and murdered: What it will take for Indigenous women to feel safe. *CBC News*. www.cbc.ca/news/aboriginal/missing-and-murdered-what-it-will-take-for-indigenous-women-to-feel-safe-1.2977136

Lamparter, J. S. (2022). Voices beyond bars: Art as a means of self-expression for incarcerated youth. In L. S. Brenner, C. Ceraso, & E. Diaz Cruz (Eds.), *Applied theatre with youth: Education, engagement, activism* (pp. 210–214). Routledge.

Lavie-Ajayi, M., & Krumer-Nevo, M. (2013). In a different mindset: Critical youth work with marginalized youth. *Children and Youth Services Review, 35*(10), 1698–1704. http://dx.doi.org/10.1016/j.childyouth.2013.07.010

Lear, J. (2006). *Radical hope: Ethics in the face of cultural devastation.* Harvard University Press.

Lévinas, E. (1989). *The Lévinas reader* (S. Hand, Ed.). Basil Blackwell.

Linds, W. (2006). Metaxis: Dancing (in) the in-between. In J. Cohen-Cruz & M. Schutzman (Eds.), *A Boal companion: Dialogues on theatre and cultural politics* (pp. 114–124). Routledge.

Linds, W., Ritenburg, H., Goulet, L., Episkenew, J., Schmidt, K., Ribeiro, N., & Whiteman, A. (2013). Layering theatre's potential for change: Drama, education, and community in Aboriginal health research. *Canadian Theatre Review, 154,* 37–43. https://doi.org/10.3138/CTR.154.007

Lyng, S. (1990). Edgework: A social psychological analysis of voluntary risk taking. *American Journal of Sociology, 95*(4), 851–886. https://www.jstor.org/stable/2780644

Lyng, S. (1993) Dysfunctional risk taking: Criminal behaviour as edgework. In N. Bell & R. Bell (Eds.), *Adolescent risk taking* (pp. 107–130). Sage.

Machamer, A., & Gruber, E. (1998). Secondary school, family and educational risk: Comparing American Indian adolescents and their peers. *The Journal of Educational Research, 91*(6), 357–369. https://doi.org/10.1080/00220679809597565

Mackey, C. (2010). *Random acts of culture: Reclaiming art and community in the 21st century.* BLT Books.

MacMaster, S. (2004). Harm reduction: A new perspective of substance use services. *Social Work, 49*(3), 356–363. http://doi.org/10.1093/sw/49.3.353

Madison, D. S. (1998). Performance, personal narratives, and the politics of possibility. In S. J. Dailey (Ed.), *The future of performance studies: Visions and revisions* (pp. 276–286). National Communication Association.

Makofane, M. D. (2014). A conceptual analysis of the label 'street children': Challenges for the helping professions. *Social Work, 50*(1), 134–145. http://dx.doi.org/10.15270/50-1-20

Marlin-Curiel, S. (2002). Truth and consequences: Art in response to the Truth and Reconciliation Commission. In R. Cándida Smith (Ed.), *Art and the performance of memory: Sounds and gestures in recollection* (pp. 37–62). Routledge.

Marsh, K. (2012). 'The beat will make you be courage': The role of a secondary school music program in supporting young refugees and newly arrived immigrants in Australia. *Research Studies in Music Education, 34*(2), 93–111. http://doi.org/10.1177/1321103x12466138

Martin-Smith, A. (2005). Setting the stage for a dialogue: Aesthetics in drama and theatre education. *The Journal of Aesthetic Education 39*(4), 3–11. https://doi.org/10.1353/jae.2005.0044.

Maslow, A. H. (1943). A theory of human motivation. *Psychological Review, 50*(4), 370–396. https://doi.org/10.1037/h0054346

Matanovic, M. (2002). Turning the sword. *YES! Magazine* [Art and Community]. (Summer), 12–15. https://www.yesmagazine.org/wp-content/uploads/2021/09/22-Art-and-Community_small.pdf

Mate, G. (2008). *In the realm of the hungry ghosts: Close encounters with addiction.* Alfred K. Knopf.

McCreery, K. (2001). From street to stage with children in Brazil and Ghana. *The Annals of the American Academy of Political and Social Science, 575,* 122–146. https://www.jstor.org/stable/1049184

McDonald, D., & Wilson, D. (2013). *Poverty or prosperity: Indigenous children in Canada.* Canadian Centre for Policy Alternatives. https://www.policyalternatives.ca/publications/reports/poverty-or-prosperity

McLaren, P. (1994). Multiculturalism and the postmodern critique: Toward a pedagogy of resistance and transformation. In H. Giroux & P. McLaren (Eds.), *Between borders: Pedagogy and the politics of cultural studies* (pp. 192–222). Routledge.

McLaren, P. (1998). *Life in schools: An introduction to critical pedagogy in the foundations of education.* Longman.

McLaughlin, K. (2016). *Empowerment: A critique.* Routledge.

Moreno, J. L. (1977). *Psychodrama: First volume* (4th ed.). Beacon House.

Mukhopadhyay, S. (2012, 13 February). This Valentine's Day, occupy the romantic-industrial complex. *The Nation.* https://www.thenation.com/article/archive/valentines-day-occupy-romantic-industrial-complex/

Murray, R., Caulier-Grice, J., & Mulgan, G. (2010). *The open book of social innovation.* The Young Foundation. https://youngfoundation.org/wp-content/uploads/2012/10/The-Open-Book-of-Social-Innovationg.pdf

Mutz M., & Müller, J. (2016). Mental health benefits of outdoor adventures: Results from two pilot studies. *Journal of Adolescence, 49,* 105–114. https://doi.org/10.1016/j.adolescence.2016.03.009

National Inquiry into Missing and Murdered Indigenous Women and Girls (MMIWG). (2016). https://www.mmiwg-ffada.ca/

Native Land Digital. (2023). https://native-land.ca/

Neugebaur, R. (Ed.) (2000). *Criminal injustice: Racism in the criminal justice system.* Canadian Scholars Press.

Newman, B. M., Lohman, B. J., & Newman, P. R. (2007). Peer group membership and a sense of belonging: Their relationship to adolescent behavior problems. *Adolescence, 42*(166), 241–263.

Nicholson, H. (2005). *Applied drama: The gift of theatre.* Palgrave Macmillan.

Nicholson, H. (2011). Applied drama/theatre/performance. In S. Schonmann (Ed.), *Key concepts in theatre/drama education* (pp. 241–245). Sense Publishers.

Nicholson, H. (2014). Theatre and joyful encounters. *Research in Drama Education: The Journal of Applied Theatre and Performance, 19*(4), 337–339. http://doi.org/10.1080/13569783.2014.954810

Noble, W. C., & Filice, M. (2016, 14 March). The Neutral Confederacy. *The Canadian Encyclopedia*. The Canadian Encyclopedia. https://www.thecanadianencyclopedia.ca/en/article/neutral

Noddings, N. (1984). *Caring: A feminine approach to ethics and moral education*. University of California Press.

Nunkoosing, K. (2005). The problems with interviews. *Qualitative Health Research*, *15*(5), 698–706. https://doi.org/10.1177/1049732304273903

O'Connor, P., & Anderson, M. (2015). *Applied theatre: Research: Radical departures*. Bloomsbury Methuen Drama. https://login.ezproxy.library.ualberta.ca/login?url=https://search.ebscohost.com/login.aspx?direct=true&db=cat03710a&AN=alb.9531725&site=eds-live&scope=site

Office of the Correctional Investigator Canada. (2006). Report finds evidence of systemic discrimination against Aboriginal inmates in Canada's prisons. http://www.oci-bec.gc.ca/cnt/comm/press/press20061016-eng.aspx

Ogg, A. (2015, 9 August). Cree names of Cree-speaking communities across Canada. Cree Literacy Network. https://creeliteracy.org/cree-place-names/cree-place-name-project/

Online Etymology Dictionary. (2014). Aesthetics. Retrieved 6 February 2023. https://www.etymonline.com/search?q=aesthetic

Online Etymology Dictionary. (2019). Mimesis. Retrieved 21 March 2023. https://www.etymonline.com/word/mimesis

Ottaway, N., King, K., & Erickson P. G. (2009). Storying the street: Transition narratives of homeless youth. *Medical Humanities*, *35*(1), 19–26. http://dx.doi.org/10.1136/jmh.2008.001362

Panel on Research Ethics. (2022). *Tri-Council policy statement: Ethical conduct for research involving humans*. Government of Canada. https://ethics.gc.ca/eng/policypolitique_tcps2-eptc2_2022.html

Park, P., Brydon-Miller, M., Hall, B., & Jackson, T. (Eds.). (1993). *Voices of change: Participatory research in the United States and Canada*. Bergin & Garvey.

Perkins, D. D., & Zimmerman, M. A. (1995). Empowerment theory, research and application. *American Journal of Community Psychology*, *23*(5), 569–579. https://doi.org/10.1007/BF02506982

Phelan, J., Link, B. G., Moore, R. E., & Stueve, A. (1997). The stigma of homelessness: The impact of the label 'homeless' on attitudes toward poor persons. *Social Psychology Quarterly*, *60*(4), 323–337. https://doi.org/10.2307/2787093

Plato. (2003). *The republic* (D. Lee, Trans.). Penguin. (Original work published ca. 375 B.C.E.)

Poulin, C. (2006). Harm reduction policies and programs for youth. Canadian Centre on Substance Abuse. https://policycommons.net/artifacts/1220109/harm-reduction-policies-and-programs-for-youth/1773185/

Prendergast, M., & Saxton, J. (2009). *Applied theatre: International case studies and challenges for practice*. Intellect.

Prendergast, M., & Saxton, J. (2013). *Applied drama: A facilitator's handbook for working in community*. Intellect.

Prendergast, M., & Saxton, J. (2015). Seduction of the real: The significance of fiction in applied theatre. *Research in Drama Education: The Journal of Applied Theatre and Performance*, 20(3), 280–284. http://dx.doi.org/10.1080/13569783.2015.1059747

Prenki, T., & Selman, J. (2000). Defining popular theatre. In T. Prentki & J. Selman (Eds.), *Popular theatre in political culture: Britain and Canada in focus* (pp. 8–14). Intellect.

Prentki, T., & Preston, S. (2008). Applied theatre: An introduction. In T. Prentki & S. Preston (Eds.), *The applied theatre reader* (pp. 9–15). Routledge.

Preston, S. (2008). Introduction to ethics of representation. In T. Prentki & S. Preston (Eds.), *The applied theatre reader* (pp. 65–69). Routledge.

Provincial Advocate for Children and Youth. (2014). Feathers of hope: A First Nations youth action plan. https://cwrp.ca/sites/default/files/publications/en/Feathers_of_Hope.pdf

Public Health Agency of Canada. (2006). *Street youth in Canada*. Government of Canada. https://www.phac-aspc.gc.ca/std-mts/reports_06/pdf/street_youth_e.pdf

Pura, T. (2002). *Stages: Creative ideas for teaching drama*. J. Gordon Shillingford.

Rappaport, J. (1995). Empowerment meets narrative: Listening to stories and creating settings. *American Journal of Community Psychology*, 23(5), 795–807. https://doi.org/10.1007/BF02506992

Reason, P., & Bradbury, H. (2008). Introduction. In P. Reason & H. Bradbury (Eds.), *Handbook of action research* (2nd ed., pp. 1–13). Sage.

Rhoades, R. (2018). Intersectionality and solidarity in curriculum-making theatre encounters with marginalized youth researcher-artists. *Journal of the Canadian Association for Curriculum Studies*, 16(1), 185–198. https://jcacs.journals.yorku.ca/index.php/jcacs/article/view/40358

Robinson, D., & Martin, K. (2016). Introduction: 'The body is a resonant chamber'. In D. Robinson, K. Martin, & D. Gareau (Eds.), *Arts of engagement: Taking aesthetic action in and beyond the Truth and Reconciliation Commission of Canada* (pp. 1–20). Wilfred Laurier University Press.

Rohd, M. (1998). *Theatre for community, conflict & dialogue: The hope is vital training manual*. Heinemann.

Rynor, B. (2023, 5 April). 'Don't just publish another paper. Let's do something', says scholar advocate Cindy Blackstock. *UA/AU University Affairs*. https://www.universityaffairs.ca/features/feature-article/dont-just-publish-another-paper-lets-do-something-says-scholar-advocate-cindy-blackstock/

Salverson, J. (1996). Performing emergency: Witnessing, popular theatre, and the lie of the literal. *Theatre Topics*, 6(2), 181–191. https://doi.org/10.1353/tt.1997.0012

Santiago-Jirau, A. (2022). Queering applied theatre: Working with LGBTQ youth to dismantle systems of oppression. In L. S. Brenner, C. Ceraso, & E. Diaz Cruz (Eds.), *Applied theatre with youth: Education, engagement, activism* (pp. 119–127). Routledge.

Sapiro, B., & Ward, A. (2020). Marginalized youth, mental health, and connection with others: A review of the literature. *Child and Adolescent Social Work Journal*, 37, 343–357. https://doi.org/10.1007/s10560-019-00628-5

Schechner, R. (1985). *Between theater and anthropology*. University of Pennsylvania Press.

Schechner, R. (2003). *Performance theory*. Routledge.

Scott, J. (1990). *Domination and the arts of resistance: Hidden transcripts*. Yale University Press.

Simons, H., & Usher, R. (2000). Introduction: Ethics in practice of research. In H. Simons & R. Usher (Eds.), *Situated ethics in educational research* (pp. 1–11). Routledge/Falmer.

Simpson, L. B. (2016). Indigenous resurgence and co-resistance. *Critical Ethnic Studies*, 2(2), 19–34. https://doi.org/10.5749/jcritethnstud.2.2.0019

Shakespeare, W. (2014). *Romeo and Juliet*. Lerner Publishing Group (Original work published in 1597)

Shaughnessy, N. (2005). Truth and lies: Exploring the ethics of performance applications. *Research in Drama Education*, 10(2), 201–212. https://doi.org/10.1080/13569780500103877

Shaughnessy, N. (2012). *Applying performance: Live art, socially engaged theatre and affective practice*. Palgrave MacMillan.

Shaughnessy, N. (2015). Dancing with difference: Moving towards a new aesthetics. In G. White (Ed.), *Applied theatre: Aesthetics* (pp. 87–122). Bloomsbury.

Shawyer, S., & Shively, K. (2019). Education in theatrical intimacy as ethical practice for university theatre. *Journal of Dramatic Theory and Criticism*, 34(1), 87–104. https://doi.org/10.1353/dtc.2019.0025

Sheridan, J. W., & Longboat, D. R. (2014). Walking back into creation: Environmental apartheid and the eternal – Initiating an Indigenous mind claim. *Space and Culture*, 17(3), 308–324. https://doi.org/10.1177/1206331212451536

Sinding, C., Gray, R., & Nisker, J. (2008). Ethical issues and issues of ethics. In G. Knowles & A. Cole (Eds.), *Handbook of arts in qualitative research* (pp. 460–469). Sage.

Sloan, C. (2018). Understanding spaces of potentiality in applied theatre. *Research in Drama Education: The Journal of Applied Theatre and Performance*, 23(4), 582–597. https://doi.org/10.1080/13569783.2018.1508991

Smith, L. T. (1999). *Decolonizing methodologies: Research and Indigenous peoples*. Zed Books.

Smyth, P., & Eaton-Erickson, A. (2009). Making the connection: Strategies for working with high-risk youth. In S. McKay, D. Fuchs, & I. Brown (Eds.), *Passion for action in child and family services: Voices from the prairies* (pp. 119–142). Canadian Plains Research Center. https://cwrp.ca/sites/default/files/publications/prairiebook2009/Passion_for_Action_in_Child_and_Family_Services.pdf

Spolin, V. (1986). *Theatre games for the classroom*. Northwestern University Press.

St. Pierre, E. A. (2011). Post qualitative research: The critique and the coming after. In N. K. Denzin & Y. S. Lincoln (Eds.), *The SAGE handbook of qualitative research* (pp. 611–625). Sage.

Stuart Fisher, A. (2008). Bearing witness: The position of theatre makers in the telling of trauma. In T. Prentki & S. Preston (Eds.), *The applied theatre reader* (pp. 108–115). Routledge.

Sweenie, R., De Keyser, H. H., Gutiérrez-Colina, A. M., Brammer, C., & Ramsey, R. R. (2022). Adherence and self-management interventions among systemically marginalized and under-served youth with asthma. *Clinical Practice in Pediatric Psychology, 10*(4), 394–408. https://doi.org/10.1037/cpp0000462

Tanner, J., Hartnagel, T., & Krahn, H. (1995). *Fractured transitions from school to work: Revisiting the dropout problem.* Oxford University Press.

Tate, J. K. (2022). Stargate: A theatre company of imagination, hope, life skills, and quality art for justice-involved young men. In L. S. Brenner, C. Ceraso, & E. Diaz Cruz (Eds.), *Applied theatre with youth: Education, engagement, activism* (pp. 197–205). Routledge.

Taylor, P. (2002). Afterthought: Evaluating applied theatre. *Applied Theatre Research*, (3), Art. 6. https://www.intellectbooks.com/asset/774/atr-3.6-taylor.pdf

Taussig, M. (1993). *Mimesis and alterity: A particular history of the senses.* Routledge.

Taussig, M. (2020). Mimetic excess. In M. Taussig, *Mastery of non-mastery in the age of meltdown* (pp. 5–9). University of Chicago Press.

Tedford, A. (2022, 7 June). Indigenous water activist Autumn Peltier honoured for her activism. Royal Rhodes University. https://www.royalroads.ca/news/indigenous-water-activist-autumn-peltier-honoured-her-activism

Thompson, J. (2003). *Applied theatre: Bewilderment and beyond.* Peter Lang.

Thompson, J. (2008). The ends of applied theatre: Incidents of cutting and chopping. In S. Preston & T. Prentki (Eds.), *The applied theatre reader* (pp. 116–124). Routledge.

Thompson, J. (2009). *Performance affects: Applied theatre and the end of effect.* Palgrave MacMillan.

Thompson, J. (2011). Performance of pain, performance of beauty. *Research in Drama Education: The Journal of Applied Theatre and Performance, 11*(1), 47–57. https://doi.org/10.1080/13569780500437689

Tuck, E. (2009). Suspending damage: A letter to communities. *Harvard Educational Review, 79*(3), 409–427. https://www.hepg.org/her-home/issues/harvard-educational-review-volume-79-issue-3/herarticle/a-letter-to-communities_739

Tuck, E., & Yang, K. W. (2012). Decolonization is not a metaphor. *Decolonization: Indigeneity, Education & Society, 1*(1), 1–40. https://jps.library.utoronto.ca/index.php/des/article/view/18630

Tuck, E., & Yang, W. K. (2011). Youth resistance revisited: New theories of youth negotiations of educational injustices. *International Journal of Qualitative Studies in Education, 24*(5), 521–530. https://doi.org/10.1080/09518398.2011.600274

Turner, V. (1982). *From ritual to theatre: The human seriousness of play.* Performing Arts Journal Publications.

Turner, V. (1986). *The anthropology of performance.* PAJ Publications.

Tyler, S. (1987). *The unspeakable: Discourse, dialogue, and rhetoric in the postmodern world.* University of Wisconsin Press.

Unger, M. (2012). *The social ecology of resilience: A handbook of theory and practice.* Springer.

United Nations. (2007). United Nations Declaration on the Rights of Indigenous Peoples. https://www.un.org/development/desa/indigenouspeoples/declaration-on-the-rights-of-indigenous-peoples.html

University of Alberta. (2023). Acknowledgement of traditional territory. Marketing and Communications. https://www.ualberta.ca/toolkit/communications/acknowledgment-of-traditional-territory

van Fossen, R., & Ndejuru, L. (2017). Terms of engagement: The ethics and aesthetics of artistic experimentation in the Rencontres/Encounters Project. A dialogue of sorts. *Canadian Theatre Review*, (172), 77–81. https://doi.org/10.3138/ctr.172.017

Vettraino, E., Linds W., & Jindal-Snape, D. (2017). Embodied voices: Using applied theatre for co-creation with marginalised youth. *Emotional and Behavioural Difficulties*, 22(1), 79–95. https://doi.org/10.1080/13632752.2017.1287348

Visenor, G. (1994). *Manifest manners: Postindian warriors of survivance*. Wesleyan University Press.

Visenor, G. (2008). Aesthetics of survivance: Literary theory and practice. In G. Vizenor, *Survivance: Narratives of native presence* (pp. 1–25). University of Nebraska Press.

Wagamese, R. (2019). *One drum: Stories and ceremonies for the planet*. Douglas McIntyre.

Wager, A. (2015). Hidden pedagogies at play: Street youth resisting within applied theatre. In A. Babayants & H. Fitzsimmons Frey (Eds.), *Theatre and learning* (pp. 97–114). Cambridge Scholars Publishing.

Weber-Pillwax, C. (2004). Indigenous researchers and Indigenous research methods: Cultural influences or cultural determinants of research methods. *Pimatisiwin: A Journal of Aboriginal and Indigenous Community Health*, 2(1), 76–90. https://journalindigenouswellbeing.co.nz/volume-2-1-spring-2004/indigenous-researchers-and-indigenous-research-methods-cultural-influences-or-cultural-determinants-of-research-methods/

Weinblatt, M., & Harrison, C. (2011). Theatre of the oppressor: Working with privilege towards social justice. In T. Emert & E. Friedland (Eds.), *Come closer: Critical perspectives on Theatre of the Oppressed* (pp. 21–31). Peter Lang.

Werner, E. E., & Smith, R. S. (1982). *Vulnerable but invincible: A longitudinal study of resilient children and youth*. McGraw-Hill.

Wessels, T. (2013). *The myth of progress: Towards a sustainable future*. University Press of New England.

Westley, F., Zimmerman, B., & Patton, M. Q. (2007). *Getting to maybe: How the world is changed*. Vintage Canada.

Wikipedia. (2022). Sagging. Retrieved 28 June 2019. https://en.wikipedia.org/wiki/Sagging_(fashion)

Wilkinson, S., & Kitzinger, C. (2008). Representing the other. In T. Prentki & S. Preston (Eds.), *The applied theatre reader* (pp. 87–93). Routledge.

Whitfield, T. W. A. (2005). Aesthetics as pre-linguistic knowledge: A psychological perspective. *Design Issues*, 21(1), 3–17. https://www.jstor.org/stable/25223975

Willis, P. (1977). *Learning to labour: How working class kids get working class jobs*. Columbia University Press.

Wilson, S. (2008). *Research is ceremony: Indigenous research methods*. Fernwood Publishing.

Young, I. M. (1986). The ideal of community and the politics of difference. *Social Theory and Practice*, *12*(1), 1–26. https://www.jstor.org/stable/23556621

Youth Uncensored Evaluation Video (YUEV). (2012). University of Alberta.

www.ingramcontent.com/pod-product-compliance
Ingram Content Group UK Ltd.
Pitfield, Milton Keynes, MK11 3LW, UK
UKHW052113030225
454636UK00010B/132

9 781835 950791